Praise for *Putting Away Childish Things:*

"A superb way of involving the reader emotionally and imaginatively in these important issues. Indeed, it is probably the only way of doing so. As we follow Kate's journey we become aware of the paradoxes and difficulties of faith in the modern world, and appreciate the way these affect our spiritual, intellectual, and professional aspirations at every level. At the end of the novel, Borg is thus able to lead his readers to the crucial insight that religious commitment is more than belief."

—Karen Armstrong, author of *The Case for God*

"With a novelist's gift for creating plot and character, the distinguished New Testament scholar and theologian Marcus Borg has written a book that succeeds not only as a work of fiction but as an exploration of the kind of religious and social issues that divide many Christians today. I recommend it not only as an insightful exploration of contemporary Christian thought but as a consistently lively and engaging story."

—Frederick Buechner, author of *Secrets in the Dark*

"Professor Borg spins a fine yarn and teaches much in the process, yielding a whole cloth of integrated and inquiring Christianity. Let's hope there is a second tapestry to come!"

—The Most Rev. Katharine Jefferts Schori, Presiding Bishop and Primate of The Episcopal Church

"We all know that Marcus Borg is a gifted teacher, biblical scholar, and writer of nonfiction, but it turns out that he's a master storyteller, too. In *Putting Away Childish Things,* we encounter thoughtful and conflicted characters talking honestly and intelligently about God, faith, doubt, sex, food, and life's big decisions. A rewarding read!"

—Brian D. McLaren, author of *A New Kind of Christianity*

"*Putting Away Childish Things* is a page-turning tale grappling with issues of faith confronting today's church. An inspiring and compelling story that will be treasured and revisited, Borg's illuminating insights and all-too-human characters make theology accessible to all."

—Julia Spencer-Fleming, award-winning author of *One Was a Soldier*

"Emily Dickinson said 'tell all the truth, but tell it slant,' and Marcus Borg does just that. With his trademark pith and lucidity, Borg gives us a novel with meat on its bones: his story of theology professor Kate Riley's vocational and spiritual journey has something for the inquirer's intellect, the lover's heart, and the seeker's soul. Through his compelling story, he invites us to explore new truths that help us navigate a clear path through the culture wars and hot-button issues of our day. This is a feast for mind, heart, and spirit."

—Anne Sutherland Howard, author of *Claiming the Beatitudes* and Executive Director of The Beatitudes Society

"The form is different with Marcus Borg's insightful new novel, but the reader's experience and payoff are the same as with his many excellent nonfiction books: this is a great read that leads to a deeper, more hopeful understanding of the meaning and possibilities of Christian faith today."

—Tom Krattenmaker, USA Today Board of Contributors, author of *Onward Christian Athletes*

PUTTING AWAY CHILDISH THINGS

PUTTING AWAY CHILDISH THINGS

A NOVEL OF MODERN FAITH

MARCUS J. BORG

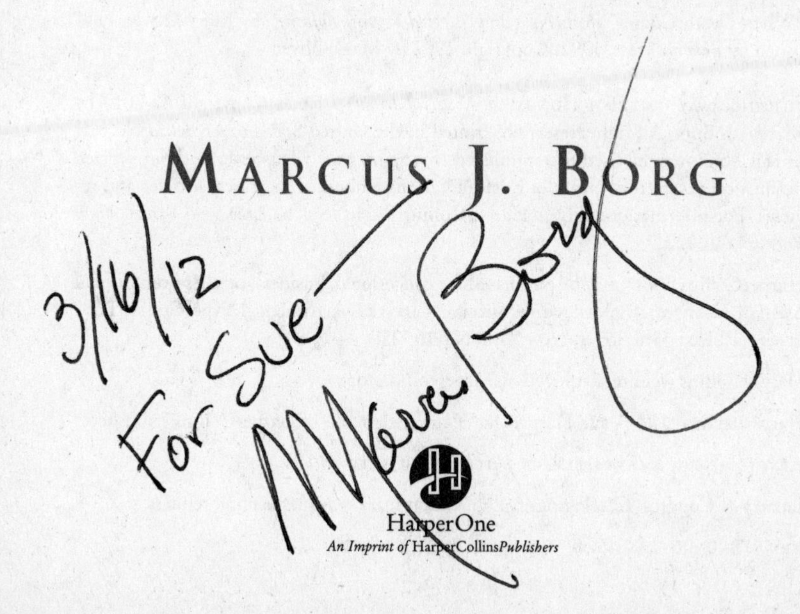

HarperOne
An Imprint of HarperCollins*Publishers*

HarperOne

Every effort has been made to obtain permissions for pieces quoted in this work. If any required acknowledgments have been omitted, or any rights overlooked, it is unintentional. Please notify the publishers of any omission, and it will be rectified in future editions.

"The Avowal" by Denis Levertov, from *The Stream and the Sapphire,* copyright 1984 by Denise Levertov. Reprinted by permission of New Directions Publishing Corp.

"When Death Comes" from *New and Selected Poems, Volume I* by Mary Oliver. Published by Beacon Press, 1992. Copyright 1992 by Mary Oliver.

FIRST HARPERCOLLINS PAPERBACK EDITION PUBLISHED IN 2011

Library of Congress Cataloging-in-Publication Data is available upon request.

ISBN 978–0–06–188816–8

11 12 13 14 15 BV 10 9 8 7 6 5 4 3 2

1

On a Saturday in mid-December, Kate Riley locked the door of her office at Wells College in Willow Falls, a small town in central Wisconsin. Behind her, the click of the key in the lock signaled a final good-bye to a successful fall term. She had just finished assigning course grades to the students in her religious studies classes. Before her was a three-week break until winter term began. She relished the prospect of unscheduled time.

Stepping outside, Kate was struck by the winter afternoon sunlight, pale, luminous, and lemony, as if the sun were shining through water. She stopped and simply looked. *If I ever move,* she thought, *I will miss this.*

She loved this time of year. In the small town in Min-

nesota where she had grown up, the earlier and earlier descent of darkness as the days of December shortened had been magical and mysterious. She remembered how twilight had turned to dark as she walked home from school, streetlights coming on, light spilling from the windows of houses. It had felt exciting to be out in the dark, even though it was not yet time for supper.

The deepening darkness had also meant Christmas was near. She recalled the cartoon figure on the front page of the daily newspaper counting down the shopping days until Christmas and her impatience as the number moved so slowly from double digits to single digits and then finally reached the magic number one.

For almost as long as Kate could recall, the season also meant the coming of the second longest vacation of the year. She had been in school most of her life, except for about a decade after graduating from college. Then she had returned to school—five years of graduate study followed by almost five years of teaching at Wells. The academic calendar had become her calendar.

After a minute or so, she crossed the parking lot and got into her car, a red Volvo sports sedan. Purchased the previous fall, her first new car had been a budget-stretching indulgence. She had long loved cars, and the performance of the Volvo's turbocharged engine delighted her. And its all-wheel drive was very useful in this wintry part of the country, the final rationalization with which she had justified the extravagant expense.

Shifting through the gears and feeling the power of the motor's low-end torque, she couldn't imagine why anybody would want an automatic transmission. Crossing the bridge over the frozen river at the edge of town, she pulled into the parking lot behind Murphy's Tavern, where last night's snowfall lay mounded in the corners.

Murphy's was another indulgence. Most days she stopped for a pint or two of Guinness on her way home from the college. Bad habit or perfectly fine? She went back and forth.

She preferred to think of Murphy's as a pub rather than a tavern, but that was a stretch. Worn and tired, it had an air of shabbiness that verged on seediness. Its lack of curb appeal was a large part of what attracted Kate to the place. A couple of miles from campus, it was far enough away that it was seldom frequented by students or faculty. In the late afternoon, it was most often almost empty—a handful of regulars seated at the bar, the booths and tables usually unoccupied. She could count on being alone here.

Kate sat down in her favorite booth next to a window, from which she could see the river—today mostly covered with snow except where the gray ice had been exposed by the wind. Arthur, the bartender, a short British fellow in his sixties, came to her booth. Smiling, he asked, "How's the professor today?" He always called her that.

And, as always, she smiled back and said, "I'm doing well, Arthur. And you?" Then, also as always, she ordered a pint of Guinness and a pint of ice water, the latter to slow the pace at which she drank the former.

She lit a cigarette—another reason for being fond of Murphy's. And another indulgence, Kate thought, even though she rationed herself to six a day. One in the morning with coffee, two saved for the evening, which meant she could smoke as many as three here.

She couldn't smoke at the college, of course. Its buildings had been smoke-free for years. Moreover, she was embarrassed to be seen smoking by people who knew her. No standing outside a college building and lighting up. Murphy's was perfect.

From her leather backpack that served as a briefcase, she took out her journal. Kate almost always spent some of her Murphy's time writing in her journal. It had become a kind of spiritual practice. When she neglected to do so for three or four days, she would find herself becoming scattered, unappreciative, closed down—even grumpy and impatient. So journaling mattered, and she jour-

naled best in a place that was neither work nor home. Writing the date at the top of a fresh page, she paused and then began:

Fall term all wrapped up. Loved the feeling of freedom as I left my office, relishing the prospect of unscheduled days for almost three weeks. And the light. Grateful. Grateful for this time and place.

Yet realizing that my days aren't completely unscheduled. Need to prepare syllabi for winter term. And beginning on Monday, a week with lots of radio interviews about my new book. My "unscheduled" three weeks suddenly seem crowded.

But still, more time than usual for just being—that delicious spaciousness of time I sometimes feel when there's nothing scheduled in a day. I don't want to let myself feel crowded. Mom always used to say, "It's always the devil who tells you there's not enough time."

Kate paused again, then added:

And now that the end-of-term rush of exams and papers and grading is over, I want to pay attention to Advent.

Advent—the season of the church year that began four weeks before Christmas—had become important to her only a decade ago. As a child, she really hadn't known about Advent—her Irish Catholic father and Swedish Lutheran mother had compromised on their faith differences by not attending church. Kate had had only the vaguest sense of what Christianity was about. She knew about the "big days" of Christmas and Easter, from childhood friends and from her parents' secular observance of them, but that was about it.

Then, about a dozen years ago, shortly before Kate began graduate school, she had a series of experiences that made God real to her. She recognized them as a variety of mystical experience. They startled her, even as they were also the most wondrous and wonderful experiences of her life.

She became curious about church and attended a variety of worship services, including, one Sunday, an Episcopal church. To her surprise, she found the liturgy deeply moving: a group of people saying and singing traditional words together, listening to ancient texts from the Bible read and sometimes chanted, kneeling for prayer, making the sign of the cross, hearing the Eucharistic liturgy sung by a woman priest, going forward to receive bread and wine, smelling the wine as the chalice was lifted to her lips. She felt as though she had come home.

So she became an Episcopalian and, among other things, learned about the seasons of the church year: Advent, Christmas, Epiphany, Lent, Holy Week, Easter, Pentecost, and the long season from Pentecost to Advent known as "ordinary time." A rather exquisite phrase, she thought.

Now it was Advent again. She wrote in her journal:

Advent—"ordinary time" is over. Recalling the rich themes of Advent: darkness and light; yearning and fulfillment; exile and return; a way prepared in the wilderness; pregnancy and birth. All this as preparation for the coming of Christ: "Be born in us today."

Want to live Advent and not just let it pass by. So what is it about for me this year, at this time in my life?

"Ahem."

Startled, Kate looked up.

Fred Burgoyne, one of the senior members of the religion department at Wells, looked down at her, his expression a mixture of surprise and bemusement. "Hello, Kate. Didn't expect to see anyone I knew here. Mind if I join you?"

He didn't wait for her to respond, sliding into the cracked leather seat across from her and settling his large bulk with a thud.

Kate tried to hide her annoyance at the interruption. "Hello, Fred. What brings you here?"

"Actually, my car broke down a block over. Just waiting for the tow truck to come and ducked into the nearest warm place."

Arthur hurried over. "Professor, you okay?"

"Yes, thank you, Arthur."

Arthur looked at Fred, his face revealing a mixture of curiosity and distrust. He was protecting her privacy, Kate realized.

"Ready for your next Guinness, Professor?" he asked.

About two inches of her Guinness remained. Arthur consistently timed his requests to about five minutes before Kate would finish her first pint for, as they both knew, it took about five minutes to draw a Guinness properly. She had learned this from a friend who had been in Ireland, where he had first become fond of the dark stout beer, originally a Protestant beer in a Catholic land, he'd said. Usually she was grateful to Arthur for his solicitousness, but now she wondered what Fred might think.

"No, thank you, Arthur. Fred, would you like anything?"

Fred looked at the table for a menu. Finding none, he glanced back at Arthur, who waited with that same mistrusting expression. "Do you have a good single-malt scotch?"

"No, but we've got a blend."

"What's the brand?"

"I don't know. Nobody's ever asked me. They just order scotch."

"Well, I suppose that'll have to do."

Arthur nodded and turned without another word.

Fred raised an eyebrow at Kate. "Rolling the dice asking for that in a place like this. So, it seems like you come here often?"

Kate didn't want to admit to him that he'd invaded her secret place, but she didn't want to lie to Fred either. "Sometimes," she said finally.

Fred looked around at the peeling paint, the dim lighting, the serious drinkers hunched over the bar with an incredulous expression on his face.

Kate felt the need to defend herself and Murphy's. "I find it a good place to write," she said, nodding at her open journal.

"Ah," Fred nodded and shifted into mentor mode, looking over his glasses at her in a way that made her feel she was one of his students. "I hear you've gotten quite a bit of publicity for your latest book."

"I do have several radio interviews lined up for next week. It will be a busy Advent for me."

"Advent? So you follow the church calendar then?"

Kate was taken aback. "Well, yes. I especially enjoy Advent. I like the idea of"—she was about to say "preparing for Christ," thought better of it, and said instead, "a season of reflection."

Fred frowned. "That reminds me, Kate. I've been thinking about whether it's such a good idea for you to be focusing on such Christian ideas in your published work."

Although Kate knew she and Fred didn't see eye to eye on matters of faith, this remark struck her as completely out of left field. Trained in process philosophy and theology, Fred had lately developed what Kate saw as a somewhat eccentric interest, namely, the question of whether Jesus ever existed. His recent publications, consisting of a few articles and the occasional letter to the editor of the area's newspaper, argued that early Christianity was a myth invented by Paul and others. His prose was not only provocative but pugnacious—he seemed to delight in stirring the pot. But in person he had always been gentle and playful and seemingly supportive of her work, at least until now.

"Why do you say that, Fred?" she responded, trying to keep the surprise out of her voice. "I don't see my work as any more Christian than that of many other biblical scholars."

"Well, your first book was fine. A very nice treatment of James. But then you did this new book with its focus on the birth narratives and their meaning for church people today, and now I hear

that you might be doing a book on C. S. Lewis. Don't you worry that your interests are becoming a little, well, popular?"

What was that supposed to mean? Now she really wanted a second cigarette, but she didn't want to smoke in front of Burgoyne. She overheard a conversation between two women at the bar as Arthur washed a couple of glasses. One said, "You just shut your mouth." Her companion said, "Well, I'll shut my mouth if you'll just shut your legs." They laughed.

Kate returned her attention to Fred. "I'm just writing about what interests me. What do you mean exactly by my interests becoming too popular?"

Now Fred looked reluctant. "Nothing. Let's talk about something else. Other than your book commitments, what are you doing for the break? Visiting family?"

Kate winced slightly. Her fingers itched for her second cigarette. "No, I've decided to spend Christmas alone this year." Kate's parents had died in a car accident when she was a senior in high school. Since that time, she had sometimes spent Christmas with aunts and uncles or with friends. Though she still had standing invitations to spend Christmas with relatives and several friends on the faculty had told her that they would be happy to include her in their Christmas festivities, she had decided over two years ago, after Peter, to be alone at Christmas. After all, she was alone.

Feeling as though she had to add something to her statement, she pulled a couple of books out of her bag. "Plus I'm looking forward to diving into these."

Fred picked up the first, *Wittgenstein's Poker*. "Ah yes, this is a good one. Wittgenstein and Popper and their historical meeting at the Cambridge Philosophical Society in the mid-twentieth century."

"I'm interested in the way the eyewitnesses differ about what exactly occurred," Kate said. "Did Wittgenstein threaten Popper

with a fireplace poker or did he just hold it up? It raises the question of what memory is. When we remember, what are we doing? Are we going back in time so that we are present once again at the event, at 'what happened'? Or are we remembering the last time we remembered it or told the story of it, so that memory is a series of veneers laid over the past?"

"Interesting," Fred said, his tone implying that it was not, in fact, all that interesting.

Kate felt another rumble of irritation as he picked up the second book, a detective novel by Julia Spencer-Fleming entitled *In the Bleak Mid-Winter*.

"I haven't heard of this one," he said.

"It's from a series about a woman Episcopal priest in upstate New York."

"Ah, back to the church again," Fred said.

"I guess," Kate shrugged. *Why is he harping on that subject?* she wondered.

She glanced at her watch and pretended it was time for her to go. She gathered her books and journal and slipped them into her backpack, then fumbled in her wallet for money, regretting that she'd never gotten to order a second Guinness. "Sorry, Fred, I need to leave. I have a dinner commitment. Can I drop you anywhere?"

"No, no," he said. "I'm sure the tow truck will be here momentarily, and I want to go to the auto shop and make sure they take good care of my baby."

"Ah, I understand that," Kate smiled, relieved by his refusal. "Well, enjoy your break."

"You too," Fred said. "You too."

2

Troubled by the strange conversation she'd had with Burgoyne, Kate tried to distract herself with NPR as she drove to Geoff's house. Realizing that she would be early, she drove around for a while, taking one of the country roads that led up into the forested hills surrounding Willow Falls. Nothing comforting in the evening news, however. The war in Iraq continued to go badly, and the title of Bob Woodward's book *State of Denial* floated into her mind.

It was a relief when she arrived at Geoff's house. The newest member of the department, Geoff Cooper was in his second year at Wells. His area was Asian religions with a specialty in Buddhism. She enjoyed him, and he had become her best friend on the faculty. In addition to their everyday contacts at the college, they had dinner together once or twice a month.

They were the only single members of the department. He was about her age—a couple years younger. Handsome, though he didn't look as though he worked out. Soft mouth that smiled easily. Gray-green eyes. Salt and pepper hair—though more pepper than salt. Probably everyone would have thought they were a couple, except for the fact that Geoff was gay, which she hadn't guessed until about the third or fourth time they'd had dinner together a year ago.

She knocked at Geoff's back door and walked in without waiting for him to answer. Geoff was in the kitchen. He looked up at her, smiled, and asked, "Shall I open a bottle of wine?" as he peeked into a pot on the stove.

"Not yet, at least not for me," Kate said as she slipped off her coat and unwound her scarf. "I've already had a Guinness. But some sparkling water, some *Sprudel,* would be nice." She enjoyed the sound of the German word and the way she had to push her lips forward to say it, as if she were kissing somebody.

"You betcha," Geoff said, teasingly using one of her Midwestern expressions. He poured a glass of sparkling water for her and a glass of Russian River California chardonnay for himself. He sipped. "Pretty nice. Don't miss it."

"I'll try some with dinner, after that Guinness has settled a bit. Speaking of that Guinness, you'll never guess who I ran into at Murphy's."

"An old boyfriend?"

Kate grinned. "No. I wish. Fred Burgoyne."

"That is strange. Why wasn't he home with his family?"

"His car broke down."

Geoff laughed. "That's how most people end up there, I think."

"Hey," Kate raised her hands in mock protest. "I know you're not the biggest fan of Murphy's, but I like it. And I have to admit, I was dismayed to have my private place invaded by somebody from the department. He said the strangest thing." She took another sip of her sparkling water. "He said that my scholarship was too Christian, too 'popular.' What do you think he meant by that? Do you think they've been talking about my tenure chances?"

Geoff perched on a stool next to her.

"I haven't heard anything, although I doubt that I would; I'm the low man on the totem pole, and they all know that we're close friends. But what problem could they have with your scholarship? Your new book's gotten great endorsements and *Publishers Weekly* gave it a starred review."

"I know, but he made several comments about the church. I set him off by mentioning Advent. I think he's concerned that I'm letting my faith dictate my scholarship."

Geoff set down his wineglass. "That's ridiculous. Surely his areas of interest are dictated at least partly by his own faith or lack of it. Our beliefs affect everything we do. If they let the fact that you're a practicing Christian interfere with your tenure chances, I will personally place the call to the ACLU."

Kate laughed, his remark dispelling any lingering uneasiness. "I think we're getting ahead of ourselves. I probably just overreacted. How has your day been?"

"Pretty ordinary." Geoff brightened. "Hey, did you hear that the Chinese government has just passed a law against unauthorized reincarnation? I'm not sure I've got all the details right, but I think they're going to require a license for reincarnation."

Geoff was a self-professed news junkie. He always had some kind of interesting tidbit to share with her. Sometimes Kate suspected he focused on the news of the weird because he didn't want to talk about his personal life. Or then again, perhaps he didn't feel that his personal life was very interesting. Kate could relate to that sentiment. She smiled at him. "Really? That's bizarre."

"Well," Geoff continued, "they're thinking of the Dalai Lama's successor—they don't want another troublemaker. So they want to be in charge of who it is."

"Kind of like the Roman Empire in the first century requiring a license for resurrection—no unauthorized resurrections allowed?"

"Exactly," Geoff grinned.

"So," Kate said, "I have something to celebrate: I'm done with end-of-term chores. Free as a bird. How about you?"

"I finished yesterday, so me too. But I don't feel free as a bird. I've only got four days before I leave to be with my folks for Christmas. And this year I agreed to stay for two weeks. Brothers and sisters and nieces and nephews coming, but at staggered dates. So, a flow of relatives. Like a parliament of owls—did you know that's what a group of owls is called?"

"My favorite is an exaltation of larks."

"That's a good one too. Anyway," Geoff continued, "when I get back, I won't have a lot of time before the start of next term, so I want to get a lot of preparation done before I go. So, a couple of days of writing syllabi. Plus I need to do some Christmas shopping. Then, getting on a plane—feels like a lot."

He peered at the clock over Kate's head. "Time to check the stove."

"What are we having?"

"Duck à la Geoff," he said. "Duck quarters browned and then simmered in white wine with onions, shallots, garlic, and herbes de Provence. Simmered so long it falls off the bone."

"You've served it before. I love it."

Geoff dished out two servings of the duck and, plates in hand, they moved to the table. By unspoken agreement they both bowed their heads for a silent blessing before they began to eat.

"So," Geoff said, putting his napkin in his lap, "I've told you about my next few days. What do yours look like?"

"Well, I'm spending Christmas alone again this year. So I'm basically going to be at home—with myself. I mostly love the thought. Except next week won't feel exactly alone—I've got all those radio interviews to do on my book. Fourteen—that's a lot."

"Good for you," Geoff said. "Your publicist has done a good job."

"Yeah, I guess so." Kate paused to take a bite. "But still, I wish there weren't quite so many. This duck is fantastic as usual, Geoff."

"Thank you. Are you nervous about the interviews?"

"No, not really. These will be my first book interviews, but I've done interviews before. In my late twenties, I worked part-time as an interviewer on an NPR station. Mostly I was the interviewer, of course, but near the end I got interviewed about some of the stories I did. So I've been on both sides of the mike, and I'm not uncomfortable about doing them. It's just that they seem like such interruptions. One of the joys of my life is a completely unscheduled day—and they're pretty rare. And to have two or three interviews a day—that's a lot of interruption."

She shook her head. "But enough about me." She looked at his dear face. "You know, there's something I've been wanting to ask you. Are you ready for a personal question?"

Geoff cocked his head. "Maybe."

"Well, we've known each other for over a year, and I've known that you're gay for much of that time, but I've never asked you if you're in a relationship. The other day it struck me that if you were a woman friend, we would have talked about this a long time ago. So, do you mind? Do you have a secret life I don't know about?"

Geoff took a sip of wine. "Well," he said, "no. Not for about ten years. I had a number of relationships in my twenties—not very many, actually. But there were two that were relatively long-term, two or three years each. There was Robert." His eyes went far away for a moment, obviously recalling some fond memories. "You could call him Robert or Rob, but never Bob. And there was Thomas—and he wouldn't answer to Tom. Perhaps I'm attracted to formality. I enjoyed them. Good guys. Lots of caring and companionship and fun. But they didn't last. I'm not sure why. Of course, there wasn't much support for gay relationships not so long ago. But I don't know if that would have made the difference."

"So you've been celibate for what—ten years?"

"Yes, ma'am."

"Is that hard?"

"Well, it doesn't matter all that much most of the time."

"Is that because you've got a Buddhist attitude?"

Geoff smiled. "Perhaps. Of course there are a lot of married Buddhists. But, yeah, I think Buddhism is right about grasping being the source of our suffering. And there's a lot of grasping in sexuality, whether we're in a relationship, or not in a relationship and wanting one. I suspect sexuality that isn't grasping is very rare.

"I do know that my life has been more peaceful without it. I can really understand priestly celibacy, even though I think it's become counterproductive for the Catholic Church. They'll have to give it up soon, or there won't be enough priests. Already there aren't. They'll need to start allowing priests to marry, or ordain women—don't know which would be harder for them."

He raised his eyebrows. "But I do understand the wisdom of celibacy. If you've let go of thinking about sex, it gives you all kinds of time for other matters."

"Is that the way it is for you? That you don't even think about it?"

"Mostly. Sometimes I think it would be nice to have a companion.

Not just a sexual companion, but a companion, and sex would be part of it. But I don't spend a lot of time on it. How about you?" he asked Kate. "Do you have a secret life?"

"Actually, I'm quite a bit like you. I've had some interesting flings and one sort of long-term relationship in my twenties—a guy named Erik. But right after I began graduate school, I decided that I wouldn't have casual sex or an affair—that I'd become involved with someone only if it looked like it could be a marriage. And then a few years ago, there was Peter."

Geoff reached for the wine bottle and poured himself a second glass, then a glass for Kate. "What made you come to that decision? About only becoming involved with someone if you saw marriage potential?"

Kate smiled. "You would zero in on that. I had a brief affair with a professor from my undergraduate college, a man named Martin. It didn't happen until the year after I graduated. But he was married at the time, and I just decided I was never going to do anything like that again." She laughed, the sound hollow and self-conscious even to her own ears. "It sounds kind of sordid now, I guess, but at the time it didn't feel that way at all."

Geoff looked at her closely, but didn't press the issue. "What about the other two relationships? Erik and Peter?"

Kate was relieved not to have to talk more about Martin. "Okay, Erik. Well, let's see—that relationship lasted almost two years. I was twenty-four and he was twenty-nine. His wife had divorced him—fell in love with an Irish poet. Erik thought of himself as a nerd, and in any case no competition for an Irish poet. So he just gave up, didn't fight the divorce at all.

"We met in church, of all places. I didn't go very often in those days—just a few times a year. I thought he was interesting, and the more we talked, the more I enjoyed him. He was bright, funny, and not on the make—he couldn't imagine that he was attractive.

It just wasn't in him. But we started seeing each other. Finally, after a couple of months, I asked him, 'Erik, would you like to go to bed with me?' I knew he would never take the initiative. I think he was stunned. But he was definitely interested. We were great lovers. It was as if everything was brand-new for him—and it was, mostly, for me too. He told me he had done the 'wild thing,' as we called it, only with his wife—and I guess it wasn't very wild.

"Soon we started living together, and our evenings were mostly filled with making love, usually more than once. We listened to Elton John, the Moody Blues, Cat Stevens, and Van Morrison. James Taylor, Judy Collins, and Joni Mitchell were for afterwards. And we often made love when we woke up in the morning, and sometimes had a quickie in the afternoon. It was really nice—he wasn't greedy, just lost in delight. I loved it."

"I had no idea you were such a sex kitten," Geoff said.

"Well, I have been." Kate laughed.

"So what happened to the relationship?"

"Well, he was transferred away from Chicago, so we decided to try a long-distance relationship."

Kate took a sip of chardonnay. "It worked for about six months and then fell apart. He was too worried about whether or not I was being faithful. It even began to spoil the one or two weekends we did spend together each month. I was being faithful, but I guess because he knew firsthand how much I enjoyed sex, he couldn't imagine that I could get along very long without it.

"It almost drove him crazy. He had anxiety attacks and started seeing a therapist. During one two-week crisis period, he saw his therapist every day. One day he even saw him twice. It was terrible. He made it seem as though I was putting him through all of this pain, but I really wasn't. Then I did have an affair, a pretty meaningless one. I think he did too, and so we both suspected the other of what we ourselves had done. It got terribly complicated.

And we couldn't work it out. It was so very sad. He was actually very sweet.

"But it was very good while it lasted. I still wonder if he didn't have enough courage or if I didn't have enough patience. We might have been able to make it. And if we had stayed together, I probably would be a mom by now with a couple of teenagers."

They were silent. Geoff said, "So do you have a secret life now?"

"No—at least not of a sexual kind. But a couple of years ago, I guess I did. In the spring of my first year here at Wells, I met a guy named Peter at the regional conference of the American Academy of Religion. He teaches religion at Fillmore College, about three hundred miles from here—do you know it?"

"I've heard of it," Geoff said. "A small liberal arts college, even smaller than Wells. And named after Millard Fillmore? Kind of weird."

Kate laughed. "Actually, yes. Anyway, Peter and I hit it off pretty well at the conference, and we started to e-mail afterwards. After a couple of months, we decided to spend a weekend together—and we were real clear that it would be chaste—no sexual expectations. Well, we had a good time—we could really talk to each other. A couple of months later we had another weekend together, and then another, and on the fifth weekend we decided to sleep together. Well, it was nice—and so we started to see each other at least one weekend a month, and sometimes two."

Kate paused. "And then, about two years ago, we had to decide whether this was a long-term relationship—you know, whether this was about marriage. And we realized that neither of us was willing to move to be with the other one. The issue was jobs—you know how hard it is to find a teaching position in a college or university these days. I guess we each wanted a career more than each other."

She took another sip of the chardonnay. "This is nice. So, anyway, Peter and I drifted apart. We still talk on the phone once in a while. But we haven't seen each other for two years. So that's how long I've been celibate—not a record for me, but close."

"How's that been?"

"Okay," Kate said. "I haven't met anybody here who tempts me—except you. You know, it took me about four months to figure out that you're gay. And I thought, 'Damn.'" She grinned at him. "But you know that."

She looked at her watch. "It's nine o'clock. It used to be that Saturday night was only beginning at nine. We grow old, we grow old. I need to leave soon—church tomorrow, you know. Let me help you with the dishes."

"No—it will take me less than five minutes to load them into the dishwasher. Just let yourself be a guest tonight."

"That's a lovely notion. Thank you for that and for a wonderful evening." Kate found her handbag and her coat, Geoff kissed her on the cheek, and she headed out into the wintry night.

She arrived home after a silent drive through empty snow-bordered streets. She turned the kettle on and put a bag of PG Tips into a small teapot. While the tea brewed, she took off her turtleneck and slipped into a worn red-checked flannel shirt.

Then she got out her *Book of Common Prayer.* She loved the words of Compline, the night service. She read its opening line aloud: "The Lord Almighty grant us a peaceful night and a perfect end." Then a few psalms; she was especially fond of Psalms 31 and 134. But it was the prayers at the end of the service that were most dear to her:

> Be our light in the darkness, O Lord, and in your great mercy defend us from all perils and dangers of this night.

> Keep watch, dear Lord, with those who work, or watch, or weep this night, and give your angels charge over those who sleep. Tend the sick,

> Lord Christ; give rest to the weary, bless the dying, soothe the suffering, pity the afflicted, shield the joyous; and all for your love's sake.

And then:

> Guide us waking, O Lord, and guard us sleeping; that awake we may watch with Christ, and asleep we may rest in peace.

Instead of the peaceful feeling she normally experienced after reading the prayer, she found herself replaying the strange conversation she'd had with Burgoyne. She'd never expected that her faith could become a stumbling block in her academic career; she'd always viewed it as enhancing her area of study. In fact, Kate had always thought that seeing God as real—being passionate about God—gave her an edge over scholars who treated religion as some kind of relic from a bygone era. Thinking it over convinced her—she still believed that to be true. Returning to the prayer, she repeated it twice. Soon she was in bed, asleep.

3

On Monday morning, while it was still dark, Kate sat in the breakfast nook of her small rented house on the edge of town, sipping her second cup of coffee. She opened her *Book of Common Prayer* to the morning service. She said the opening line in the language of the older prayer book, which she occasionally preferred to the revision done in the late 1970s: "O Lord, open thou my lips." It seemed a fitting way to begin each day.

Since she was alone, she also said the response: "And my mouth shall show forth thy praise." In her mind she heard, as she often did, an Oxford college choir singing the phrase with tightly controlled joy. So British, so Anglican.

She read two of the four biblical readings assigned for the

day. She had tried for a time to read all four texts every day, but found that she always felt a bit rushed and her mind easily wandered off. Pacing mattered.

Then, as she often did, she read a prayer from another book, today from *Prayers for a Planetary Pilgrim:*

> The part of this earthen plane in which I live is wrapped in winter as this new day dawns for me. The winter earth leans away from the sun, and I miss its light and warmth. How easily I also lean away from you, Beloved God, and your warmth. How readily I lean toward other things and so find the cold touch of winter upon my words and deeds. How often I forget you, who formed my being and who shaped the cosmos, sending spinning suns by the billions into the winter wasteland of empty space.
>
> I dedicate this winter day to you, as I now enter into the chapel of my heart to sit in stillness with you. May I leave outside this circle of silence all my worries and concerns for this day, as I enter into prayer.

She sat in silence for a number of minutes and then said, "Amen." Returning to the *Book of Common Prayer,* she concluded with its prayer for guidance:

> Lord God, in you we live and move and have our being: we humbly pray you so to guide and govern us by your Holy Spirit, that in all the cares and occupations of our life we may not forget you, but may remember that we are ever walking in your sight; through Jesus Christ our Lord. Amen.

A few minutes before nine, Kate went into her study. It had been the second bedroom in her house, but she had made it an office, installing bookshelves, a desk, and an overstuffed easy chair. She settled herself in the easy chair, a copy of her new book, a glass of water, a notepad and pen, and her speakerphone arranged on the table beside her. Now she just had to wait for the phone to ring. She consulted the list her publicist had sent her. First up, KBNK, an NPR affiliate in Seattle. Host: Jeff Reed. It was seven in the morning out there—she wondered who would be listening. She focused on her breathing to calm herself. She had told Geoff the truth: she felt fairly comfortable about radio interviews, but she still experienced a flutter of nerves as she waited for the station to call.

She picked up her book and flipped idly through it, wondering what questions the interviewer would think to ask. And if he had read any of it. Her first book, a scholarly treatment of the New Testament letter of James based on her doctoral dissertation, had made a small splash in the academic world, but was too specialized to attract media attention. But this book was on the stories of Jesus's birth and so was, her publisher insisted, of general interest. And so fourteen interviews on radio stations around the country had been arranged for this week, three of them this morning. A couple would be as brief as ten minutes, some would take a full hour.

The phone rang. She answered, "Good morning. This is Kate Riley."

A voice at the other end said, "This is station KBNK. Please hold on for your interview with Jeff. It will begin in about two minutes."

"Thank you. I'm looking forward to it," Kate said, but the voice was already gone. Instead, she heard some music, station identification, a weather forecast, and advertisements for a restaurant, a mattress store, and a quick-lube chain.

Then the host's voice introduced her: "Our guest today is Professor Kate Riley, a biblical scholar who teaches at Wells College in Willow Falls, Wisconsin, and author of a new book about the birth of Jesus. The title is *Two Stories, One Birth.* A timely topic at this time of the year. Thank you for taking time to be on our show today."

He paused. Kate took it as a cue to respond: "Well, you're welcome, and thank you for having me."

"Professor Riley—or may I call you Kate?"

"Yes—that would be fine," Kate said, wondering whether he would have asked a male author that question. Like saying to Stephen Hawking, "May I call you Steve?"

He continued, "Kate, as you emphasize in the title of your book, there are two stories of Jesus's birth in the New Testament, in Matthew and Luke, and they're quite different from each other. I admit that, until I read your book, I didn't realize how different they are—I've always heard them together as one story. So maybe we should begin there."

"They are quite different." Kate hesitated for a moment, gathering her thoughts. It was difficult sometimes to condense her answers down to the sound bites she knew radio people wanted to hear. "Matthew's is much shorter—if you subtract the genealogy from the beginning of his gospel, his story of Jesus's nativity is only 31 verses long. Luke's is much longer, 132 verses, so it's four times as long." A doubt stabbed her. *That's right, isn't it? Or is it 32 verses in Matthew and 131 in Luke? Oh well, let someone call in and correct me if I'm wrong.*

She continued, "And the tone of the stories is very different. Matthew's is dark and threatening—it's dominated by King Herod and his plot to kill Jesus. Even the story of the wise men following the star is part of that plot.

"Luke's story is basically joyful. There's no plot by Herod to kill Jesus; instead, there are hymns filled with joy sung by Mary and Zechariah and Simeon. And by angels in the night sky to shepherds. You know, if we were to do a Christmas pageant based solely on Luke, it would be kind of a musical, with lots of arias."

"A musical?" Jeff queried, his tone doubtful. Kate wondered if she should explain more. Probably it wouldn't be helpful for her to break into "Singing in the Rain." She smiled to herself as he continued, "Are there other differences?"

"Yes. One of the more interesting ones is whether Jesus was born at home or in a stable a long way from home. In Matthew, it happens at home—Mary and Joseph live in Bethlehem, Jesus is born there, and the wise men come to their house, their home.

"But in Luke, Mary and Joseph live in Nazareth—that's where the angel Gabriel comes to Mary and tells her that she will become pregnant by the Holy Spirit. But even though they live in Nazareth, Jesus is born in Bethlehem because of a Roman census that requires everybody to return to their ancestral birthplace. So we have the famous story of Mary and Joseph journeying to Bethlehem, where there's no room in the inn, and that's why Jesus is born in a stable and placed in a manger. But none of that's in Matthew—no journey, no stable, no manger, because Bethlehem is home."

The host spoke again. "So, with these differences—and some sound like contradictions—are you saying that these stories maybe aren't historically factual? I think most Christians believe that they are—that these things did happen. But if they didn't happen this way, why should people take them seriously?"

"Well," Kate hesitated, "that depends upon how we *see* these stories. If we see their purpose as historical reporting, to tell us what happened, then the question of factuality matters a great deal. People often get fixated on factuality: either things happened this way, or these stories aren't true. They're no better than fables or 'pious frauds,' as one scholar recently put it.

"And it's not surprising that some people have difficulty believing in their factuality. There's lots of spectacular happenings in them. A divine conception. A magic star that behaves with the precision of a global positioning device, leading the wise men to Jerusalem and then turning left to lead them south to Bethlehem, where it stops above exactly the right house. Lots of angels—they appear to Joseph and Mary and Zechariah, and a multitude of them fills the sky and sings to shepherds. No wonder people ask whether things like this ever really happened. So in my book I present a different option for seeing these stories, one that moves beyond the question of historical factuality, namely, that we see them as parables and overtures."

Jeff broke in. "What exactly do you mean by parables and overtures?"

Perfect, Kate thought. He was leading her right where she wanted to go. "Let me begin with why I call them overtures. The musical analogy is very deliberate. Just as an overture to a symphony typically introduces the central themes of the symphony as a whole, so the birth stories in Matthew and Luke are overtures to the gospels that follow. And just as the overture to a symphony is the symphony in miniature, so the birth stories are the gospel in miniature. They sound the central themes of the gospels, and they seem to have been deliberately composed to do so.

"And I also see the stories as parables. Think of the parables of Jesus, like the good Samaritan and the prodigal son. I don't know anybody who thinks that Jesus was simply reporting something that happened the other day. Or that if these stories didn't happen, they're not true, no better than pious frauds. Everybody recognizes that their point is their meaning—that's their purpose. To argue about whether or not there really was a good Samaritan would completely miss the point.

"Parables are about meaning, not factuality. And the truth of a parable is its meaning. Parables can be truthful, truth-filled, even while not being historically factual. And I apply this to the birth stories: we best understand them when we see them as parables and overtures, and when we don't worry or argue about whether they're factual."

"Very interesting," Jeff said. "So how far do you take this? As I understand your book, you're saying that it doesn't matter whether there was a star of Bethlehem or wise men bringing gifts, or whether Jesus was born at home or in a stable, or whether angels sang to shepherds, or even whether Jesus was born in Nazareth or Bethlehem. Would you extend this to the virgin birth as well—that it doesn't matter whether it happened? That's pretty important to a lot of Christians."

The big question. Kate took a breath. "Well, my emphasis as a historian is on the meaning of a story of a divine conception in the context of the first century, not on whether it happened."

"So, what does the story of the divine conception of Jesus mean?"

"More than one thing." Kate was talking faster now. She wanted to get to everything before they had to end the interview. "There is a Jewish context. In the Jewish Bible, the Christian Old Testament, there is a tradition of special births made possible by God, beginning with the birth of Isaac to Sarah and Abraham, the mother and father of Israel, when she was ninety years old and he a hundred. And there are more stories of such births, almost always when the future of Israel was at stake.

"And there's a Roman context. The Roman Empire had a theology, which scholars call Roman imperial theology. Within this theology, Caesar Augustus, the greatest of the Roman emperors, was said to have been the product of a divine conception—conceived by the god Apollo in the womb of his mother, Atia. And so he was 'Son of God.' He had other titles as well. Augustus was also called 'lord,' 'savior of the world,' and the 'bringer of peace on earth.' So were his successors. These adulations were on coins and temples and public monuments—as omnipresent in the first-century world as advertising is in ours."

Kate continued, again wondering if her response was getting

too long. "And of course, this is language that the followers of Jesus used about him—in the gospels and the rest of the New Testament, and in the birth stories. So when we put these stories in their first-century context, they counter Roman imperial theology at point after point. Jesus is the product of a divine conception, the true Son of God, the true Lord, the true savior of the world, the one who really brings peace on earth. Jesus is all of that—and the emperor is not. The story of Jesus's divine conception is part of that larger meaning. Jesus is Lord—empire is not."

The host interjected, "One last question. What you're saying sounds pretty political. Are you saying that these stories are more political than religious?"

"How much time do I have?" Kate asked.

"Oh—about two minutes."

"Okay. Well, not *more* political than religious. They're both. You know, religion and politics are consistently intertwined in the Bible, from beginning to end. Think of ancient Israel's story of its origins, the most important story in the Jewish tradition: Moses and the exodus from Egypt. Is that story religious or political? It's both. It's about God and God's passion—what God is passionate about—and it's a story of a liberation that is political and economic as well as religious.

"This connection between religion and politics continues in the Jewish Bible—think of the prophets. God's passion in the Bible is that the world be a different kind of place. Their passion, and God's passion, is justice and peace. I see the stories of Jesus's birth as continuing this emphasis. Of course, they're about more than politics. They have themes that touch our personal and spiritual yearnings as well. They're about light in the darkness—the magic star in Matthew, the glory of the Lord shining in the night sky as angels sing to shepherds in Luke. They're saying that Jesus is the light in our darkness, the light of the world.

"Then there's the theme of fulfillment of our deepest yearnings. Matthew does this by citing the fulfillment of prophecies, Luke by echoing the language of hope and fulfillment in the songs in his story of Jesus's birth.

"And they are about God's passion for a different kind of world. They're about all of this. Even the themes of light and fulfillment are political as well as religious. They are the gospel in miniature. And just as the gospel—the good news about Jesus—is both religious and political, so are the Christmas stories." Kate stopped, thinking that the time was probably up and that this would be a good place to end.

She was surprised when Jeff said, "We have about thirty seconds, so let me ask you one more question. What should this mean for Christians and politics in America today?"

In thirty seconds, and now less, what should she say, and how bland or bold should she be? It felt as if she thought for at least five seconds, leaving a period of dead air bordering on the unacceptable. Finally, she said, "Well, as a country, we are the empire of our time, the Rome of our time—and we go around pretending that we're Jesus."

"Okay. Well, that's all the time we have," the host said. "Thinking about *that* should make for an interesting Christmas. Thank you, Kate Riley, talking about her new book, *Two Stories, One Birth.* You can buy it at most bookstores and, of course, on the Internet." Before Kate could say, "Thank you," another advertisement came on.

Those last words of hers about our country as Rome pretending to be Jesus had been pretty ballsy, but she was pleased with having come up with the line. It was new; she had not said or thought that before. The interview as a whole had gone well.

She relaxed back in her chair and glanced at her watch. She had just a few minutes before her next interview. She scanned her schedule again. KJCS in western Minnesota. Hosts: Steve and Debra Hastings. She wondered if that was a husband and wife team. Her home state, but she didn't recognize the call letters. Probably not an NPR affiliate this time.

She got up, stretched, and jotted a few brief notes about her last interview before the phone rang again. "Hello, this is Kate Riley," she answered.

"I'm Audrey. I'm the producer for the KJCS *Rise and Shine* show. You'll be on air with Steve and Debra in just a few moments. Do you have any questions?"

"I think I'm fine. Thank you."

"Then please hold."

And Kate was again shunted off to radio hold land where she listened to a commercial promising thicker, more luxurious hair and another promoting a Christian diet book. Then a click and she heard a male voice announcing, "And now author Kate Riley has joined us to talk about the true meaning of Christmas. She's just written a book called *Two Stories, One Birth: What the Gospels Really Say About Christmas.* Welcome. Now, shall we call you Reverend Riley?"

"Thank you. No, it's actually Professor or Dr. Riley, but Kate is just fine."

"So, Kate, tell us a little more about your book."

"Well, as you mentioned, it's called *Two Stories, One Birth.* It's about the two birth narratives in Matthew and Luke and their historical context."

A woman's voice now. This must be Debra. "One of my favorite parts of the Christmas Eve service is hearing the gospel reading about the birth story. Poor Mary, having to have her baby so far from home."

Kate hesitated. These two sounded more like hosts of a Christian talk show than of the news or book program she had expected. She wondered if KJCS meant "King Jesus Christ Savior." She probably needed to tread carefully. "You know, that's an interesting point. Only in the book of Luke do Mary and Joseph have to travel to Bethlehem to have their baby. In Matthew, Jesus is also born in Bethlehem, but Matthew's narrative makes no mention of the couple traveling there, leading us to assume that Bethlehem is their home."

Silence. Then the woman's voice again, sounding more hesitant. "Are you saying that Mary and Joseph didn't travel to Bethlehem? That's in Luke. It's very clear."

"No, no. I just wanted to point out that the birth narratives are quite different, even though we often try to synthesize the two into one seamless narrative. In my book, I try to take each story on its merits and discuss why Matthew and Luke wrote their versions the way they did." Kate felt that she'd gotten into murky water with her previous comment and wanted to explain carefully. "For example, it sounds like you relate to Mary, so probably the Luke narrative is the one you know best. In Matthew, the story is all about Joseph. Mary is hardly mentioned, and the birth itself is almost an afterthought, buried in the middle of a verse. And even then, it's mostly about Joseph. It says, 'He had no marital relations with her until she had borne a son; and he named him Jesus.'

"Indeed, the only part of Matthew that we would find familiar from our Christmas pageants is the story of the wise men—the story does not say how many—who follow the star and bring gifts to the baby Jesus. Here also we have Herod looming like a dark shadow over the first days of Jesus. When the wise men stop in and tell him they are following the star and looking for the king of the Jews, he fears for his royal authority and asks them to return to him and tell him the location of the baby. He says he wants to worship him, but he really plans to kill him. Then an angel tells Joseph of Herod's plans, and he flees to Egypt with his family. Herod orders the slaughter of all the babies in and around Bethlehem.

Some years later, after Herod died, we are told, Joseph returns with his family, and they settle in Nazareth.

"Luke is the narrative most people know best. It is much longer and contains most of the details we see in our Christmas pageants—Mary's visit from the angel, the trip to Bethlehem, the manger, the shepherds, and choirs of angels. But there is a lot more here. Much of this birth narrative is devoted to Elizabeth and Zechariah, the parents of John the Baptizer. Women figure much more prominently in this story—Elizabeth, Mary, and later Anna, who sees the baby Jesus in the Temple. Here also we have the decree from Augustus that causes Mary and Joseph to travel to Bethlehem from their home in Nazareth. Here they must stay in the stable because there is no room at the inn, and Jesus is born there and visited by the shepherds amid choirs of angels."

Kate paused, sitting back in her chair. She had gone on a little longer than she probably should have. On the other end, silence.

Finally the male host, Steve, spoke. "Any perceived discrepancies in those two stories are, I'm sure, just errors in our understanding. There are lots of people out there grasping for anything to try to debunk the truth about Jesus."

"That is certainly not my intention," Kate said. "I do not point out the differences to say that the stories are false. I just think it's important for all of us—especially people of faith—to know what the gospels really say."

Now Debra broke in. "That sounds like you're a Christian at least. Are you?"

Kate hesitated. She didn't like the direction this interview was taking. "Yes, I am a Christian."

"Okay," said Debra. "But what I want to know is, don't you believe in the virgin birth?"

"I think these stories are beautiful, and I prefer to view them as parables. Or to think of them as the overtures that give us a hint as to the character of the gospels that follow—"

"But you don't *believe* them, do you?"

"Well, that's not really what the book is about. My interest is in the idea of divine conception and its context, not whether it literally happened."

"How can you call yourself a Christian and not believe it is important whether they are true?" The woman's voice was rising.

Kate was sitting up straight as a post. "I do believe they are true." She hesitated, tempted for a moment to let her statement stand, intuiting that it would lead the interview down an easier path. But she dismissed the temptation. It wouldn't be honest. She had to explain. "But I don't necessarily equate truth with factuality."

"What exactly do you mean by that?" Steve again.

"I mean that something doesn't have to have happened to be true. For example, take the parables." She could only hope this point would work as well here as it had in the previous interview. "Just about every Christian agrees that Jesus's parables express truth, but I don't know anyone who worries about whether or not there actually was a prodigal son, for example. The birth stories can express truth about Jesus—namely, that he was the true king of the Jews, as opposed to Herod, and the true Lord as opposed to the Roman emperor—even if there wasn't a star or a choir of angels or a journey from Nazareth to Bethlehem."

Steve cut in. "I'm sorry, but there is a difference here. Jesus never presented the parables as literal truth. He made it clear that they were teaching stories. It's not the same with Jesus's birth. Either he was the Son of God, or he wasn't. Either he was a lunatic, or he was who he said he was."

Kate recognized C. S. Lewis's famous argument. Should she counter? Well, why not? She wasn't likely to get these two on her side anyway. Might as well go all the way. "Actually, I would argue that Jesus never said he was the Son of God."

Debra gasped. "How can you say that? Jesus repeats that statement many times in the Gospel of John."

"John is so different from the first three gospels. I would argue that of the four gospels, it is likely the least based on historical fact, although, again, that doesn't mean that it isn't filled with truth. Throughout the gospels, Jesus refers to himself most often as the Son of Man, a very different term indeed."

"For our listeners, I would just like to say here that *I* believe in the virgin birth, and that Jesus is the Son of God." Debra's voice shook with emotion.

"Yes," Steve added, "and I think it's also important to make it clear at this point that the views expressed on this program are not necessarily the views held by this station or the views of Debra and myself."

Kate sighed inwardly and wondered if she would be better off just to hang up. After two more sermonettes, the interview finally ended, and Kate dropped back into her chair, feeling physically battered. What had her publicist been thinking, setting her up with a show like that? It was clear that no one at that station had read a page of her book. And that had only been her second interview. What if there were more disasters lying in wait? The phone rang again, and Kate groaned even as she reached out to answer it. *Here I go again.*

Kate settled into her usual booth at Murphy's on Friday afternoon with a sigh. She hadn't been in all week—the interviews had lasted late into the afternoons, the final ones between five and six on the "going home" shows. And she had no interest in going to Murphy's in the evenings—too noisy and she couldn't be sure of getting her favorite booth. But today her last interview had ended at three. So

To Julia Roller, my editor for this book,

and to Dr. Judy Ringle, my colleague and assistant for more than a decade

PREFACE

This is my first novel. My previous books have all been nonfiction—to the extent that is possible. They have been about religion, mostly about Jesus, the Bible, God, and Christianity.

I candidly acknowledge that this is a "didactic" novel, a teaching novel. It is the only kind of novel I can imagine writing. I have been a teacher all of my life. My characters wrestle with issues of religion today, and in particular with what it means to be an American Christian in a time of major conflicts, both theological and political.

I am aware that I may not have a novelist's imagination or gifts. And I am aware that if I were not an already somewhat established author, this novel might not have been published. It's not easy to find a publisher for a first novel.

I have wanted to write a novel for a long time. I am not sure why. My motive may be an impression that being a novelist is better than being an author of nonfiction. Why I should think that is not clear. An additional motive is curiosity. What would it be like to write a book in which I am making everything up?

It is common for novelists to say that all of their characters are fictitious and that any resemblance to people living or dead is purely coincidental. In my case, it is more truthful to say that any resemblance to people living or dead is completely unavoidable, even though no character should be identified with a particular "real" person. We write about what we know.

All of the characters are made up. The exceptions are occasional historical and contemporary figures from the world of religion and scholarship. But they are not really characters, just people to whom my characters refer. The events in my characters' lives are also made up—with the obvious exception that they are engaged with the history of our time.

Finally and gratefully, some thank-yous:

- To the staff and management of the Ambassade Hotel in Amsterdam, where I began writing this novel and where, a year later, I completed it.
- To my editor, Mickey Maudlin, and my publisher, Mark Tauber, at HarperOne for their encouragement and uniformly helpful suggestions.
- To production editor Lisa Zuniga, copyeditor Ann Moru, and proofreader Annette Jarvie.
- Above all, to Julia Roller, an exceptionally fine editor and "coach" who helped me in many ways; whatever the quality of this novel, it is much better than it would have been without her.

she had put her journal and notepad into her backpack, wrapped herself in her coat, got into her Volvo, and enjoyed driving across town. She noticed that the snow of a week ago looked almost unchanged. The week had been dry and cold.

Her Guinness beside her, she wrote the date at the top of a fresh page in her journal and jotted some thoughts about the interviews she'd done, all of which had been a great improvement on the disaster with KJCS.

The only other hiccup had been a host who'd announced simultaneously to Kate and the audience that the regular host had called in sick, so he was filling in and had had no time to prepare. Then he said, "Our guest today is a professor named Kate Riley." Then, to Kate, "So who are you, and why are you on this show?" And she had thought, *Oh my God, this is an hour-long show.* But she had discovered that the substitute host seemed willing to go where she led him. So after she had given a brief introduction about the book, she started saying things like, "Would you like me to tell you more about the two stories?" or "Would you like me to provide an illustration or two of what I've just said?" Consistently and apparently gratefully he had said, "Oh, that would be good," or "Yes, please do." In the end, she had rather admired the guy for simply getting out of the way.

Her cell phone rang, and she frowned at it. Kate didn't receive many calls or even use her cell much. Her close friends were mostly of the Luddite variety who stuck to home numbers. She picked it up and glanced at the display. Geoff. She flipped it open. "Hello?"

"Hi, Kate. Are you at Murphy's?"

"Yes." She felt confused, even a bit annoyed. It was nice to hear from Geoff, but they'd just talked the night before. And if he'd guessed she was at Murphy's, where he knew she liked to be alone to write, then why would he bother her?

"I thought so. I tried your home phone first. Look, I don't know how to tell you this, but I think you should go home pronto and turn on Freedom News Network."

"What?"

"Yeah. One of the talk-show hosts, this guy named Bob Bradley, he, uh, mentioned you in his show. And since we're an hour later here at my sister's, if you get home you can see it for yourself."

"Mentioned me? Whatever for? Are you sure it was me?"

Geoff sighed. "Oh, I'm sure. Look, just go home and watch it, okay? You can call me afterwards."

"You're scaring me, Geoff."

"I don't mean to. I just think you should watch it for yourself. And then call me. If you want."

"Okay," Kate said slowly. She had never heard Geoff rattled; a kernel of fear formed in her stomach. "If that's the way you want it. I'll call you back in a little while."

"Ye-es." Geoff sounded slightly hesitant now. "I do think it's best. Talk to you soon."

Kate flipped the phone shut, crammed her things into her backpack, and rushed home, hoping that whatever she was about to see wasn't as bad as her intuition told her it probably was.

4

Kate slid into her usual pew three rows back from the front for the midnight service at St. Columba's on Christmas Eve. She normally enjoyed this vantage point, because she liked to be near what was happening, but also wanted to see people in front of her so that she had a visual sense of being part of a congregation gathered together. Tonight, however, she kept wondering if any of the other parishioners had seen Bob Bradley's show and were staring and whispering behind her.

The show on the Freedom News Network had been horrible. She'd never seen Bradley's program before, but apparently he always presented a list of the five "Most Un-Americans" of the week. The "honorees" were usually liberal politicians, but this week she had been number one.

Her cheeks burned as she thought about the unfairness of it. Brandishing a copy of her book, Bradley had gestured to her author photo on the screen behind him and said something along the lines of, "Kate Riley, liberal professor at a *liberal* liberal arts college, announced this week while talking about her secular humanist apology of a book that, although she professes to be a Christian, she can't be bothered to believe in little details like the virgin birth or indeed the gospels, which she passes off as 'beautiful stories.' Beautiful stories, indeed, ladies and gentlemen! One of the most sacred parts of our country's Christian heritage, a heritage that just about everyone in America holds dear. Where is your respect, Kate Riley? At Christmas, of all times! Shame on you!"

Kate had been beyond floored. She had barely managed to call Geoff back. "Where did he get all that? What gives him the right?" she had whispered. After talking it through, she had realized that he must have heard about her radio interview at KJCS. Perhaps those sermonizing hosts had sent him a transcript. Geoff assured her that she probably didn't even know anyone who listened to Bradley's inflammatory rhetoric. "Except me," he had added weakly. And she had thought, *Oh my God. What is this going to do to my career?*

She had called her publicist and told her she wanted to make a response, and the young woman had dissuaded her, assuring Kate that a back-and-forth was just what Bradley wanted and that he would only twist her words, that it was better just to let it go. If anything, she had said with a note of optimism, it would help book sales, because viewers would be curious about what was so awful in her book. And sure enough, sales had shown a bump over the week, although whether it was attributable to last-minute gift buyers or Bradley's show was hard to know.

Kate had thought of little else the past two days, her much-anticipated leisure time consumed by second-guessing and worry.

Coming on the heels of Burgoyne's strange comments in Murphy's the other day, she couldn't shake the feeling that she was going to feel some repercussions from Bradley's singling her out. The local paper had called her, asking for a comment, and she had declined, thinking that she might write a letter to the editor in a day or two, knowing that was the only way to guarantee that her words were printed in context and, she hoped, in entirety. She'd even stayed away from Murphy's, fearing that someone there would have seen the show and ask her about it.

But she couldn't let that ranting jerk scare her away from her favorite Christmas service at St. Columba's, the Episcopal church in Willow Falls. Kate had become part of it soon after arriving at Wells almost five years ago.

St. Columba's was a congregation of about two hundred, but on Christmas Eve and Easter attendance swelled to around three hundred, straining the capacity of the lovely stone church built over a century ago in, it was said, late medieval English Perpendicular Style. The rector was Fredrika Adams, a woman in her fifties who had been a priest for about twenty years and whose preferred form of address was "Freddie." Kate didn't think the diminutive name fit the strong, confident priest, so with permission she called her "Fredrika." Since Kate had joined the congregation, she and Fredrika had become friends, and they had dinner together every month or so. Kate thought of Fredrika's priestly vocation as the road she herself had not taken.

The usher appeared next to Kate, motioning her forward to receive the Eucharist. She rose and proceeded down the center aisle to accept the moistened wafer from Fredrika, who said, "The Body of our Lord, for you," with a smile. Feeling calmed by the familiar ritual, she settled back into her seat and watched the other members of the congregation file forward and then down the side aisles to return to their pews. Kate had spent Christmas Eve in this church all but one of the last five years. The exception had been two years ago when she and Peter had gone to New York City for Christmas. Over the years, she had observed that the Christmas Eve congregation tended to be made up almost completely of families or at least couples. Hardly anybody was alone.

Kate felt her solitude and it was okay—being here alone combined the perspective of a cultural anthropologist watching other people doing interesting things with the freedom of not paying attention to anybody's consciousness except her own. Tonight she felt especially grateful to be part of this community and also, she noted with relief, content to be alone.

The service ended with the hymn "O Come All Ye Faithful." Kate knew she could not sing it all the way through without her voice choking up with feeling:

O come all ye faithful, joyful and triumphant,
O come ye, O come ye to Bethlehem;
Come and behold him, born the king of angels.
O come, let us adore him, O come let us adore him,
O come let us adore him, Christ, the Lord.

Kate lost her voice on the second "O come let us adore him," then regained it, and lost it again in the final verse:

Yea, Lord, we greet thee, born this happy morning;
Jesus, to thee be glory given.
Word of the Father, now in flesh appearing.
O come, let us adore him, O come let us adore him,
O come let us adore him, Christ, the Lord.

At the end of the service, she stayed in the pew for a while, her head bowed, until she felt a gentle tap on her shoulder. Kate glanced up to see Fredrika's kind face, and her eyes welled up. Embarrassed, she quickly ducked her head again.

"I wanted to congratulate you, Kate," Fredrika said.

Kate's head snapped back up. "What?"

"I heard you were mentioned on Bob Bradley's show," Fredrika continued, "and anyone he singles out has to be doing something right in my book, so, congratulations."

Kate stared and finally smiled. Fredrika had a gift for knowing the right thing to do and say. It was part of what made her such an exceptional priest. "Well, you're the first to congratulate me."

"No one listens to that man," said Fredrika, her voice softer. "He's nothing but a troublemaker, trying to stir up chaos where there is none. But I am so, so sorry that his vitriol landed on you. You didn't deserve that."

"Thank you," Kate said again. "I appreciate hearing that. It's been a long couple of days."

Fredrika rested her hand on Kate's shoulder. "If you ever want to talk about it, I'm always available."

"Thank you, Fredrika." Kate stood and clasped her friend's hand. "Merry Christmas."

"Merry Christmas, Kate. Peace be with you."

5

On a Tuesday in January, the first day of the Wells winter term in her senior year, Erin Mattson shook the snow off her boots before going into Edwards Hall. She glanced at her schedule again, trying to be discreet. She didn't want to look like a freshman, but she'd never had a class in the religious studies and philosophy building before, and she didn't know exactly where Edwards 205 might be. She climbed the stairs to the second floor and walked down the hall until she spotted 205.

She pushed the door open, slipped off her duffel coat, and slid into a chair in the last row. *If it's not good, I'll just drop it,* she told herself. "Religion and the Enlightenment," taught by Kate Riley, was said to be a great class, although not by her friends in The Way, a Christian group on campus that she belonged to.

Erin glanced around the room. A couple dozen students, as large as a class got at Wells. There was a low buzz in the classroom; many of the students knew each other and were catching up after Christmas vacation. She recognized about half of them. In the front row were two women she knew as acquaintances, Fiona Amundson and Allison Wainwright, both senior religious studies majors. They had people over to their apartment most Tuesday nights to talk about religion. Erin had gone a couple of times, but still didn't feel entirely comfortable with them or, certainly, their beliefs. She recognized several people she had met there in the classroom today.

Across the room was Jonathan Maxwell, whose appearance couldn't have screamed football player any louder than if he had actually been wearing his helmet. Well over six feet tall and two hundred pounds, he was one of the team's stars, an All Conference linebacker, whatever that meant. Football was no big deal at Wells. Rumor had it that he was good enough to have played in the Big Ten or the Pac Ten, and maybe even had a future in the NFL if he wanted it. But he had chosen to come to this small college because of its academic reputation. In their few encounters at Fiona and Allison's, he had forced Erin to reevaluate her stereotypes about jocks. After a flirtation with geology, he had declared a double major in history and religious studies.

She groaned to herself when she saw Andrew Murray, the complete opposite of Jonathan. Slender—maybe skinny was the right word—he was about a foot shorter than Jonathan, had dark hair down to his shoulders, wore a beret, and sported a goatee. Erin found his self-conscious philosophizing annoying. She thought he tried way too hard to project the image of the "young philosopher," down to the worn copy of Nietzsche he liked to carry around. Plus he made no secret of thinking all religions and their adherents were misguided, and he was only too delighted to jump on that soapbox anytime religion was mentioned.

Then Amy Reynolds appeared in the door, seeming to hesitate. Erin was surprised to see her friend, but recovering quickly, she raised her hand in a wave. Amy smiled and headed toward her, claiming the seat next to Erin.

"I've never even been in this building before," Amy whispered. "I wasn't sure exactly where the room was."

"Me neither," Erin said. "I didn't realize you were taking this class too."

"I decided at the last minute," Amy said. "I needed to fulfill my integrative studies requirement, and this was one of the only classes that didn't conflict with my internship." She glanced over at Erin, who felt the unspoken question.

"I need to fulfill that requirement too, and I guess I was interested to see what the class would be like," Erin said. "I've heard Professor Riley is really good."

"Mm-hm," Amy shrugged. "I just hope it's not too crazy. Like, I don't want to have to bring my Bible and correct her."

Erin nodded, but felt her stomach clench slightly at Amy's words. It was nice to have a friend from The Way in the class; Erin had been sure she would be the only one. Most of the members of their campus group steered well clear of the religious studies department. They saw the religion faculty as liberals (at best) who encouraged skepticism and often seemed anti-Christian.

So although Erin was glad to have a buddy in the class, at the same time she couldn't help but feel that Amy would be watching her for signs of doctrinal slippage to report back to Peter and their other friends from The Way. She hoped it wouldn't interfere with her real reason for taking the class: the hope that Kate Riley would address some of the issues that had been bothering her lately.

As Erin glanced over the class again, she saw Fiona nudge Allison and whisper something, eyes on Erin. They were probably wondering what she and Amy were doing here too.

Two other students walked in the door. A guy named Josh whom Erin also recognized from Fiona's. He was walking with a girl Erin didn't know. She watched Fiona notice them too and frown as Josh placed his hand on the back of the girl, a very pretty brunette, to guide her to a seat. Erin had thought Josh and Fiona were together. Guess not. Erin really liked Josh. He was scary smart, but also seemed to listen to other people's opinions, something Erin appreciated.

The buzz faded as Professor Kate Riley walked into the room. Although Erin had never taken a class from her before, she'd noticed her around campus. Kate Riley stood out among all the tweed and the beards on the faculty—a woman, younger, tall and trim, dark hair just touching her shoulders. Today she was dressed casually, as usual. She favored jeans and off-white sweaters or white button-down shirts. Her trademark was red shoes—running shoes, ballet flats, open-toed shoes with low heels, hiking boots, even tall high-heeled leather boots—all red. And red earrings. Erin had seen her on campus during the last week of fall term in early December wearing Christmas wreath earrings with lights that blinked on and off. Today she wore large red hoop earrings to go with her red hiking boots.

It seemed to Erin that the guys in the class sat up a little straighter as Professor Riley entered the room, walked to the blackboard, and wrote, "Religion and the Enlightenment." Professor Riley turned back to the class and said, "As I assume you all know, this is Religious Studies 411, and this is the title of the course. Anybody want to get out of here because you thought it was going to be calculus?" A few students chuckled, but nobody left.

Professor Riley moved from the blackboard and sat on the table at the front of the room, her feet not quite reaching the floor, her ankles crossed above her red hiking boots. "I'm Professor Kate Riley. Call me whatever you're comfortable with: Professor Riley, Dr. Riley, Ms. Riley, Fraulein Doktor Professor Riley—though that might be a bit much. Or just Kate would be fine."

Erin and Amy exchanged glances. Even at a small place like Wells, calling teachers by their first names was not the norm.

"How many of you have had a course from me before?" About half raised their hands, including Fiona, Allison, Jonathan, Josh, and Andrew. "Well, you know what's coming next—and for those of you new to my courses, listen up. I want you to rearrange the chairs so that you are in a double horseshoe, with the open part toward me. I don't want any of you to be more than one row back from the action. And I want you to do this each day."

Erin and Amy moved their chairs, both choosing by unspoken agreement to be in the second row of the horseshoe. Erin felt a little out in the open, stripped of the security of the last row. From here she could see just about everyone, and they could see her too. She noticed that Fiona and Allison had both chosen front-row center.

Then Kate distributed the syllabus—fourteen pages long, the longest one Erin had ever received from a professor. The reading assignment for each class period was described in meticulous detail—what to look for, what to pay attention to, what to reflect about before class.

Then there was a description of Kate's criteria for grading papers:

Clarity: I should always be able to understand what you're saying.

Organization: Within the paper as a whole, and within each paragraph, I should always be able to understand why you're saying what you're saying in the order that you're saying it, and be able to see how it fits into the whole.

Economy: No "puffy writing"—I am an expert at spotting wordiness.

Comprehension: I want to see evidence that you have done the reading and thought carefully about the author's argument—what is the author saying?

The instructions on the syllabus continued:

You are free to be critical of the author's argument, but the price you must pay is to show me that you have thoroughly understood what the author is saying.

Erin shifted uncomfortably as Kate finished her concise comments on the syllabus, underlining her expectations and the course requirements. Erin was a mostly "A" student, but she had heard that Professor Riley was an exceptionally tough grader.

"Okay," Kate said. "I know that you each have different reasons for taking this course. Some of you are majors or minors, and some of you are here because this course satisfies the college's requirement for an upper-division course in the integration category—a course that integrates a number of disciplines in the study of cultural history. And we will do that by focusing on how the scientific Enlightenment of the seventeenth and eighteenth centuries has affected Western religion, using its impact upon the Bible and Christianity as a case study."

She rose and passed out some sheets of paper. "What I want you to do next is to introduce yourself to me with a brief writing exercise. I'd just like to know a few things about you and your previous study of religion. And because much of this course concerns the Bible, the second section says 'Me and the Bible.' I'll give you about ten minutes to think and write about what comes up. All of you, whether or not you grew up Christian, have some impression of the Bible. You might want to do this as a memory exercise—your early memories associated with the Bible. Or you may want to tell me what your impressions of the Bible are now. Or both. There are no right or wrong responses—simply your associations with the Bible."

Erin received her paper from the guy on her left and started filling in the blanks:

Name: Erin Mattson

Hometown: Kalamazoo, Michigan

Year: Senior

Major: Psychology

She paused at the next line, and then went ahead and filled it in:

> *Previous study of religion:* No formal academic study, but I have participated in Bible studies, read many books by theologians, and I attend The Way campus group.

Ah, the next one was an easy one:

> *Do you consider yourself religious?* Yes, very.

The last heading, halfway down the page, was "Me and the Bible." Erin hesitated again. Then she wrote:

> *Me and the Bible:* I accept the Bible as inerrant. I had a conversion experience here at a meeting of The Way. So I study it and believe that it is the source of all truth.

Erin wondered how honest she should be. Glancing at Amy, who was absorbed in her own paper, Erin decided to write what she was thinking:

> Lately, I'm not so sure. I don't know what to think of some of the passages in the Bible, like the passages in the epistles that say women shouldn't wear gold or braid their hair and should be silent in church. But I don't want to become a cafeteria Christian, picking and choosing what to believe. Yet it seems to me that everyone else is kind of doing that already. I'm really confused about the passages about homosexuality too.

Glancing over at Amy again, Erin considered whether she should scratch out that last part, but decided to let it stand. She continued:

> The Bible is very clear that it's wrong, but it also says clearly to love your neighbor and to take care of the plank in your own eye before pointing out the speck in your neighbor's, and it seems to me that a lot of other things the Bible seems to accept as just fine, like slavery, we all agree now are wrong. So I guess I'm open to some other interpretations.

Erin set down her pen, moving her notebook to cover her paper. Now she could just hope that Kate wouldn't ask them to read their thoughts aloud.

Fiona Amundson had just stopped writing when Kate said, "Well, that's the amount of time I set aside for this. I want you to get into small groups of four or five to share with each other what you've come up with." Fiona and her roommate, Allison, deliberately moved their chairs in opposite directions. They liked to join separate groups, so they could share with each other what was being said in each of their groups.

The group Fiona joined included Josh, the pretty brunette who had come in with him, Erin, and Amy. Fiona knew Erin, but wasn't sure of Erin's friend's name; she thought she was probably also from The Way.

After they had formed their desks into a circle, there was a moment of silence as everyone looked at each other. Fiona decided to take charge. "I'll go first," she said. "My name's Fiona Amundson. I'm a senior from Chicago. My major is religious studies, and my previous religious study consists of basically all of Kate's classes, plus Intro to World Religions and a few others. Am I religious? Yes, I'm definitely very interested in religion. As for 'Me and the Bible,' that's a little harder. I wrote down some of my memories. Sunday school in the Methodist church I grew up in. Stories of Adam and Eve, Noah and the ark, Joseph and his coat of many colors. Moses as a baby hidden in the bulrushes to save him from being killed by Pharaoh, the exodus and the parting of the Red Sea, Mt. Sinai and the Ten Commandments. David and Goliath. And, of course, stories about Jesus.

"And then, in middle school and high school, I started wondering about the stories in the Bible—did all of that really happen? Then here in the introductory religion course, I read other sacred scriptures—like those from Lao Tzu, the Buddha, and Muhammad. And I started wondering: What if the Bible was like those texts—full of wisdom and also the product of a particular time and place? I became convinced that it was." She shrugged. "Josh, you want to go next?"

"Sure," he said. "My name is Josh Patterson, and I'm from Minnesota. I'm a senior and a major in religious studies. I've taken several classes from Kate. Do I consider myself religious? Yes. I'm actually thinking about becoming a priest—Episcopalian, not Catholic. I don't think I could handle celibacy. But I'm not sure."

Although Josh hadn't shared anything she didn't already know, Fiona found herself dwelling on Josh's comment about celibacy. Did he mean that especially for her or for that girl next to him? Josh was Fiona's best male friend. Maybe the brightest person she knew—other than Kate, of course. And he was nice—attentive, a good listener, and worth listening to. There was nobody better with whom to have a deep conversation, intellectual or personal. True, he wasn't good at small talk and was very serious—to an extreme. Josh didn't use his brightness to make clever or playful remarks. Though he could join laughter, he was seldom its source. And, Fiona had become aware, he didn't dance—indeed, avoided it.

She often wondered if Josh wanted more from their relationship. He had never said so, but she sometimes sensed a longing. Occasionally she wondered whether she wanted more, but she wasn't sure. He was okay-looking, but nothing special—and every time her thoughts traveled down this path, she felt vaguely ashamed that she thought about looks at all. Perhaps the problem was that there was not much chemistry, even though she felt very close to him, even intimate. And more than once she had thought that if anything happened, it might spoil the relationship they did have. But she hadn't liked seeing him walk in with that girl, and her reaction had surprised her. Was she really jealous? If so, what did that mean?

Josh turned to the girl, and Fiona tuned back in.

"Well," she said in a soft voice, "My name is Amanda Collins, and I'm from here in Wisconsin. I'm a sophomore, and I still haven't decided on my major. I haven't taken any other religion classes. I guess I would say I'm more spiritual than religious. I don't really go to church. And the Bible? Honestly, I don't know much about it other than some of the stories I remember from way back when—Adam and Eve, and the guy in the fish." She seemed to be unsure about whether that was enough and looked at Josh, who smiled at her and patted her hand.

Fiona felt annoyed and also surprised by her feelings. But she set them aside for now. She was really curious about what Erin and her friend would say.

"I'm Erin," Erin said. "I'm from Michigan. I'm a senior and a psychology major." Erin didn't glance at her paper as she spoke as the others had. Fiona noticed that Erin had folded it in half so that none of her writing was visible. *I wonder why?* thought Fiona. Fiona had met Erin a few times around campus and had invited her to some of the Tuesday night gatherings she and Allison hosted. Erin had come a couple of times, but had never said much.

"Uh," Erin continued, "I haven't taken any formal religion classes, but I have studied the Bible and participated in Bible studies at The Way. And that probably answers the next question. Yes, I consider myself very religious. As for the Bible—" She seemed to hesitate. After a couple of beats, she said, "I guess I would just say that it's central in my life." She glanced at her friend.

"I'm Amy. I'm a junior, majoring in economics. This is my first religious studies class, although I've studied the Bible, read lots of theology, and studied Greek in The Way. I would also say that I'm very religious. And I believe that the Bible is God's word, that it is inerrant, and that it is the foundation of my life." She made this last statement with a slight air of defiance.

Fiona nodded. Neither Amy nor Erin had said anything that surprised her, but she still wondered about Erin's folded paper. She made a mental note to invite Erin for tonight. Fiona glanced at Kate and saw that she was reading a letter at her desk. Perhaps feeling Fiona's gaze, Kate glanced at her watch. She frowned. "Time! Sorry, that was actually a little more than fifteen minutes. Please pass your papers in to me. Let's regather in our double horseshoe shape, and I'll quickly give you a preview of what this course will be about.

"As you know, our subject is the impact of the Enlightenment on Religion. I presume that you all know in a general way what the Enlightenment was. It was the period of Western cultural history beginning in the seventeenth century that was marked by the birth of modern science and scientific ways of knowing. The Enlightenment is the birth of what we call modernity, which is still the dominant mind-set of Western culture, even though we may be moving into a new cultural era that we simply and vaguely call postmodernity. We don't know what else to call it yet.

"The Enlightenment—modernity—has pervasively affected how people see religion and the Bible and how the Bible is interpreted. It has affected not only those who have welcomed the Enlightenment, but also those who reject it. I think you all know that there is conflict about the Bible among Christians today. American Christianity is deeply divided, and ideas about the Bible—about what it is and how to read it—are at the center of the conflict."

As exemplified in our own cross-section of the group, thought Fiona.

"This conflict is not new, but is a continuation of what began in the seventeenth century. For a while, it was a conflict between skeptics and Christians, but it soon became a conflict among Christians as well.

"So that's our subject matter: how the modern worldview, born in the Enlightenment, has affected us—and how it has affected ideas about religion and the Bible in particular. On the syllabus, you'll see the central topics we'll be covering. Take a couple of minutes to look it over so that you can decide whether you want to spend this term studying this."

Fiona looked at the outline of topics:

1. The Enlightenment as the Birth of Modern Science
2. The Enlightenment's Collision with Common Religious Beliefs
3. The Enlightenment and Genesis: Creation and the First Humans
4. The Enlightenment and the Gospels: History, Fiction, or Parable?

The list continued, but Fiona was distracted by whispering. She looked for the source of the sound and saw Amanda leaning close to Josh's ear and saying something. *Damn, what's going on?*

Before Fiona could redirect her attention to the syllabus, Kate began to speak again. "There are a few more comments I want to make on this first day of class. This is a course in historical imagination. We will not only study but need to imagine a world very different from our own—the pre-Enlightenment world of late medieval and Reformation Europe.

"In that world, the Bible was still the foundation of life for most people. It provided them with a picture of the way things are. Its truth was taken for granted, including its stories of creation and the flood and early human history, its stories of miracles, and its overarching story of the relationship between God and Israel, culminating in the story of Jesus. Its ethical truth was also taken for granted; its laws were thought of as the basis of society's laws.

"There was little reason to question it, and few did. This way of seeing the Bible was the conventional wisdom of Western culture. In an important sense, it didn't take faith to believe that it was divine revelation of the way things are. Everybody did. To appreciate the impact of the Enlightenment, we need to imagine a world like that. And then we can imagine—and understand—why the conflicts that followed were so intense.

"And this leads to a second comment. This is also a course in the conflict of ideas. We sometimes think that ideas aren't very important—that they don't affect life very much compared to what we call real stuff. But ideas matter—especially the ideas lodged deep within us about what is real, what is possible, and what life is about. The Enlightenment generated a conflict of ideas—about what the Bible is and, even more foundationally, about what I will describe later as a religious worldview versus a nonreligious worldview.

"And finally," Kate said, "this is a course in critical thinking. Those of you who have taken a course from me before know that I say this at the beginning of every term. To cite one of the best-known sayings from Socrates, the founder of Western philosophy: 'The unexamined life is not worth living.' "

She continued, "If we do not examine our lives—if we do not examine the messages that we receive from our culture, the understandings and values that we got from our socialization, from our growing up—we will simply live out those messages. We will live our lives on autopilot. In learning how to think critically about the big questions, nothing less than our freedom is at stake."

Kate paused. "Well, that's it for today. I look forward to seeing you on Thursday."

The students gathered up their belongings and began to leave. Fiona watched Josh and Amanda walk out together and then hurried to catch Erin to invite her to that evening's gathering.

6

Kate left campus and drove to Murphy's. She settled into her booth as Arthur began to pour her Guinness and took out the letter she had opened while her afternoon class was talking in small groups. Its return address—Office of the President, Scudder Divinity School—had attracted her attention as she sorted through her mail, tossing, as always, anything that wasn't first-class. She wondered why mass-mailing marketers—or was it marketeers?—hadn't figured that out. She read the letter again.

Dear Professor Riley,

I am writing to you personally to invite you to apply for a one-year visiting professorship at Scudder Divinity School during the next academic year. One of our New

Testament professors is retiring at the end of this year. Rather than immediately beginning a search for his replacement, we will take a year to evaluate our staffing needs. In the meantime, we need a temporary appointment.

We are impressed with the reputation you have earned as a scholar and author. In addition, Martin Erikson, one of our most distinguished professors, speaks very highly of you.

The more specific details of the appointment and information about Scudder can be found on our Web site. For now, we want you to know that the appointment includes:

1. *A teaching load of two courses per semester. In each semester, one course will be our "Introduction to the New Testament," required of all students. The second course will be decided upon by the appointee in consultation with the Academic Dean and the biblical faculty.*

2. *A compensation package consisting of a salary of $72,000 plus benefits, moving expenses, a partially furnished faculty apartment at no cost, and funding for professional travel.*

The application deadline is February 1. We know this is only three weeks away, and we apologize for the short timetable. Our plan is to narrow the field to three finalists and then bring them to Scudder for interviews beginning the second week of February. Our goal is to make our decision by March 1.

If you are interested, as we hope you will be, your application should include: (1) your curriculum vitae; (2) a two- or three-page narrative describing your interest in teaching at Scudder and the courses you would like to teach in addition to the two sections of New Testament Introduction; and (3) three or four letters of reference that comment upon your scholarship and teaching.

If you have any questions, please feel free to call or e-mail our Academic Dean, Alberto Gomez. We think you would be an excellent choice for this position. If you decide to apply, you may be certain that your candidacy will be given the most serious consideration.

Dr. Leitha Debnar
President, Scudder Divinity School

Kate knew about Scudder. A progressive and quite prestigious divinity school—if not among the top five in the country, close to it. Founded as an Episcopal seminary and now with an ecumenical student body, it was named after Vida Scudder, a professor of English at Wellesley College in the early- to mid-twentieth century. Scudder was an activist Episcopal theologian and author known for her advocacy of the "social gospel" with its emphasis upon economic justice and peace.

A decade ago when Kate had considered becoming a priest, she had thought of going to Scudder. Then she decided on an academic rather than a priestly vocation. But Scudder still had allure.

A letter from the president personally inviting her to apply. That was very flattering, but then again, perhaps it was Scudder's routine way of doing things. She read the closing paragraph again.

The mention of Martin Erikson as an advocate had surprised her. She hadn't thought of Martin in some time. Then just the other night she had brought him up with Geoff, and now this. Did he really want her to teach at his school? The thought was flattering but also confusing. They had ended things rather abruptly. As a matter of fact, she had ended things by moving away, and just about all she'd known of him since then was from reading the dozen books he had written since she had been his student.

And she couldn't help but wonder if they knew about the Bob Bradley show. That seemed to have died down. She had decided not to write that letter to the editor after all, not wanting to alert anyone who didn't know about what Bradley had said about her. Come to think of it, no one at Wells had mentioned a thing about it today. Kate started to feel hopeful that perhaps very few people knew about the show, or that if they did know, they felt the same way as Fredrika.

Feeling cheered, Kate looked at the compensation package again. As uncomfortable as it felt to admit it, the money made a difference. She still had five years of student-loan payments, and her salary at Wells, though adequate, was just enough to get by. She did the calculations: the salary listed was $15,000 more than her current salary, plus free housing—that totaled about $25,000 more than her present income. Of course, going there would mean moving out of her house and storing all her stuff—or maybe she could find somebody to sublet. Catching herself, she said aloud, "Slow down."

Kate slipped the letter back into the envelope and turned to her journal. She decided to be brief, for she wanted to look over her students' papers before she drove home.

Haven't journaled since Saturday. Yesterday spent much of the day thinking about how I wanted to start classes today. Sunday was Epiphany Sunday—loved Fredrika's sermon about the voice from heaven in the story of Jesus's baptism telling him, "You are my son, my beloved," and her suggestion that this might have been a mystical experience that Jesus had. And her echoing an Old Testament passage: "O that today you would hear my voice." That's what I want.

Today, first day of classes. Liked the students. Lively buzz as they talked to each other. Nice to see a lot of familiar faces and quite a few new ones.

And an invitation from Scudder to apply to be a visiting prof for a year. Interesting, exciting. Need to think about it. I would need a leave of absence. Wonder if the department will feel okay about that.

As this was her fifth year at Wells, she would come up for tenure next year. Would that be a problem if she were elsewhere? And what about Fred Burgoyne's words about her scholarship being too Christian? What would he think if she accepted a position at a seminary, of all places? She thought about it for a few moments, then added "Soon to Geoff's for dinner," and closed her journal. Removing a folder from her backpack, she began to read her students' thoughts about "Me and the Bible."

After opening the door in response to Geoff's, "Come on in," Kate hung her parka in the entryway closet and walked into the kitchen. He turned on a gas burner under a large Calphalon pot filled with water.

"So, what are we having tonight?"

"Pasta," he said. "With a puttanesca sauce."

"Doesn't that mean 'whore's sauce'?"

"Yeah—but it's really good. And it's not a comment about anybody here tonight."

"That's good," Kate said as she sat down on a kitchen stool. Geoff pointed to his glass of wine. "Want some?"

"Sure, why not. How did your vacation end up?"

"Pretty good," Geoff said. "Two weeks with the family went better than I expected."

"How are your mom and dad doing?"

"Fine. You know, it's still hard for me to believe that they're in their late seventies. I was their baby—my sibs are in their fifties, and their kids—my nieces and nephews—are in their twenties. But my folks are still trucking along. They look older, but no health crises yet. I keep wondering when I'll have to deal with their decline. But so far, so good."

"And your difficult brother-in-law?"

"Oh, you mean Calvin. Well, he's still not sure that it's really okay that I'm gay. But he was decent. We watched some NFL play-off games together and talked about shotgun formations and three-wide-receiver offenses, nickel defenses and nose guards. So he thinks I'm kind of a guy."

"No discomfort about tight ends?"

"Didn't come up."

"Well, it's good to have an evening with you again."

The water reached a boil, and Geoff added the pasta. "Linguine," he explained. "Just a few minutes. How was your first day of classes?"

"Fine," Kate said. "Good kids—I always like the first day of class."

"Anyone mention . . ." He let his thought trail off, but Kate knew what he meant.

"No, not a word. I'm hopeful that it all blew over, that no one at Wells has ever heard of Bob Bradley and will never be the wiser."

Geoff grinned. "I hope so too."

"I did get an interesting letter." She told him about the letter from Scudder.

"The president of Scudder said she was *personally* inviting you to apply?"

"Yes."

"Sounds like Scudder is courting you."

"Well, maybe. But it could be just the way she writes letters."

"Well, I suppose. But I've never had the president of a college personally invite me to apply for a job. So what do you think? Are you going to apply?"

"It would be interesting." Kate paused. "Maybe 'interesting' is too weak. I think it would be exciting to be there. I'd love to teach seminarians, at least for a year. And one of my old professors from my undergraduate years is on the faculty."

"Who's that?"

Kate hesitated. "His name is Martin Erikson." Geoff's eyebrows went up. Kate plowed on. "I don't know if you've heard of him—he's not in your field. But he's written a lot of books that are quite well known in church circles. His dissertation was on German theology in the first half of the nineteenth century, and so were his first two books—one about Friedrich Schleiermacher, the other about David Friedrich Strauss. But his last ten or so are much broader—they're about what it means to be Christian today. Not devotional or inspirational, but theological in a user-friendly kind of way. And they treat the big topics—you know, God, the Bible, Jesus, Christian practices, Christianity and politics. I guess he's what some call a public theologian."

Geoff pointed the wooden spoon at her. "Don't try to get out of this one with a lot of theological dodgery. Martin, huh? He's the one you told me about last time, isn't he?"

Kate felt her cheeks flush. "Yes. He's that Martin."

"And he wants you to come to Scudder? I think you need to tell me more."

Kate still wasn't sure she wanted to talk about Martin, but Geoff was a good listener. Maybe he could help her sort her thoughts out. "Okay," she agreed. "Well, I took a course from him my frosh year—gosh, that's soon twenty-five years ago. And what I remember most is his excitement. It seemed as if he was encountering the texts he taught for the first time—as if he was discovering their richness and power and puzzles right along with us. I caught my passion for religion from him, and I took every course he taught in the next three years. Without him, I wouldn't be a professor of religion." She smiled. "And we wouldn't be sitting here tonight."

Geoff raised his eyebrows as he dished out the linguine and sauce. "I think you're leaving something out. Didn't you mention a relationship with him?"

Kate followed him to the table. "Nothing ever happened while I was his student. I looked up to him, maybe even had a crush on him. He had all of this excitement in his classes, and it was great being with him in his office. In my senior year, I did an independent study with him and saw him in his office for an hour every week.

"There was also a touch of melancholy about him. I wondered if he was happy. I couldn't tell. And he was married."

"Oh."

"Yeah." Kate toyed with her wineglass. "After I graduated, I stayed on for a year as a research assistant. I knew I wanted to go to graduate school someday, but I wasn't sure where and what field of study, so I grabbed at the opportunity to get paid for figuring some of that out.

"I didn't work for Martin, but we began spending more time together. We went out to dinner now and then and our relationship shifted; we weren't quite equals but more like colleagues, and I found myself growing more and more attracted to him. I loved our talks, the way he made me think, and I found that I was attracted to him physically too. He was a fairly young professor at the time, in his late thirties, though that seemed old to me then. And he was also married, but he simply never spoke about his wife, and so I just assumed that things were dodgy between them, or maybe over."

Kate paused. "Finally, one night I invited him back to my apartment and seduced him."

"Even then, the sex kitten?"

Kate grinned. "My idea of seduction in my early twenties was a couple of bottles of Guinness—Martin's favorite, I owe my love of Guinness to him—but it seemed to do the trick."

"Then what happened?"

"We continued seeing each other for a couple of months, but I started to feel more and more confused about what it was we were doing. I didn't know what was going on with his marriage, and I didn't feel confident enough to ask him about it. I told myself it was just a fling he was having, and so when I was offered a job as a newspaper reporter in Chicago, I just moved away with hardly a good-bye."

Geoff frowned, a forkful of pasta halfway to his mouth. "So you never really ended things? Did you keep in touch after that?"

"Actually not for a long time. I thought it was easier to make a clean break, so I didn't call or write him. Actually, it wasn't that intentional—I just kept putting it off, and then it seemed like too much time went by. That was before cell phones and e-mail, so it was a little easier to lose touch with someone. Many years later, about ten years ago, I looked him up and wrote him asking for a letter of recommendation for grad school. He wrote it for me and that was our last communication."

"It sounds from the letter you got today like he's been following your career. What do you think about seeing him again?"

"A little confused still, but also intrigued. It has been a long time, but he was important in my life, and I think I'd really like to see him again."

"Hmmm." Geoff leaned back in his chair. "Very interesting. So what do you think? Are you going to go for it?"

Kate paused, wondering if there was a double meaning. "I don't know yet—I just got the letter today. But yes, I'm going to explore it. And of course I have to ask the department. I don't want to jeopardize my job—I like it here."

"Do you think that might be an issue?" Geoff asked.

"I don't know," Kate hesitated. "I guess I'm not sure if it's okay to ask permission to do this kind of thing—you know, go teach somewhere else for a year and then come back. I mean, does that kind of thing happen very often?

"And maybe beyond that, I'm not quite sure what our senior colleagues make of me. They're pleasant enough, and they seem proud of me, but they also seem, I don't know, maybe a bit distant and reserved. So I feel like I don't really know what they're thinking. Especially after what Burgoyne said to me in Murphy's. I still don't feel quite settled about that. I certainly hope they didn't see or hear about the Bradley thing.

"But I guess I'll get an idea soon enough—I'm going to call our dear chair tomorrow and make an appointment to see him on Thursday. I'll keep you posted. But enough about me for right now. I can tell I've been doing all the talking because you're finished and I've only had a few bites. How was your first day of term?"

"Good. Met my two classes—my standard intro course and my new upper-division course on Engaged Buddhism—you know, the one we talked about. Full house in both courses—and I'm really pleased that so many want to study the way a politically engaged form of Buddhism has emerged in the last half century. That's exciting to see."

He shrugged. "Nothing else really stands out about my day. Oh—wait, I did hear a great opening line in a country-western song. A guy is singing it: 'I didn't know we weren't talkin' till I heard about it in town.' Isn't that great?"

Kate laughed and helped Geoff to clear the plates. "Like one I remember from a few years ago—a woman is singing it: 'When we wake up in the morning, why can't you remember the things you said to me last night?' " Kate thought briefly about Martin and how they had never awakened together. He had always needed to go home.

"And so it goes," Geoff said.

"And so it goes. And probably time for me to go. A stay-at-home writing day tomorrow. And I want to get up early so I can savor all of it."

"See you later, sex kitten."

"Ha-ha."

7

Erin pulled her jacket zipper a little higher as she hurried across campus to Bible study. She jumped up the steps and into the warmth of The Wayhouse, formerly a private residence just off campus. Everyone else in her small group was already there, lounging in the living room.

"Sorry I'm late," she said as she found a spot on the floor by Amy and pulled out her Bible.

"That's all right," Peter said. The campus leader of The Way, he lived in the house and led the worship services and all the small group Bible studies. "I know that the first day of classes is a busy one. As a matter of fact, we're not going to start our new study tonight. We're just going to talk about our breaks and pray for the semester ahead. Who wants to open us in prayer?"

Amy raised her hand. "Great," Peter said. They all bowed their heads and clasped hands.

"Father God," Amy began, "I just want to thank you for watching over us during our breaks and bringing us all back here safely. I ask that you guard us, Lord, this coming semester, that you grant us wisdom and discernment in our classes, that we are able to see and understand what is true and pleasing to you and what is falsehood. I also ask, God, that you just help us to bring even more people to your saving light. There are so many on this campus, Lord, who are still walking in the darkness. Please use us however you see fit, Lord God, to bring them to you. In your name we pray, Amen."

"Amen," the others chorused.

"Thank you, Amy." Peter smiled at her, and Amy blushed. Peter had graduated from Wells a couple of years earlier, and Erin knew that Amy, like many of the young women in the group, would like nothing better than to go out with him. He was handsome, Erin conceded, in a rugged way, with dark brown hair and eyes and a touch of stubble on his face, but he was a little too intense for her.

Now that she'd started questioning some of the beliefs everyone else in The Way seemed to hold, she worried about what Peter would say if he knew. As they went around the circle, everyone sharing about their breaks and their class load for the semester, she wondered, not for the first time, what everyone would think about her religious studies class with Kate Riley.

Erin tuned back in as Mark, a junior who was premed, finished talking about the skiing he had done over the break and asked for prayer for his heavy science and lab load this semester.

Amy was next. "I had a fantastic break," she said. "Right after Christmas, I went on the mission trip to the reservation, and we worked in one of the churches there, handing out coats, boots, and Bibles. I met so many great people. It was a little hard to come back, especially because I knew this semester would be crazy. I've got four classes plus my internship and one of those classes is 'Religion and the Enlightenment' with Professor Riley. It was just the first day today, and she was already talking about seeing the Bible as a foundation for life as an outdated point of view. And the other people in there—they just hang on her every word, like she's their god or something. Right, Erin?"

Erin, although she was sitting next to Amy, was startled to be brought into the discussion in this way. She nodded automatically, although in truth she thought Amy was exaggerating a bit. Even in this first class Professor Riley—Kate—had struck Erin as an uncommonly good teacher. She too had perhaps been guilty of hanging on her every word.

"You're in that religious studies class too, Erin?" Peter's thoughtful gaze rested on her.

"Yes, I'm taking it for my integrative studies requirement."

"And what did you think?" Peter asked.

"It was just the first day. Mostly we talked to each other in groups, but I thought it was okay."

Peter nodded, his eyes still on her. "Well, I'm glad to have a couple strong Christians in that class, so that you can respond to any half-truths or lies you hear and also help others who might be led astray. People like Kate Riley are dangerous because they claim to be believers, although frankly I don't know what it is she believes in. I don't know if any of you heard about this, but she said some pretty inflammatory things in a radio interview over the break—about how some of what the Bible says about Jesus is only parable, that the virgin birth never happened."

Some of the other members of the group nodded. "Oh yeah," said a junior named Todd. "My dad asked me if I'd ever had her in class. He said he saw her on a news show—something about being un-American."

Peter continued, looking at Erin and Amy. "For both of you, remember that I'm always here if you want to talk about anything brought up in the class. Erin, why don't you go ahead and tell us about your break and what you'd like prayer for this semester."

"My break was fine. Just spent it at home with my family. There is one thing. I—I don't think I want to get into it tonight, but I'd like to ask for prayer for discernment for a family situation."

Another member of the group, Wendy, who was writing down all the prayer requests to e-mail out the next day, frowned. "Do you want to give us a name or anything?"

"No, I don't think I'm ready to say any more. Just a family situation. I may want to talk about it next time." Erin smiled apologetically. "And for school, I need to figure out what I'm going to do next year, so I'd also like to ask for prayer for guidance for that decision too."

Peter didn't say anything more, but after they'd closed in prayer, he came over to Erin and rested his hand on her shoulder. "I meant what I said, Erin. If you want to talk to me about anything, I'm here."

"Thanks," Erin said, but she was fairly sure she knew what his response would be to her questions. "I'm okay."

Peter shrugged and turned away.

Amy caught up to Erin on the sidewalk outside. "What'd Peter say to you?"

"Oh, nothing. Just that he was available if I needed to talk."

Amy grinned. "Lucky."

"You know I don't think of Peter that way."

"That's what you say!"

"It's the truth."

Amy shrugged. "Whatever. So are you going to stay in that religion class?"

"I think so. Aren't you?"

"Yeah, I have to. I need to get that integrative credit this semester. Maybe we can study together."

"Okay." Erin hoped Amy didn't notice her hesitation before she spoke. She realized they were almost to the dorm where they both lived. "Amy, I've actually got another meeting to run to, so I'll see you later, okay?"

"Uh—sure." Amy's voice reflected surprise and maybe even a little hurt that Erin didn't tell her where she was going.

It was almost eight thirty and Erin didn't want to be late to both of the evening's meetings, so she gave her friend a quick hug and hurried off.

Fiona and Allison lived in a "senior suite" in the oldest dorm at Wells, a stone structure in faux Oxford and Cambridge style. They each had a bedroom, with a sitting room in between. The bedrooms were large enough to include a desk and study area, so the sitting room could be used for social gatherings. For a party, it was capacious enough for fifteen to twenty students, provided no one wanted to sit down. But more often, as on Tuesday evenings, they hosted smaller gatherings to talk about ideas, almost always about religion.

Fiona opened a bottle of cheap merlot, and Allison set out dishes of cheese dip, hummus, and crackers. In the fridge were their other offerings: a few beers, some sodas, cranberry juice, and sparkling water. The "regulars" would be there—Josh, Andrew, and Jonathan. And Erin had accepted Fiona's invitation.

As Fiona brought the wine to the low table in the middle of the sitting room, Allison said, "I ran into Josh this afternoon and told him he could bring Amanda if he wants to."

"You did?"

"Isn't that okay?"

"Well, yeah, I guess so."

"You guess so? Would you rather I hadn't?"

Fiona was silent for a few moments. "Well, you know she's only a sophomore, and I bet she's underage. I don't know how I feel about furnishing wine or beer to minors."

"Really?" Allison glanced at Fiona with surprise. "But that's never been an issue before. We've been drinking wine at these gatherings for a couple of years, and we just turned twenty-one."

"Well, maybe I'm just getting more cautious now that I'm not underage myself."

Before they could continue, the group began to arrive. Josh arrived last, and alone. Fiona wondered if he had chosen not to ask Amanda or if she had declined.

They sat on the floor around the low table and traded stories about what each was taking this term and their first day of classes. Then Allison said to Erin, "Fiona and I were surprised to see you in Kate's class today. Don't you guys—I mean members of The Way—don't you usually avoid religion classes?"

Erin nodded. "Yeah. I was worried that some of them would give me a hard time. They're not the biggest fans of the religious studies program and tell me to be on my guard around all the liberals. I think that includes all of you." She smiled. "They think the only reason to take one of the religious studies courses is to test your faith and maybe to know your enemy. So I tell them I'm only taking the class because it fulfills an integration requirement. I have a feeling some of them are still worried about me, though."

"What are they worried about?"

Erin was quiet for a moment. "That's a good question. I think they're worried that I might change what I believe in, and to them there's not a lot of wiggle room. Or that I might get confused. Possibly that I might leave the group. But I don't see that happening. I love The Way. I go to all the meetings—we meet twice a week—Bible studies on Tuesday evenings, worship services on Thursday evenings. And I love what happens there—people taking the Bible seriously and talking about what the Lord is doing in their lives. We sing and pray and enjoy each other.

"I love the feeling of community—everybody there is accepted. It doesn't matter whether you're good-looking or brilliant or have social skills or rich parents. We really work on loving each other. There's nothing else like it on campus. And there's a lot of commitment—they stand for something, they're not just searching."

"How'd you get started going to The Way?" Allison asked.

"I had a conversion experience at one of their meetings my sophomore year. A girl I knew a little bit had invited me, so I went. During one of the songs, a strange feeling came over me—a wonderful feeling, really. And then I knew Jesus was there—he didn't say anything, and I didn't see him, but I knew he was there. And so I said, not out loud but silently, 'Where have you been?' And he said, 'I've been with you all the time.'

"It was very powerful—and so I became part of the group. And they've really helped me to deepen my walk with Jesus."

Andrew said to Erin, "Can I ask you about your conversion experience? Do you think it was real?"

"What do you mean?"

"Well, do you think Jesus really was there?"

Erin's face grew serious. After a moment, she said, "I know that it felt like Jesus was there, and I know that the experience changed me." She shrugged. "That's what I know."

Before Andrew could ask another question, which probably would have been about the ontological status of Jesus and whether it differed from that of, say, Krishna, Allison said to Erin, "You said that you told the people in your group that you were taking the class because of the integration requirement, but it sounded like you have another reason for taking it? Is that right?"

Erin hesitated. "Well, I'm open to hearing some other ways of thinking about the Bible and about Jesus. I do have problems with a few of the things that my friends from The Way say you have to believe. You know, about taking everything in the Bible literally, about homosexuality being a sin, and that stuff about hating the sin, but loving the sinner. I haven't said anything to the group yet—I wonder if maybe the problem is with me—perhaps I just haven't understood yet what some of these things mean."

Fiona said, "The girl you were sitting next to today—I think her name is Amy? Isn't she in your group too?"

"Yes, Amy's in The Way. We're pretty good friends, and I mentioned to her that I was going to take the course, but I didn't know she was planning on taking it until she showed up in class. I don't think she's as bothered as I am by some of the things we hear in The Way. It will be interesting to me to see what she makes of all of this."

Josh asked, "So the reason you're taking Kate's course is not just to meet a graduation requirement, but to see how she thinks about some of these things?"

Again Erin paused and then said, "Yeah, you could say that. I am curious about her. The student grapevine says she's a liberal with religious convictions. I want to know what that's about. But I'd like to hear what you think. You're all fans of hers." She looked around at them. "Tell me what you like about her."

Jonathan, who had been quietly listening, began. "Well, she's a really good teacher—I mean really good. But if I had to name one thing, what I love is her passion—this stuff matters to her, and you can feel it. You know how some profs do the 'on the one hand' and 'on the other hand' routine, and it kind of ends with a shrug of the shoulders and the question 'Who knows?' Well, she does the 'on the one hand' and 'on the other hand' routine too, but then she becomes passionate about the difference each point of view makes."

"And you love her red shoes," Allison said.

Jonathan smiled. "Fair enough."

Andrew jumped in. "Well, you're right about her passion. But I think she sidesteps some issues, especially a big one. Sometimes she talks about God as if God were real, and my crap detector turns on. And when I ask her how anybody can know that, she just says something like, 'What I can tell you is how people have thought of God and, in addition to that, how I see things.' That seems to me to skip over some important questions. Like, does anything that people say about God make sense?"

Jonathan shook his head. "Oh Andrew, that's just because you've become a professional skeptic."

Fiona said, "I'm not sure about Andrew's point, but I agree with everything else that's been said. She's really good. And for me, she's what I want to be when I grow up. I'd love to be a professor and live in the world of ideas and books and do what she does. And she's sexy. I didn't know you could be both."

Erin spoke again. "Well, I'm sure it will be interesting."

They talked until ten thirty. Fiona and Allison insisted on a firm ending time for the group. They said that it provided structure, and it did, especially keeping their guests from staying much too late.

As everyone left, Fiona said to Josh, "Can you stay for a minute?"

"Sure."

Fiona said, "Let's sit down—but I don't need to keep you long." Allison disappeared into her bedroom.

Fiona looked at Josh, nervously looked away, and then looked at him again. "I want to ask you about Amanda. I saw you sitting together today, and it looked like you know each other. I didn't know that before Christmas break. So what I'm wondering is—are you guys, you know, an item?"

Josh paused. "Well, we got to know each other over the vacation. My folks and her folks know another couple in common, and the three couples rented a condo together in Colorado for the week between Christmas and New Year's. So we all spent a week together—Amanda and I were the only two kids. And," Josh continued excitedly, "I learned how to ski—I love it."

"So are you, like, together?"

"Well, maybe. Kinda. It's almost too early to know."

"Maybe? Kinda? Josh, I'm afraid of losing you."

"You won't lose me. We're best friends."

"Yeah, but if you start spending a lot of time with Amanda, you'll have less time to spend with me. And what if Amanda's not comfortable with you hanging out with me like we've done for a long time? You know, we see each other almost every other day. Is she going to like that?"

Josh looked down and was silent.

Fiona continued, "Have you slept together yet?"

"Nooooo . . ."

"Noooo?!"

"Well, no. But we've played around a bit."

"You know, she's too young for you."

Josh looked up at Fiona. "She's only two years younger than we are."

"Yeah, but at our age that makes a lot of difference. Think of all the things we've learned since we were sophomores. Think of all the things we can talk about now that we couldn't talk about two years ago."

Josh was silent again.

Fiona said, "Damn it, Josh Patterson. Aren't you afraid of losing me?"

8

Early Wednesday morning, Martin Erikson checked out of his small but classy canal-house hotel in Amsterdam, the Ambassade on Herengracht. He had been there for a week. The Ambassade had become his favorite over the last decade, during which he had visited the city almost annually. He stayed in the same room every time and thought of it as his "apartment" in Amsterdam, though it was only a large sleeping room with a fine old desk at a large window looking out on the canal.

Stepping out into the misty gray predawn light, he trailed his roller bag behind him as he walked several blocks north along the canal, turned right on Raadhuis Straat, then left on Spui Straat, and then strolled across the square in front of Central Station to catch the train to Schiphol Airport and his flight back to the States.

He had fallen in love with Europe thirty-five years ago. In his twenties, he had spent four years at Oxford. He had grown up poor and landlocked in the northern Midwest, living at home with his parents while he did his undergraduate degree.

But he had received a very generous scholarship for graduate work. And so, in his early twenties, he went to Oxford for a year. Then he spent three more years there earning a doctor's degree—a D.Phil., which to those "in the know" in the academic world meant that the degree was from Oxford, the only university that calls its doctorate a "D.Phil."

His time there had been wonderful—so much so that when he was flying back to the States after receiving his doctor's degree, he feared that the best years of his life had already been lived. He had loved the ancient colleges, the narrow cobblestoned streets, Evensong in college chapels, walks across Christ Church Meadow and Port Meadow, the latter leading to one of his favorite pubs, The Trout. In the center of the city, his pubs were The Turf, and The Eagle and Child, the latter known locally as The Bird and the Baby, where C. S. Lewis, J. R. R. Tolkien, and the "Inklings" had met weekly for more than twenty years.

His time in Oxford had also included exploring Europe. With his American scholarship, he had lived well, at least in student terms—he had enough money to eat out, buy drinks in a pub, pay for his books, and travel when he could. During the vacation breaks between Oxford's terms, he had headed to the "Continent," as people referred to it in those days. He had taken his small underpowered British car on the ferry across the English Channel to Belgium and wound his way through Germany, Denmark, and Sweden to Norway to spend Christmas with the part of his family that had not immigrated to the States—great-aunts and -uncles in their eighties and nineties and their children to the third generation. In subsequent trips, he had visited the south coast of Spain, Paris, Rome, Yugoslavia, Hungary, Czechoslovakia, and East Germany. It had been a rich time in his life.

In the last decade, his love for Europe had become focused on Amsterdam. His friends on the faculty smirked whenever he told them he was going there again. He had tried to explain why he liked the city so much. Its Old World architecture and canals. Best walking city he had ever been to, not only because of its beauty and flatness, but because there was hardly any motorized traffic—a few cars and taxis, delivery trucks, and official vehicles, but otherwise a city of pedestrians and bicycles and trams. Going for a walk was like stepping into a movie set for another time.

He loved its museums, especially the Van Gogh and the Rijksmuseum. Classical music in the Concertgebouw, one of the world's great concert halls, where he could buy a seat on the stage facing the conductor. Once he had been so close that he was seated ahead of the percussion section, the timpani slightly behind him and to his left.

The city had become familiar to him, and so going to it felt like returning to a place where he had put down a root. His colleagues would listen politely and then say, thinking of its reputation for pot and prostitution, "Yeah, sure." So he had given up explaining. Now he simply told them that he was about to go off on what he had begun calling his annual "urban vision quest."

In a way, that's what it was for him. Not that he had ever had a vision in Amsterdam, but going there was like going on a religious retreat for him—solitude in a time out of time.

Now sitting at his gate in the airport an hour before departure, he was aware of being anxious. As always, he had bought an economy ticket, but hoped to hear his name called for a complimentary upgrade to business class. It happened to him often on transatlantic flights. His airline liked him, or at least the million miles he had flown on it. But it didn't happen all the time. So he waited, hoping to hear the gate attendant announce, "Passenger Erikson—Martin Erikson—please come to the counter."

His name was called, and he felt relieved. Not just pleased, but relieved. Of course, it was very nice to be "up front," as he thought of it—more space, good food and service, a sense of being pampered. But he knew the anxiety he had felt and the relief he now felt were disproportionate to the occasion. His anxiety about being bumped up to business class was about more than comfort. He suspected it was a need to be recognized, validated, marked as "first-class," as "having made it." He wasn't comfortable with the thought—it sounded very unredeemed. The concept of being redeemed was central to Martin's faith. It meant to be set free from slavery and bondage, and surely being anxious about getting a seat "up front" was a kind of bondage.

He found his aisle seat next to an attractive and well-dressed woman in her forties. Everything about her, from face to clothing, looked expensive. After stowing his carry-on baggage in the overhead compartment, he settled into his seat and said to her, "Nice to be up front."

She looked up at him from the book she was reading and said, "Yes, I suppose it is." Then, looking back over her shoulder at the economy section of the airplane, she added, "But I've never been back there." Martin felt a bit like a peasant.

On the flight home, they didn't talk again. Martin ate, dozed for an hour, and read Philip Roth's novel *Everyman,* a seventy-one-year-old man's story of his own death—a masterpiece of aging and infirmity, memory and bafflement, letting go and oblivion. Then he began reading a book about the Nicene Creed.

By the time he landed in the States, caught a connecting flight, and then the shuttle bus to the airport parking lot, it was early evening and already dark. He began the hour-long drive home. He was tired—it had been many hours since he had gotten up in Amsterdam that morning. So, as he often did when he was tired and driving at night, he tuned the radio to a Christian station. He didn't want Christian music—that might put him to sleep. He wanted talk—perhaps a sermon or a Bible study. As he said when he explained why he sometimes listened to Christian radio, "It helps to keep the blood up."

He found a call-in show. A caller named Ray asked the host, "My question is about heaven. Will there be differences in rank when we're there? Or will we all be equal?"

Martin puzzled about why the question mattered. What was going on in this man's life that led to this question?

The host responded, "Well, Ray, the Bible teaches that we will all be equal in heaven, except for one thing. We will have different crowns."

"Different crowns?"

"Yes, Ray, our crowns will be different, depending upon our good deeds. Of course, we are saved by faith—but our crowns will be the result of how we've lived."

"So . . . will our different crowns make a difference in our lives in heaven?"

"We don't know, Ray. But we do know that the best thing we can do in heaven is to give our crowns to Jesus. We are to cast our crowns down before him around the glassy sea."

"The glassy sea?"

"Ray, it's right there in the book of Revelation, chapter 4. Some of us will have golden crowns, and we will cast them down before the throne of God."

"So we'll have different crowns—but it won't make a difference?"

"That's right, Ray. Those who have the most glorious crowns will give them to Jesus."

"Oh."

"Does that help, Ray? Have I answered your question?"

"Yes . . . I guess so."

"Thank you for your call, Ray."

Martin was bemused. He imagined people walking around heaven with different crowns, even as he also wondered how anybody could imagine that we could know things like this, or even think them.

A man named Gary called in and asked a question about an issue in his family's life. The host responded, "Well, Gary, let's see what God has to say about that," and then began quoting a passage from one of St. Paul's letters.

My God, Martin thought, *"Let's see what God has to say about that"—as if everything in the Bible came directly from God.* Not for the first time, he thought that American Christianity was so deeply divided that it was virtually two different religions, both using the same Bible and the same words. Well, it had worked. His blood was up.

Suddenly a throwaway comment the host made brought his attention back to the radio show. Had he said—surely not?

He turned up the volume, but the host was off on a tangent about submission within the Christian family. Martin could have sworn he had said something like, "Well, you know we can trust in the Bible as true, no matter what liberal college professors like Kate Riley tell us."

Kate? Had the host really mentioned her name? Whatever for? Martin listened for another several minutes, but her name was not mentioned again. If he had really heard it the first time. He must have imagined it. He had been thinking about Kate lately. Wondered if she would apply for the position at Scudder and perhaps be a colleague next year. He didn't even know if she was married. But even if not, surely a woman like her was in a relationship of some kind. He shook his head. He was being a foolish old man. Kate had left him behind long ago, and quite rightly too.

He drove his car into the parking lot under the faculty apartment building and took the elevator up to his floor. It took him only a few minutes to unpack—he traveled light. It was still only eight o'clock, too early to go to bed, even though the thought was attractive. He wasn't hungry—he had been fed twice on the flight from Amsterdam. Flying "up front" was nice.

Resolved to wait a couple hours before going to bed, Martin walked into his study. Though his apartment was comfortably large, he spent most of his time in the study. He savored the familiar space. Three walls of bookcases from floor to ceiling. The fourth wall painted deep magenta, with a bay window. Under the window, his desk. A table with stacks of papers and mail, some of which needed attention. A pair of dark brown leather chairs in one corner where he sat when he read. He had no overhead lights, only lamps, which gave everything a soft glow.

On the wall to the left of his desk, photos of his two children, now grown and on their own. A few from their younger years included his ex-wife. They had divorced not long after their younger child had left home for college. With the shared task of parenting largely gone, there was little to hold them together. After a year of marriage counseling, she decided to go her own way.

He lit his pipe. His study was virtually the only place left in the world where he could do so. The three airports he had been in today all forbade smoking. He was no longer permitted to smoke in his office at the seminary, which several years ago had proclaimed itself "smoke-free" with, he thought, more than a whiff of righteousness.

He saw the prohibition as needlessly restrictive, part of the health Puritanism infecting the country. What did it matter if he smoked his pipe in his office? Over the years when it was still okay to do so, no one had ever complained. Indeed, he had often been complimented on the good smell of his pipe tobacco and the olfactory delight of walking into his office. And how could smoking in his office create the danger of secondhand smoke? Nobody but he spent more than an hour a week there.

He recalled with amusement a story he had heard about a well-known senior professor in a nearby prestigious university who refused to obey the rule against smoking in faculty offices. He was admonished first by his department chair and then by the dean. His response was defiant: "What are you going to do about it? Fire a tenured professor for *smoking*?"

Martin admired his chutzpah, but wasn't willing to go down that road himself. Instead, he spent fewer hours in his office—six hours a week for student appointments and the hour between his two classes on Tuesdays and Thursdays. But he no longer worked in his office. His pipe was indispensable for reading and, especially, writing.

He wasn't sure if the seminary's ban on smoking applied to faculty apartments, but had decided to follow the "Don't ask, don't tell" policy. But he did restrict his smoking to this one room. And so his study had become even more his place in the world.

Martin poured himself a small glass of single-malt scotch, a Glenlivet. Feeling not quite awake enough to read, he decided to check his e-mail. He really didn't want to do much with it tonight, but thought he would get a preview of tomorrow's tasks. He grimaced as 283 new messages popped up. Not surprising really—he had deliberately done no e-mailing while he was away. He had been on retreat, after all.

He scrolled through, looking to see if there were any he wanted to read tonight. He deleted those that looked as though they didn't need reading and skipped any that looked work-related—tomorrow would be soon enough.

One of the e-mails said "Kate Riley" in the message line. He opened it up, realizing that his pulse had quickened at the sight of her name:

Dear Martin,

It's been a long time, but I wanted to send you a quick note to let you know that I received an invitation from your president to apply to be a visiting professor at Scudder next year. Her letter said that you speak very highly of me. I'm delighted to know that you remember me and think well of me. Thank you.

I would value being in conversation with you about this. Would that be appropriate? Do you have time?

Best wishes,
Kate Riley

Martin took a sip of his Glenlivet as Kate's name took him back some twenty years. The five years he had spent at Concord College, a college very much like the one where she now taught, had been the most exciting teaching experience of his life. Because his department was small, he had had to teach several courses outside of his field of study, some covering subjects in which he had never had a course himself. He remembered the repeated feeling of discovery as he read the texts he had assigned to his students, keeping one class period ahead of them. He had never had such a great sense of learning together.

They were also difficult years. His children were still at home, and he and his wife were always tired. His evenings were almost always spent preparing for class or reading student papers. Money was tight and dominated their lives more than they liked. He had found refuge in the classroom.

And Kate Riley had been part of that. He had first met her when she had taken his introductory course, in which they read

Peter Berger, W. T. Stace, Lao Tzu, the Buddha, Martin Buber, Paul Tillich, and others. A rich diet for first-year students, he realized, even more so now than then. But his students bravely soldiered on, taking it for granted that this is what it meant to go to a private college with an intellectual reputation. Kate later told him that that course required more time than any course she had ever taken. Nevertheless, she had enrolled in more of his courses at Concord and, as often happens in small colleges, they had gotten to know each other quite well, in the way that faculty and students can know each other.

He remembered her as both very bright and industrious, a combination not always found among students. Some bright students depended overly much on their natural quickness and ability to do B or A level work without working very hard. Not Kate. She read everything with care, wrote everything with care—never took a shortcut, so far as he could tell.

She had been attractive too, though she didn't try to be, indeed seemed not to know that she was. She wore loose, nondescript clothes—a lot of old slacks and baggy sweaters. She was a bit awkward, as if she were still growing into her body. Walked in a bit of a slouch, with her shoulders bent forward as if uncomfortable with her height or perhaps with her breasts. She made no effort to attract boys, and for the most part didn't. Only those with a perception unusual in young men noticed her.

Martin had noticed her, but he had always been careful to keep an appropriate distance. As an undergrad, Kate had always struck him as serious and—he wasn't sure of the right word—brave? He thought of their conversations in his office, which began her sophomore year and became more frequent in her senior year. She was willing to follow a stream of thought wherever it led, even when she wasn't sure she cared for the implications. She had once spoken of her undergraduate years as a time when everything came apart, and they had spoken semi-seriously of the malaise of epistemological anxiety. But she had never turned back.

Then after graduation she had stayed in town, working as a research assistant for one of his colleagues. Their friendship had grown. Stripped of the restrictions of the professor-student relationship, he had taken her out for dinner several times. What a pleasure it had been to talk theology with this intelligent young woman. It had been more than a little gratifying to spend time with someone so engrossed by his every word and who could argue and debate opposing views with such passion. Looking back, he could see what a contrast she had presented to his home life with his exhausted wife, who had been more interested (or at least it had seemed that way at the time) in the children and the laundry than in his ideas. So it was perhaps inevitable that one night they had crossed another line, from friendship to a sexual relationship.

It had surprised him. Though he had thought about it, he had to admit that he hadn't really imagined it would happen. She didn't have a car, so he would pick her up at her apartment and then drive her home after their evenings together. One night she said, "So, do you need to go right away, or would you like to come in for a cup of coffee—or maybe a Guinness? I've got a few in the fridge." It was about ten o'clock and he figured that his wife would be asleep, so what would another half hour or hour matter? So he agreed.

It was the first time he had been in her apartment. Though it was the whole top floor of a three-story house, it was like a large studio apartment—a small kitchen in an alcove with a dormer window, her bed in an alcove under another dormer, the largest space a living area with a small couch and a couple of chairs. Kate put on an early Tom Waits record, and they sat on the couch together and talked while they drank a couple of Guinnesses apiece.

Then she asked him, "Are you happy, Martin? I can't tell."

He didn't know what to say, so he said, "More or less."

"More or less?"

"I know that might sound a bit lame. Yes, I love my work. But . . ." He recalled not having finished the sentence.

He remembered her putting her head on his shoulder and saying, "Well, I think you should be happy. You're a really good man."

Then his memory became confused. Had he taken her hand? Or had she taken his? In either case, in a few minutes they were in her bed in the alcove, embracing and kissing. He remembered that she wasn't wearing a bra, and when he touched her breasts, he had exclaimed, "My God, they're so—" And she had said to him, "You owe that to my mom—she had a great body." And soon they were making love.

Over the next two months, they were together—how many times? Eight times? Ten? As he thought back on it, he felt confused, as he had at the time. It was the first time he had been unfaithful to his wife. Some guilt. He had been honest with his wife about having dinners with Kate, but after they became lovers, the honesty stopped. And he also felt embarrassment—she was a former student. There was an awkwardness about the disconnect between his passion and his intentions—he knew he wasn't ready to leave his wife, and even if he had been, he wasn't sure a long-term relationship with Kate would have been a good idea. There was the age difference—he was thirty-eight and she was twenty-two? Or twenty-three? And so, though he loved being with her, he couldn't do so wholeheartedly.

Then she had moved away, rather abruptly, to take a job in the Chicago area. She had promised to write when she found an apartment. But no letter came. He lost track of her. Had a vague memory of her working in journalism for a while. Then, about ten years ago, she had written to him asking if he would be willing to write a letter of recommendation for graduate school in religious studies. She had apologized for not being in touch, but said nothing about their past relationship. Of course he had been willing to recommend her.

Since then, through the academic grapevine, he knew a bit about her career. A Ph.D. in the history of Christian origins at an excellent grad school, a fine dissertation on the epistle of James that had been published, a teaching appointment at Wells, and, just now, a second book on the stories of Jesus's birth.

He also sensed that she had become more—again, he searched for the right word. Devout? He wasn't sure if that word had the right connotations. But she seemed to write not simply as scholar, but from a place of conviction. He wondered if something had happened to her.

Martin returned to her message and typed out a reply:

Dear Kate:

Very nice to have your e-mail waiting for me when I got home tonight.

I just flew in from a week in Amsterdam, so I'm soon to bed. And I know I'll be jet-lagging for a couple of days. But I do want to send you a brief response tonight.

Pleased to know that you are interested enough in the position to want to talk about it. And of course, that would be fine. There certainly is no issue of professional ethics—I am not on the search committee, and so I have no more official role in the process than any other faculty member—we each get to vote in the final selection process. Moreover, the seminary considers my relationship to you to be an asset, not a problem.

So, yes, happy to be of whatever help I can be.

All the best,
Martin

He read the e-mail again. Should he change the their "relationship"? He didn't want to imply the wror course, he hadn't mentioned anything to his colleague she had been his student and that he was highly impressed with her scholarship. He thought for a moment, then decided to let it stand. Let her take it as she would. He sent the message and turned off his computer.

Still only nine o'clock. Hoping to stay up another hour, he returned to the book he had begun to read on the plane, *The Creed,* written by Luke Timothy Johnson, a scholar whom he admired even though Johnson had been critical of some of Martin's books. In a section explaining what it means to speak of God as the creator of all that is in *every* moment of time, and not just in the past, of God continually creating, he came upon a passage that read: "The perception of existence as a gift given moment by moment by an unseen power generates in us a sense of awe and wonder, of receptivity and thanksgiving."

Martin took a puff of his pipe and a sip of his Glenlivet. *Yes,* he thought, *that's right. That's exactly right.*

He finished his drink and went to bed.

9

On Thursday morning, Kate finished her morning devotional time and then opened Mary Oliver's *New and Selected Poems.* She found one of her favorites, "When Death Comes":

When death comes
like the hungry bear in autumn;
when death comes and takes all the bright coins from his purse

to buy me, and snaps the purse shut;
when death comes
like the measle-pox;

when death comes
like an iceberg between the shoulder blades,

I want to step through the door full of curiosity, wondering:
what is it going to be like, that cottage of darkness?

And therefore I look upon everything
as a brotherhood and a sisterhood,
and I look upon time as no more than an idea,
and I consider eternity as another possibility,

and I think of each life as a flower, as common
as a field daisy, and as singular,

and each name a comfortable music in the mouth,
tending, as all music does, toward silence,

and each body a lion of courage, and something
precious to the earth.

When it's over, I want to say; all my life
I was a bride married to amazement.
I was the bridegroom, taking the world into my arms.

When it's over, I don't want to wonder
if I have made of my life something particular, and real.
I don't want to find myself sighing and frightened,
or full of argument.

I don't want to end up simply having visited this world.

She wondered whether she had thought of reading this poem because of the invitation from Scudder and her appointment with her department chair later today. Yesterday, as usual on Wednesdays, she had not been on campus—she tried to preserve Wednesdays as at-home writing days. So she had phoned her chair, Vincent Matthison, and told him briefly about the invitation from Scudder and that she wanted to see him about it. He suggested that she meet with him at eleven thirty today.

With an hour yet before she needed to leave for campus, she opened her e-mail, wondering if Martin had responded. When she saw his message, she felt an undeniable frisson of anticipation and even a little bit of nervousness. *What am I, twelve?* she thought. Determined to be businesslike, she read his response, thought for a moment, and then replied:

Dear Martin,

Welcome home from Amsterdam. Very nice to hear from you, and thanks for taking the time to reply at the end of a long travel day.

A quick message before I run off to the college. I am definitely interested. The first step is to talk to my department about it. I won't feel comfortable applying without first letting them know that I'm considering this. It's a small department—three tenured older professors, a man about my age in his second year, and me (I'm in my fifth year, and up for tenure next year).

I've made an appointment to see my chair later this morning.

Thanks for your generous offer to be in conversation. I haven't yet thought of exactly what I might want to ask you about. But when I do, as I almost certainly will, I'll be in touch.

Best wishes,
Kate

Good enough. She put Martin out of her mind and continued on to the rest of her e-mail messages.

At eleven thirty Kate met with her chair, Vincent Matthison. Like the other two senior faculty members, Vincent had been at Wells for thirty years, the three of them hired in the 1970s just before women and minorities began to enter the profession in significant numbers.

They exchanged some pleasant small talk about their Christmas vacations. Kate mentioned the radio interviews she'd done for her book. To her relief Vincent seemed to know nothing about the Bob Bradley show. Then they turned to the letter from Scudder. Kate emphasized that it was a one-year visiting appointment and that she would want, of course, to return to Wells afterward. She concluded by saying that she wanted Vincent and the department to be the first to know about the possibility and to talk with them before she did anything about it.

Vincent listened without expression. When she finished, he was silent. She was surprised—she had imagined that at the very least he would say that it was an exciting opportunity for her and perhaps even encourage her.

"Can I have a copy of the letter?" he asked.

Though Kate had not expected this request, she had copied the letter earlier in the morning. "Sure," she said uncertainly and handed him the copy.

He read it over and then raised his eyes to hers. "Are you seriously thinking of applying for this?"

His tone made her wonder if it was inappropriate, so she said somewhat haltingly, "Well, I was. I mean I am," and then added, "I think it's worth exploring."

Again Vincent was silent, slightly frowning as he usually did when he was pondering. "So if you do this, you'll be requesting a one-year leave of absence?"

Kate had wondered if that might be an issue, but she hadn't expected this to be his first response. "Yes, I guess that's what would be involved."

Vincent was silent again. Then he said, "Well, we've never had an untenured professor in this department ask for a leave of absence to be a visiting professor elsewhere. I'm not sure it's happened in the college as a whole. A leave for family reasons, yes, and for research. But this seems different.

"So I think this is a matter that the department needs to take up, and we will need to talk to the dean as well. I suggest we start with the department and talk about your request at next Tuesday's meeting. We have only a few items on the agenda, so there should be time for an initial conversation about this. I'll let the other members of the department know this will be coming up."

Vincent stopped, his face still impassive. Then, frowning slightly, he looked at his watch.

Kate took this as a signal that the conversation was about to be over. "Thanks," she murmured, restraining herself from adding, "I guess."

She left his office, now frowning herself, walked down the hall, and knocked on the door of Geoff's office, even though his door as usual was partly open. "Do you have a minute?"

"Sure—in fact, I've got ten, and then I need to go off to class."

Stepping into his office, she said, "Well, I've just told Vincent about the invitation from Scudder, and I couldn't read his response. He seemed distant, maybe even miffed. He said it's an unusual request for an untenured professor to make. Then that it's a matter for the department and the dean, as if there's a major policy issue involved and that there might be problems. So he suggested that we talk about it as a department next Tuesday."

Geoff raised an eyebrow. "Really?"

"Yeah."

"And?"

"And—I don't think I know yet." She stopped. "Sorry to blurt all this out right before you go to class. I mustn't keep you." A frown remained on her face.

"Want to talk about it later?"

"Yeah, that would be nice."

"Stop by my office after class? 'Knock me up,' as they say in England."

"Thanks, Geoff."

Still preoccupied, Kate walked up the stairs and into her classroom. She welcomed the students to the second day of class, asked if anybody was here for the first time, and did a bit of housekeeping. She took a deep breath. *Focus,* she told herself. *Don't bring anything extraneous into the classroom.*

"I think of the beginning of a term as a bit like building a fire. First we've got to gather and lay the wood, then strike a match in order to light the kindling, then blow on it for a while, until finally we've got a blaze going. Well, we're in the wood-gathering phase, which, to change the metaphor, I think of as framing the course—creating a framework within which the detailed studies we'll be doing make sense.

"I have a handout for you today. I've adapted it from a book by W. T. Stace, written about fifty years ago, called *Religion and the Modern Mind.* I'll read it aloud and then give you about ten minutes to think about it before we talk about it. It introduces the term 'worldview' and then invites you to imagine the worldview of an earlier period of Western cultural history."

> A worldview is a comprehensive picture or image of reality—a set of ideas about what is real and what is possible. It is a "big picture" of the way things are. In philosophical terms, your worldview is your metaphysics, your ontology.

Every culture has a worldview, a widely shared image of what is real and what is possible that shapes the life of the culture. And every person has a worldview, whether aware of it or not. We acquire a worldview simply by growing up within a culture. It is what we are socialized into.

Sometimes, by scholars, scientists, or philosophers, the worldview of a culture is explicitly articulated. But in most people, including sometimes the scholars who analyze worldviews, it works unseen, a dim background in their minds, unnoticed by themselves because taken for granted as "the way things are."

In the last four centuries, there has been a dramatic change in the worldview of Western culture. To see the scope of this change, I invite you to try to imagine the worldview that dominated the immediately preceding period of Western cultural history, what we commonly call the medieval period, the Middle Ages.

As recently as five hundred years ago, the geocentric theory of astronomy—the notion that the earth stands still at the center of the universe—held undisputed sway. Though some in the ancient world suggested that the earth was a moving planet, by the Middle Ages these ideas were ignored or forgotten. No one, at least no one of importance, from the rise of Christianity to the time of Copernicus in the sixteenth century, doubted that the sun and the stars and the planets revolved around a motionless earth.

This earth-centered universe was small. The heavenly bodies moved on a firmament, the upside-down bowl of the sky—for that is what the sky looks like to us. Beyond the firmament was the dwelling place of God and the angels and perhaps other spiritual powers. It was not very far away.

Moreover, the universe was not only small, but young. Estimates of its age made it only several thousand years old. Based on the genealogies in the book of Genesis, calculations commonly concluded that the world was created around 4000 BCE. Dante's estimate of the age of the earth made it slightly older. He suggested that it was created in 5200 BCE and that it would end in 1800 CE, thus lasting for seven thousand years—a Sabbath week of millennia. In the 1600s, one scholar calculated not only the year, but the day: Sunday, October 23, 4004 BCE. But these differences do not counter the dominant conviction that time, like space, was compact.

The use of the Bible to date the age of the universe points to a central feature of this premodern worldview: it was based on the Bible. The Bible not only provided information about the past—creation, the great flood in the time of Noah, the exodus from Egypt, the life of ancient Israel, the story of Jesus and earliest Christianity—but also described the drama at the center of human life.

As Augustine, the most important postbiblical Christian thinker in the first thousand years of Christianity, said in the fifth century: the whole of world history, from creation to the day of judgment, was a drama with three acts. Act one was the fall of Adam and Eve and their expulsion from the Garden of Eden. The second act was the coming of Jesus to atone for the sins of humankind that began with Adam and Eve. The third act would be the second coming of Jesus and the day of judgment, in which the living and the dead would be raised. The righteous, the blessed, would enter eternal bliss. And the wicked would experience everlasting torment.

Thus the Bible not only disclosed "what is real," but also what we should believe and how we should live. Finally, and importantly, believing this—that the earth was at the center of a universe that was small and young, and that the divine drama centering in the fall of Adam and Eve and the redemption made possible by Jesus was the most important issue in life—was easy.

Indeed, disbelieving it was difficult, for it was taken for granted by virtually everybody. Believing it did not require what we often think of as "faith." Rather, it was the conventional wisdom of the time, the cultural consensus, "what everybody knows." And there was no conflict with other ways of seeing and knowing—in particular, there was no conflict with science. In the Christian Middle Ages, religion and science agreed. Their worldview, their picture of reality, was a harmonious whole.

Kate finished reading the handout, paused, and looked up at her students. "Okay. Now, I'm going to give you about ten minutes to think about this excerpt and write a brief response. I want you to try to imagine that this was your worldview—that you lived in a culture that saw things this way, as our ancestors did not many centuries ago. You may want to read the excerpt again. What I want you to do is to try to imagine what your life would be like if you—and everybody you knew—saw things this way."

Some of the students began to write immediately, while others looked thoughtful. At the end of ten minutes, Kate put them in small groups of four or five and said, "Here's what I want you to do. Go around your group, and each of you simply report what you've come up with—you can read it or just speak it. No conversation at this point—your job is to hear each other well. Then, when you've finished your go-around, use the rest of your time to talk about what you've heard from each other—something you want to ask about, or add to, or something you thought of because of what you heard. Take about fifteen minutes."

When the fifteen minutes were up, Kate said, "Now let's do some large-group conversation. I want to hear from a number of you—and don't worry about repeating what you said in your small groups."

The students began to respond. One said, "It seems to me it would be a pretty secure world in which to live. Think of it—we are at the center of everything, because God has put us there. And God has told us how to live. You would know the purpose and meaning of life—there wouldn't be questions like, 'What's this all about?' "

Another said, "Well, maybe. But it occurred to me is that it might be pretty scary, you know, that there would be a lot of fear in it. I mean, how many people were confident they were right with God—that they were saved? And if you weren't confident of that and worried that you might go to hell—that sounds pretty scary to me."

A third commented, "Yeah, it would be fearful. And I think I would feel confined. Think about it—all these conventional understandings seen as the way God has set things up. Sounds oppressive to me, and I bet the authorities used it to keep people in line. It seems like such a narrow view, and you'd have to conform to it or be in deep trouble."

Josh said, "I get your point—but I'm not sure that what we think now is that much better. You know, so many people today think that life is about this world only—that it's all about getting as much as you can and enjoying it while you can. At least those earlier people thought life was about more than that."

Andrew responded, "But we don't and can't think like that. We know better—we aren't the center of the universe. I mean, isn't the worldview of the Middle Ages gone? Who thinks that way anymore? There's a lot of ignorance in it, but it's not their fault—how could they think otherwise? But we know better—isn't that what the Enlightenment is about?"

Fiona said, "But the Enlightenment is such a mixed blessing. Think of the twentieth century and all its nihilism. So much of twentieth-century art and literature is about a loss of meaning. You know, we don't have a clear sense of what life is about. We have to make up our own meaning, and that's hard."

There was a short pause. Then Erin spoke. "Some things about that worldview aren't that different from my own—for example, the Bible being at the center. But most of the ideas were so hard to relate to. Not just the science, but also the fact that everyone's religious views were the same. It was a stretch to imagine living within a worldview like that one—or probably to imagine living within the worldview of any culture other than our own."

Another student said, "Yeah—I got in touch with how hard it was to imagine seeing things that way." He paused for a moment, seemingly looking for words. "And, well, it made me wonder how much of what *we* think, and how much of what *we* take seriously, is the product of *our* worldview. And, does everybody see through the lens of a worldview? Is there any other way of seeing? And if so, what does that mean for how much we can actually know?"

"Ah," Andrew said, "epistemology raises its head."

Kate broke in. "In case epistemology is a new word for any of you, it's the branch of philosophy that deals with the question of knowing—how do we know? What's involved in knowing something? What counts as knowledge?"

Jonathan said, "Well, I think we can to some extent get beyond our worldview by realizing that there are other worldviews. At the very least, knowing about another worldview relativizes our own. For example, like Erin said, unlike the people of the Middle Ages we know that we live in a world filled with lots of views about God, and understanding differences like that can help keep our worldview from being an absolute." Now looking at Andrew, he added, "And that seems like at least a modest epistemological accomplishment."

Fiona spoke up. "I've had a couple of courses from Kate—I mean, Professor Riley—before. And one of the things I've learned is that we need to set aside our worldview if we're going to understand other worldviews, other times and places. I'm not sure where that leads—I just know that there are a lot of different ways of seeing."

A student replied, "But surely we see things more clearly than previous cultures did. Look at all that we've been able to accomplish since the Enlightenment—doesn't this suggest that we've got a better take on the way things are?"

Andrew said, "But you must know that our way of seeing things is just one among many. How do we know it's any better? Imagine a hundred or a couple hundred years from now. I'm sure that people then will see things very differently than we do now. There's no one true way of seeing—there are only *ways* of seeing. Isn't that obvious? And if you take that seriously, it means we can't really know anything for sure."

The class became silent again. Then Erin said, "Well, I think Andrew's talking about relativism. I belong to a Christian group, and we talk about relativism a lot—you know, that so many people today think that everything is relative. And we don't believe that. We think there are some absolutes, that there have to be. Otherwise, anything goes."

"And where do you get your absolutes?" Andrew asked.

Erin cleared her throat. "Well, we—the group I'm part of—get them from the Bible. We—at least most of us—think the Bible is infallible, because it's inspired by the Holy Spirit. And we think that if you don't think that way, then the Bible is just another book, and you get to pick and choose what you like and don't like in it. That's called cafeteria Christianity."

Kate noticed the girl sitting next to Erin, Amy, nodding as Erin spoke.

"So," Andrew said, "in a sea of relativity, the Bible is an absolute? The Bible is the exception?"

Again, some silence. Kate spoke, "This is a good place to stop and think for a moment. What Erin and Andrew have just been talking about is the central question of the course: What happens to the Bible and Christianity within the framework of modern thought? It applies to other religions as well, especially those that claim a revealed scripture. What has happened to the notion of sacred scriptures and sacred traditions over the past three centuries because of the encounter with the Enlightenment?

"And we will set this in the broadest context of the Enlightenment. It involved a massive questioning of traditional authority—religious, intellectual, political, and economic. It's no accident that the intellectual revolution of the Enlightenment was followed by political and economic revolutions. The questioning of traditional authority is the beginning of the modern world, the beginning of our world."

Kate led them through a discussion of the other readings. With about five minutes left in the class period, she said, "I want to conclude today's class with a poem, 'Dover Beach.' Many of you may already know it. It was written by the British poet Matthew Arnold in 1870. It's considered to be a classic poem about the change in Western culture brought about by the Enlightenment. So, listen to it in our context. Listen to its images; visualize them:

The sea is calm tonight.
The tide is full, the moon lies fair
Upon the straits; —on the French coast the light
Gleams and is gone; the cliffs of England stand,
Glimmering and vast, out in the tranquil bay.
Come to the window, sweet is the night-air!
Only, from the long line of spray
Where the sea meets the moon-blanch'd land,
Listen! you hear the grating roar
Of pebbles which the waves draw back, and fling,
At their return, up the high strand,
Begin, and cease, and then again begin,
With tremulous cadence slow, and bring
The eternal note of sadness in.

Sophocles long ago
Heard it on the Aegean, and it brought

Into his mind the turbid ebb and flow
Of human misery; we
Find also in the sound a thought,
Hearing it by this distant northern sea.

The Sea of Faith
Was once, too, at the full, and round earth's shore
Lay like the folds of a bright girdle furl'd.
But now I only hear
Its melancholy, long, withdrawing roar,
Retreating, to the breath
Of the night-wind, down the vast edges drear
And naked shingles of the world.

Ah, love, let us be true
To one another! for the world, which seems
To lie before us like a land of dreams,
So various, so beautiful, so new,
Hath really neither joy, nor love, nor light,
Nor certitude, nor peace, nor help for pain;
And we are here as on a darkling plain
Swept with confused alarms of struggle and flight,
Where ignorant armies clash by night.

As the students left, Kate noticed that Josh and Fiona walked out together. As she was about to gather up her notes, Erin, the last to leave, stopped at the table at the front of the room. "Could I come and see you in your office sometime?"

Kate looked at Erin and thought how much she liked what she had glimpsed of this lively and lovely young woman. Smiling, she said, "Of course—that's what my office hours are for. And if they don't fit your class schedule, I'm sure we can find another time."

"So, should I just come by, or make an appointment?"

"Either would be fine."

"Okay," Erin said. "And thanks—I'll let you know."

Kate took her notes back to her office and then walked down the hall to Geoff's office. She peered through the partially open door and saw that he was alone. She walked in, plopped down in a chair near Geoff's desk, and sighed.

Geoff took one look at her and got up. "I'm gonna close the door. Don't get to do that with students anymore, but it's got to be okay to close my door to talk to a colleague, even though she is gorgeous. Good thing I'm gay or there'd be stories."

Kate smiled. "Thanks. But I'm weary, and your flattery leads nowhere."

"So," Geoff said, "sighs and weariness. Talk to me. Or maybe you haven't had time to think about it—you're just out of class."

"Not thought about it? I can do two things at once. Besides, my class spent some time in small groups, so I thought about it then."

"And?"

"Well, I've figured out that I'm confused."

"Really?"

Kate sensed a whiff of sarcasm. "Okay, so that's obvious. And just so you don't think I'm a complete moron, I think I've figured out what the confusion is about. But I'm not real sure, so feel free to help me out."

Geoff was still, looking at her expectantly.

Kate continued, "I'm confused by Vincent's response, because it wasn't what I expected. I don't think I had a specific idea of how it would go, but I certainly didn't anticipate what happened. I'd always thought Vincent thought well of me. When I had my three-year review right before you came, it was very positive—he and the department said my teaching evaluations were excellent, that they were impressed that I had already published a book and was working on a second, and that students thronged to my courses. Sounded pretty good to me. So I thought, 'They like me.' And so I realized that I expected Vincent to be at least somewhat supportive and to say that he and the department would do what they could to make this possible." Kate paused. "Maybe I even imagined that that they would want to keep me happy."

"So you were surprised?"

"Kind of," she said. "Maybe a lot. But not completely. I've wondered for the past year—since soon after you got here—whether something has changed. They're pleasant enough, but seem more distant. Almost as if they're not quite sure about me. And after that oh-so-positive three-year review, that's been confusing. I think today maybe I saw that my uncertainty wasn't simply something I was creating. But I don't know—maybe Vincent's just being Vincent. You know how important procedures are to him."

"Yeah, I do," Geoff said. "So what's different in the last year or so?"

"Well, I've just told you. Vincent and the others seem different—no longer proud of me, but, I don't know, maybe like they're suspending their judgment. Like they're not sure anymore what they make of me."

"I get that," Geoff said. "But has anything changed about you? Not that it's your fault—I don't want you to misunderstand what I'm asking. But if you're right that they're changing their minds about you, is it just them or is there something different about you?"

"What do you mean?"

"Well, it's not that I've noticed anything. But I've only known you for just over a year—about, let's see, seventeen months now. So you're the Kate I know. But I'm just wondering if that's the same Kate our colleagues thought they knew. Do you know what I mean?"

"Yeah, I think I do."

10

As Kate walked into class on Tuesday, Erin noticed that she was wearing "dress up" clothes—her usual crisp white button-down shirt, but with a knee-length charcoal pencil skirt and low heels. Red, of course. In front of her in the double horseshoe, Fiona whispered to Allison, "Look how she's dressed—I bet she has a meeting today."

"I want to begin today with a poem," Kate said. "It's by Naomi Shihab Nye, and it's called 'Missing the Boat.'"

It is not so much that the boat passed
and you failed to notice it.
It is more like the boat stopping
directly outside your bedroom window,

the captain blowing the signal-horn,
the band playing a rousing march.
The boat shouted, waving bright flags,
its silver hull blinding in the sunlight.
But you had this idea you were going by train.
You kept checking the time-tables,
digging for tracks.
And the boat got tired of you,
so tired it pulled up the anchor
and raised the ramp.
The boat bobbed into the distance
shrinking like a toy—
at which point you probably realized
you had always loved the sea.

Erin closed her eyes. She loved the imagery of the boat outside her window, horn blowing and flags waving, but in the end the poem was so sad—regret, a missed opportunity. Was the poem talking about a chance to expand her faith, to listen to some other ways of believing? It did feel daunting to set out on a journey like that, especially when it felt as though her friends really wanted her to stay with them and wait for the train. Was it possible she could miss her chance? Could she become so set in her group's way of doing things that she could never think critically about their ideas again? A sense of unease settling in her stomach, she opened her eyes to find Kate's gaze resting on her. Erin's cheeks grew warm. She felt as if Kate had caught her taking the poem too personally.

But Kate just smiled briefly and addressed the class. "Now, to today's topic. What your readings for today are about, and what I want us to talk about, is the cumulative understanding of religion that has emerged in the academic study of it since the Enlightenment.

"I want to provide you with an advance summary before we

turn to discussing the way your reading develops these points. I've put it on a handout to make it easier for you to follow along. I think the language is clear, but I know it's also dense—each paragraph carries a lot of intellectual freight. So listen up, or read along."

> The basic claim: religions are human constructions. They are human historical products. In one sense, what this means is obvious: all of the world's religions emerged in particular times and places. As products of those times and places, of those cultures, they of course used the language and symbols of those cultures, even as they often challenged the cultures in which they originated. But they nevertheless are historical and cultural products—in short, human constructions.
>
> Moreover, religions address obvious human needs: our desire for explanations, our yearning for security and protection, our anxiety about death, our need for social order and social control, and our desire for meaning. Thus, from an Enlightenment perspective, it's not only that religions look like human constructions because they reflect particular times and places, but it also looks like these constructions have been shaped to serve central human needs.
>
> It is this cumulative understanding of religions as human constructions that most differentiates the modern period from the premodern period. Prior to the Enlightenment and modernity, the divine origin of religion was taken for granted. Christianity, Judaism, and Islam all saw their sacred scriptures as divine revelation, as coming from God in a way that no other writings had. Christians, Jews, and Muslims agreed: each saw its own scriptures as a divine product. This is why their scriptures and their religions had authority—they were not human products, not human constructions, but divine revelation.
>
> The conflict between these two ways of seeing is part of what is often called the conflict between reason and revelation—a conflict about how we know things, and a conflict about authority. Should epistemology and authority be grounded in reason and investigation? Or should they be grounded in sacred scripture and tradition?

"So, that's what I want you to see today: the cumulative understanding of religion within an Enlightenment framework, and how that comes into conflict with pre-Enlightenment understandings of religion. Your readings for today talk about this. So, to begin our conversation, I'm going to ask you to take five minutes to respond to two questions. If you have time, say something about both—but do at least one.

"The first is: What do you make of the central argument—that religions are human constructions? How persuasive is the argument? Any parts of it that you want to comment on or ask about? And the second one: What do you make of the conflict between this and premodern ways of seeing religions? Have you thought about it before? Do you see it around you? How important does it seem to you? Is it illuminating to be aware of it? So take five minutes to think and write about one or both of those."

Erin stared at her notebook. Her sense of unease had returned. The idea of seeing Christianity as a human construction unsettled, maybe even frightened, her. If Christianity was just something people had made up to explain the world around them, then what did that mean for her faith? What was the point? Did that mean there was no heaven? No point in praying? That her relationship with Jesus was all in her head? It seemed to take all that she thought she understood about the world and put it on its head. And that was what had happened to people during the Enlightenment, she knew. But it didn't make it feel any less scary or challenging.

It made her remember one of the things that was so great about believing everything they taught in The Way. It was so reassuring to have everything spelled out, to know that she was saved and to be grateful for it. She hadn't even minded how they put everyone in categories of us (members of the group, those who were saved) and them (those who weren't Christian or didn't believe the right things and weren't saved). At least, she hadn't really minded until she'd realized that her parents and now her brother were definitely in the latter category, according to her friends in The Way.

She realized she was growing increasingly tired of the warlike mentality their categories seemed to foster. They were always praying to bring more people into their camp. They didn't seem to want to listen to others' points of view, except to try to convert them to their own way of seeing things. Even Peter's reaction to Erin and Amy's taking Kate's class—he had acted as if they were there as soldiers to protect the other students from Kate's point of view. Something in Erin was starting to rebel. She didn't see Kate as the enemy. She liked Kate and the way she made her think. She wanted to know more about how you could be a believing Christian and not see the Bible as literal truth, not divide the world into us and them anymore.

Erin started when Kate called them to move into their small groups. She hadn't managed to put anything down on her paper. But she moved her chair obediently, noticing that Amy moved in the same direction again. Great. She'd have to watch what she said again. She wished Amy would join another group just once so that she could talk more freely.

At three thirty Kate walked into the department's seminar room, a handsome high-ceilinged room with books on three walls and tall narrow leaded-glass windows above walnut paneling looking out on one of the college's snow-covered playing fields. Paul Messer and Geoff were already there, seated on one side of the long table and talking about an article they had read about similarities between the Buddha and Jesus. Kate sat down across from them and, as the three of them exchanged greetings, Vincent Matthison and Fred Burgoyne entered together.

Over the weekend, she had continued to puzzle about Vincent's response and considered what she knew about him and the other two senior faculty. She had realized some time ago that she knew them only in the context of departmental activities. Their social circles didn't overlap, except for the large faculty gatherings hosted at the president's house twice a year.

But she knew that they had been not only colleagues for three decades, but friends. She rather admired that—she had known more than one man who said he didn't really have any male friends. Couples, yes, but not a male friend you'd see on your own, the way women do with their friends. And she had heard of more than one department in which rivalries and antagonisms were rife. But they got along. And they seemed like nice guys.

Like faculty in small departments generally, each taught a variety of courses even as each had his own specialty. Fred Burgoyne taught mainly philosophy of religion classes, although his latest interest seemed to be the question of whether Jesus had ever existed.

Vincent's graduate work had been in theology, and his thesis was on the "death of God" movement that had enough impact in the 1960s to make the cover of *Time* magazine. He retained an interest in it, seeing it as an epiphany of a dramatic change in Western culture. Kate valued his cultural insights—something of major significance did happen to the notion of God in the twentieth century. But she thought they saw the content and meaning of the epiphany quite differently. They had sometimes talked about it, rather enjoyably, Kate thought.

Paul Messer's area was world religions. He taught courses on non-Western religions and Islam. Though he was trained as a historian of religions, his interest in religion was more philosophical. His thesis had focused on the relationship between monotheism and polytheism in Hinduism. His passion was "the one and the many." Of the three, Kate felt as though she knew Paul least well. Within the department, he was a peacemaker, a conciliator—not that peace or reconciliation often needed to be made. But it was hard to know what he himself thought.

Students seemed to appreciate them. Majors regularly talked about what a "good department" it was. Only a couple of times in almost five years had she heard a student make an unfavorable remark about one or another of them.

Her attention came back to the present as Vincent sat down at the head of the table, with Fred to his right. Vincent smiled and said affably, "Well, we're all here, so let's begin. Always nice to be together again after a vacation. And our agenda is quite short—some announcements, a few housekeeping details to take care of, and then some discussion about the possibility that Kate may request a leave of absence for next year. With any luck, we can be done in less than an hour."

After he had moved quickly through the announcements and housekeeping, Vincent said, "It's time now to consider Kate's"—he paused—"I guess 'opportunity' is the best word. I've told you that she has been invited to apply for a one-year appointment as a visiting professor at"—here he looked at his notes—"Scudder Divinity School. And, quite rightly, she thought the first step was to talk this over with us.

"I've already told Kate that a request for leave by an untenured professor may be irregular—that there's no precedent in the department, and maybe not in the college as a whole. I talked to Dean Robinson yesterday, and she doesn't know of any. Of course, she's only been here for two years, as she pointed out, so she's not certain about what may have happened in the past. So she's going to check and get back to me. And there's also the question of what we as a department think about this. So, even though we don't know if this is a real possibility, it might be good to talk about it and see where we are—whether it seems a good idea to us. So I invite your comments. And," Vincent added as he gestured at Fred and Paul, "one more thing. I think it's only fair to mention that the three of us who are tenured have had some informal conversation since you spoke to me last Thursday, Kate. I'm sure that's not unexpected."

After a brief silence, Fred spoke. "Vincent, I think you're right to call this an opportunity for Kate and also a compliment. Depending on how we read the phrase in the letter 'I am personally inviting you to apply,' it sounds like a recognition of Kate from beyond our walls, and I think you should feel good about that, Kate, whatever happens.

"Vincent is also right, of course, that, given that we know of no precedent, it may be irregular for an untenured professor to receive a leave to teach elsewhere. But I think the issue isn't simply whether Dean Robinson might allow this, but whether we as a department think this is a good idea. I think we need to take seriously that sometimes there are good reasons why something hasn't happened before.

"I can think of at least two reasons why a department might not wish to grant a leave under these circumstances. First, doing so would involve the department—in this case, us—in the time and expense of securing a one-year replacement. We would need to advertise, do interviews, bring candidates to campus. It's a lot of work.

"Moreover, one-year replacements aren't usually as good as the person they replace. If they were, they'd have a job. And even if the replacement should be a good teacher, it takes a year or more to learn what our students are like. And we need to think of our students."

Kate winced. She knew that Fred would not be saying this unless he had gone over it before with Vincent. Had they already made up their minds not to let her do this?

Vincent looked at Kate and added, "There may be a further

issue—a minor one, I think, but one we need to consider. Next year will be your sixth year here, and of course that means it's the year for your tenure decision. Since we spoke last Thursday, I've been puzzling about what your being away might mean for that process. Do we do the tenure evaluation in your absence? That seems a bit awkward, and maybe not even politically wise—after all, the college personnel and tenure committee ultimately decides on whatever we recommend, and they might consider it odd that the candidate for tenure isn't even here. The other option would be to delay the tenure decision for a year, and that would probably be possible. But as I say, it's another detail to be considered."

He paused and steepled his fingers. "And Kate, I debated about whether to bring this up today, but since this is a small department and we're all friendly colleagues here, I want to bring your attention to a potential complication with your being granted tenure." He paused again. "I gather that comments you made in some radio interviews over the holiday garnered some, uh, should I say, considerable media attention. And that you were even, uh, mentioned on a right-wing news show. I don't know if you're even aware of this, Kate, but some parents who saw this news program have begun circulating an online petition entitled 'Deny Kate Riley Tenure.' "

Kate's mouth dropped open. This was the last thing she'd expected to hear today. "What?!"

Vincent nodded gravely. "Yes, it seems that some of our Wells parents feel that it is not appropriate for a professor in the religious studies department to be overtly Christian. Not all of our students are Christian, you know. Indeed, I suspect that fewer than half are."

Kate couldn't have been more shocked if he'd just opened his jacket to reveal four sticks of dynamite. Geoff looked as startled as she felt. It hadn't even occurred to Kate that anyone would react in that way to her statements. She'd assumed that if anyone had any kind of a reaction, it would be from a perspective similar to Bob Bradley's—that she was some kind of a liberal heretic. She'd expected the department to fully support her on that front; they'd never stand for something that smacked of censorship. But for parents to complain that her faith was a problem for the classroom . . . she'd never seen that coming. And it was exactly the kind of thing the tenured members of the department would shy away from. Kate felt she was getting fired on from all sides.

Fred leaned forward. "Of course, tenure is a decision to be made strictly within the department. Yet I think the parents have a point that is worth discussing. Kate, I've heard that you've started thinking of a new book, even though you just recently published your second one. Very impressive. I wonder if you could tell us a bit about it."

Kate blinked. She wanted to ask more about the petition, but at the same time she didn't care to discuss it any further in front of the whole committee. What was Vincent thinking, waiting until they were gathered as a group before bringing it up? And now Fred wanted her to present her new book idea? *Kick me while I'm down, why don't you?*

"Well," she said, "it's about C. S. Lewis." She knew that Fred wouldn't like that. He didn't care for Lewis—thought his arguments were cheap and manipulative. Yet she believed her idea was a strong one, so she directed her words primarily to Vincent, Paul, and Geoff. "It's about his theological development—I think there's a major theological shift between the early Lewis and the later Lewis. A number of biographers and scholars of Lewis have noted such a change, and I want to explore the significance of that change."

"And why does this matter?" Fred asked.

Am I on trial here? she thought. But Kate answered his question with the attention it probably didn't deserve. "Well, it matters because the early Lewis, the one most people know, is a hero for many conservative Christians. Of course, Lewis is also well known for *The Chronicles of Narnia* and his science-fiction novels, but I'm talking about the overtly theological Lewis. Lewis had a brilliant and creative mind, and the early Lewis used his mental powers to make a tight rational case for what he saw as traditional Christianity. We see this in the books he wrote in his forties, like *Mere Christianity, Miracles, The Problem of Pain, The Screwtape Letters,* all of them widely read by conservative Christians today.

"But I think those scholars who perceive a significant change in his later books are right—*Surprised by Joy, The Four Loves, Until We Have Faces,* and *A Grief Observed* were all written in the last decade of his life, and they're quite different from his earlier books. Indeed, in the last of them, *A Grief Observed,* he refers to his earlier theological construction as a house of cards that God had blown down."

Vincent cut in. "And, to return to Fred's question, why does this matter? You've said that other writers have made this case. So why another book on it?"

Now Vincent's challenging me too? Kate struggled to keep her tone even. "I see it as potentially a bridge book. I want to put the later Lewis in conversation with the earlier Lewis. I think this conversation is going on in the minds of many thoughtful Christians, and I think Lewis's development can be helpful to Christians for whom the confident affirmations of his early books no longer work very well—people whose lives are leading them through a similar transition."

Fred spoke again. "So it's a book for Christians?"

Kate hesitated. Should she say, "Yes—and so?" Or was it a jab that she should parry?

Before she could reply, Vincent intervened in a gentle voice. "I think what Fred is getting at is that we have a concern that your work is perhaps becoming too broad and perhaps too Christian. Your book on James was a superb example of scholarship. Your book on the stories of Jesus's birth in Matthew and Luke was, as we say, more popular—really written for a general audience and thus not filtered through peer review. This popular focus has resulted in this unfortunate publicity problem for the department and the college. And now a book on C. S. Lewis . . . We fear that this might suggest to some people a lack of, shall we say, scholarly focus—that you are broad, but not deep. We live in an age when academic specialization is valued, as you know.

"Now," Vincent continued, "if, in addition to a book on Lewis for Christians, you were to spend next year as a visiting professor in a seminary, it might open you up to further criticism of the kind voiced in this unfortunate petition. It might also suggest to some people in the college that your heart is really elsewhere—in the church and not here in the academy."

Paul broke in, "Would it be accurate to say, Vincent and Fred, that our concerns are about the possible effects of her going on leave for her professional future? That our concern is really about what's best for her?"

Vincent said, "Well, of course." He looked slightly irritated, and Kate wondered why. Because it was yet one more of Paul's habitual conciliatory interjections, or because he felt put on the spot? To Kate, Paul's words only served to point out just how much the discussion had felt like a personal attack.

Vincent continued, "As I mentioned, Fred and Paul and I have talked about this. And what we've been doing in this meeting is simply naming the issues that occurred to us and that we think need to be thought through. Nothing we've said should be heard as pointing toward disapproval. We intend it as counsel from three older academics to a younger one."

Geoff still looked puzzled. He hadn't jumped in to defend Kate, but she hadn't expected him to. He obviously hadn't been privy to the conversations the others had had over the weekend, and as the most junior member of the faculty, he usually deferred to the others in their meetings.

He cleared his throat. "I came to this meeting expecting that giving Kate a leave so that she could teach at Scudder for a year would be a routine matter. But now I see that there are some issues to be resolved, and that we won't be able to do that today. So what's next? Where do we go from here?"

In all the discussion about her books and shock of hearing about this online petition, Kate had almost forgotten the purpose of the meeting—her request to pursue the appointment at Scudder.

"Well," Vincent said, "I think I should talk some more with Dean Robinson and find out if this is even possible. If she says it's against college policy, that would settle it, and we wouldn't need to discuss it any further. But if she says it's possible, then the ball's back in our court, and we'll need to continue this conversation and at some point make a recommendation to her. So, unless somebody has something to add, I'll talk to her in the next couple of days and let you know what she says. Anybody have anything to say before we adjourn?"

Fred leaned back in his chair and said, "One more thing. Kate, why do you want to do this? I gather that you do, or you wouldn't be talking to us about applying and a leave if you're offered the position. So, why do you want to do this?"

Kate realized she didn't know what to say. She hadn't even thought about it—it had been so clear to her that she did want to. She had only thought about things that might get in the way—

whether the department would be a problem and whether Scudder would choose her. Now the whole issue felt like a minefield. Finally, after what seemed to her an interminable pause, she said, "Well, because I think it would be interesting."

"And why do you think it would be interesting?"

Again sifting through various possibilities, Kate said, "I—I don't know. I guess I just think it would be interesting."

Silence in the room. Vincent waited a few moments, looked around, and asked again, "Anything else?" Silence again. "Then we're adjourned."

11

As they walked down the hall on the way back to their offices, Geoff caught up with Kate and asked, "Want to talk?"

"Yeah—how would you feel about going to Murphy's? You could follow me there in your car."

"Murphy's is pretty smoky."

"I won't smoke—and there are hardly ever many people there this time of day. If there are any smokers, they'll be at the bar."

They arrived at Murphy's and sat in the booth by the window overlooking the river. Arthur came over and asked, "The usual, Professor?"

Kate nodded.

"And your friend?" he asked, looking at Geoff.

"What kind of white wine do you have?" Geoff asked.

"One," Arthur said. "And I don't know what kind it is."

"I guess that'll be fine then," Geoff said uncertainly.

As soon as Arthur was a safe distance away, Geoff leaned forward. "Okay, Kate, what the hell just happened? A *petition*? Did you know about that?"

Kate shook her head. "No, that was the first I'd heard of it. And I was just in Vincent's office. I can't believe he'd drop something like that on me in that way, in front of the entire department. I went into that meeting thinking that we'd just talk about the procedure for requesting a leave, and all of a sudden there's a petition about denying me tenure."

She reached toward her backpack to get a cigarette and then remembered her promise not to smoke. She straightened back up, put her elbows on the table, and clasped her hands under her chin. "Oh God. Or ah Jaysus, as my Irish dad used to say." She took a deep breath and let it out noisily. "Not very good.

"Why would someone start a petition about me? Oh, Geoff, I was really thinking that this whole Bob Bradley situation had blown over, and everyone had forgotten what a dangerous liberal I was, and here we are with parents who don't want me teaching their kids because I *am* a Christian? And not only did my colleagues not offer me any support; they actually seemed to side with the parents! Their tone was so formal. And the way they spoke about the possibility of my taking leave . . . Did you catch their language—the 'irregularity of this possibility'? You know, they could have spoken about it being special—that it's *special* that Kate is being offered this opportunity. Instead, it's irregular. And all that talk about whether there's a precedent and other problems—even hinting that it might not be good for my career.

"Not to mention that they seemed to be using it all as an excuse to list objections to my becoming tenured—that my work is perhaps too broad and thus not truly scholarly, and that I'm more interested in what all of this means for Christians than I am in the academic study of religion for its own sake. And applying for a leave to take a teaching position in a seminary would confirm this."

She paused. "I'm wondering if this might be a kind of test. Maybe I'm supposed to tell Vincent, 'You know, I've been thinking about what you all said at the meeting, and I've decided not to apply to Scudder.' And if I do apply, I wonder if they would hold that against me. I'm really starting to feel that Fred almost has it in for me for some reason. Or maybe I'm just being paranoid.

"I keep thinking of what they could have said— like, 'Well, there are some things to check out, and we'll get to work on them and do everything we can to see if we can make this work for you.' Think of how affirming that would have been. Instead, it's, 'We need to think this through.' Are they simply being anal retentive, wanting to make sure that rules and policies are clear and clearly followed? Or are they saying to me, 'If you think this through, you'll see that it's not a good idea'?"

Geoff said, "It was hard to read them. Were they saying they'd rather you *not* do this, and that they think it's—what? Odd that you would even think of doing this—maybe even impertinent or presumptuous? Or were they saying that they need to be thoughtful and careful about *how* to do this?"

He took a tentative sip of the wine Arthur had just brought and winced, hastily setting the glass back down. "Did you notice how Vincent responded to Paul's peacemaking remark? I couldn't tell if he meant, 'That's so obvious it doesn't even need to be said,' or if he thought Paul's conciliatory remark was deflecting the conversation away from matters that he and Fred wanted to emphasize."

Kate was silent. "There's something more," she said. "You know, when Fred asked me why I want to do this, I realized I hadn't really thought about it—I just knew I did. And I didn't know what to say. I didn't want to babble on about possible reasons when I hadn't thought it through myself. So I censored myself, and all I could think to say was, 'Well, I think it would be interesting.' And when Fred asked his follow-up question about why I think it would be interesting, I ended up repeating myself. God, I felt so lame."

"That almost made me smile."

"Smile? Why?"

"Well, it was so unlike you—to see you kind of speechless. Made you more human, you know. But I also felt for you, because I imagined you were probably feeling pretty uncomfortable."

"Yeah." Kate paused. "You know, even though I felt put on the spot by Fred's question and embarrassed by my response, it's actually a good question. And I know I need to think about it."

"So," Geoff said, "what do you think? You can think out loud with me."

"Well, let me tell you some of the things that went through my head in those few seconds while I was figuring out what to say to Fred. Is it the extra money? I think I've told you that with free housing, it would be about $25,000 more than I make here. A chance to get away for a year? But if so, why? Because it's flattering, because I like the feeling of being sought after? For professional achievement? Scudder's a reasonably prestigious place, even though it's only for a year. Is it that I really want to teach in a seminary? And I sure didn't want to ramble through a list like that with the department listening in, and then end up with a line like 'So it could be any of those things—I don't know.' I'd rather sound lame than like an airhead."

"So what do you think now?"

"Well, I don't really think it's very much about the money, even though it would be nice. I don't think I would consider going to another college like ours for a year just to make more money. And I don't think I would do that just for the sake of getting away for a year." She paused again. "Well, maybe I need to think a little bit more about that. It wouldn't just be about getting away—again, I don't think I would go to another small college like ours for the sake of getting away for a year. But maybe I do think going to Scudder might increase my chances of meeting a guy. You know, it's in a city, and there are lots of schools and academic types there, and some of them must be single. There's nobody here I'm interested in except you. And you're useless."

"You're very kind," Geoff said.

Kate smiled and continued. "Flattered? Me, not you. I suppose I am, but that doesn't seem very important. And I don't think it's about the prestige of being at Scudder for a year. I don't think I need that. And that leaves one—namely, because I really want to teach in a seminary for a year, especially a good one. And I think that's the big reason."

She stopped, began to reach for her backpack and cigarettes again, remembered, and pulled her hand back.

Geoff asked, "Does that surprise you?"

"Well, not really. I guess maybe deep down I knew that I really want to teach in a place of faith—about topics that matter to the community of faith. But I hadn't realized it with this much clarity until now." Ruefully she lifted her glass, looked up at the ceiling, and said, "Thank you, Fred." She drained her Guinness.

Arthur came by, noting Kate's empty glass and Geoff's nearly full one. "Another round?"

Kate and Geoff looked at each other. Geoff said, "Up to you. I'll even let you smoke if you want to stay. Want to talk more?"

Kate looked at her watch. "No, I'd better be getting home. I've got a lot of work to do tonight." She sighed. "Thanks for listening, Geoff. The irony is that as I realize how much I want this opportunity and why, I am also realizing that pursuing it is going to seriously jeopardize my position here."

Geoff reached for her hand across the table. "Just remember, Kate, it has to be your decision. Don't let them decide it for you."

Kate couldn't help herself. As soon as she got home she logged on to the Internet and typed in "Petition to Deny Kate Riley Tenure." The first hit was for a site called www.petitiononline.com, and there she saw the petition. A sick feeling began to settle in her stomach.

Below the title, "Deny Kate Riley Wells College Tenure," was a short paragraph:

> Wells College Assistant Professor of Religious Studies Kate Riley should be teaching critical thinking about religion to our children, but instead is indoctrinating them with her own Christian beliefs. A glance at her scholarship makes it clear that she is a believing Christian rather than an objective teacher. Moreover, she also emphatically said on a recent radio show that she's a Christian. Riley is up for tenure next year. Join us in telling Wells College that we want to keep religion out of the classroom.

There was no indication of who had written the paragraph, but below it ten people had listed their names. Two sets shared the same last names, seemingly indicating that they were husband and wife, but ten people—that would mean they were parents of at least eight students. She scanned the last names, but didn't see any she recognized for sure. Then she saw that some of the names were underlined. She clicked on one, Frank Mitchell, and saw that the underlining meant that they had written a comment.

Mitchell had written:

> I'm not paying this kind of tuition for Sunday school. I thought they were supposed to be studying religion from an analytical standpoint.

Another underlined signer, Sarah Reynolds, had written:

> My daughter Amy is in Professor Riley's class this semester, and far from keeping religion out of the classroom, she is seeking to convert her students to her own radical beliefs. She can call herself whatever she wants, but she's not a true Christian, and I think it's highly inappropriate to use the classroom as a pulpit for her own liberal half-truths.

Reynolds. Amy Reynolds. Kate remembered her now. She was the quiet girl who sat next to Erin Mattson. So it wasn't just the parents who thought she was too religious; it was also parents who thought she was too radical.

Against her better judgment she bookmarked the petition so she could come back to it and see if any other parents had signed it. Disheartened and confused, she decided to turn in early instead of working. That night Kate had a dream:

> *I am wearing a clergy shirt and clerical collar. I can't recall being ordained, but I'm pleased. It is night and I am walking down a highway in a drizzle. Must be out in the country—forest on both sides of the road, and no lights to be seen. I wonder how I got here. It is very dark, the pavement black and slick. I see headlights coming toward me in the dark. The car is weaving, and I can't tell what lane it's in. It's getting closer.*

She woke up, her heart pounding.

12

On Tuesday evening, Martin slid into a pew near the front of a church not far from Scudder. He had come to hear a concert by a Lutheran college choir on its annual winter tour.

Martin had grown up Lutheran, though he had become an Episcopalian some twenty years ago. But he continued to love the Lutheran choral tradition, especially sung a cappella. "A Mighty Fortress Is Our God" continued to be one of his favorites, and he found the Lutheran melody for "Wake, Awake, for Night Is Flying" so much more joyful than the melancholic version in the Episcopal hymnbook.

He had drunk deeply of Luther's emphasis on justification by grace through faith and the contrast between "living under the law" and "living by grace"—though it had taken him more than thirty years to begin to see what it meant. Through his adolescence and early adulthood, he had experienced the opposite of grace—namely, a deep anxiety that he didn't believe strongly enough to be justified "by faith." Believing had become the new "law," the new "work." Ironically, the Lutheran emphasis on grace had not delivered him from the "law," but had left him living under the "law of believing."

But in his mid-thirties, he felt that he began to understand grace for the first time: that we are accepted by God, affirmed by God, beloved by God just as we are. Life is not about the anxious project of measuring up, but about living one's life grounded in God's grace.

By that time, he was no longer Lutheran. He thought back to when it had happened. He commonly said that he was Lutheran until he was about thirty, but in more precise retrospect, he realized that the change had begun earlier. In his first year in seminary, at age twenty-two, he had requested a "field work" placement in a church of color and was assigned to a Presbyterian church in a multiracial neighborhood. Its mostly black and Hispanic congregation had been very good to him, a racially naïve young man from a very white part of the northern Midwest. So for a year he had worshiped and sometimes led worship in a Presbyterian setting.

The next year, shortly after he arrived in England, he went to the only Lutheran congregation in Oxford and discovered that it was made up mostly of aging German immigrants, some of whom had left Germany in the 1930s; others left in the early postwar years. He may have been the only person under sixty in the small gathering. He didn't go back. Now, in hindsight, he wished he had sought out their stories.

So during his years at Oxford, he attended Anglican services, especially Evensong on weekdays in the chapels of Christ Church,

New College, and Magdalen. When he returned to the States and for most of his thirties, he hadn't been part of a church at all. As he neared forty, and in part because of undergoing Jungian therapy for several years in the troubled second half of his thirties, he began worshiping in an Episcopal church. Within a couple of years, he was confirmed as an Episcopalian.

Martin's musings about his Lutheran past came to a halt as the choir entered the chancel and arranged itself on the risers. He was initially startled at how white and blond they were. Not all of them—but a much higher percentage than Martin had become accustomed to seeing. He was immediately taken back to the white, blond Lutheran world of his childhood and youth, visually and musically.

As Martin had hoped, the concert ended with his favorite piece of choral music: "Beautiful Savior" as arranged by F. Melius Christiansen. It had become Martin's favorite the first time he heard it sung forty years ago by another Lutheran college choir. It moved him, and had done so ever since.

He listened, eyes closed, as the choir wordlessly harmonized the melody. Then a young female soloist sang the first verse:

Beautiful Savior, King of Creation,
Son of God and Son of Man!
Truly I'd love thee, Truly I'd serve thee
Light of my soul, my joy, my crown.

The choir sang the next verses:

Fair are the meadows, Fair are the woodlands,
Robed in flowers of blooming spring;
Jesus is fairer, Jesus is purer,
He makes our sorrowing spirit sing.

Fair is the sunshine, Fair is the moonlight,
Bright the sparkling stars on high;
Jesus shines brighter, Jesus shines purer,
Than all the angels in the sky.

As they sang the last verse, the choir's volume progressively increased:

Beautiful Savior, Lord of the nations,
Son of God and Son of Man!
Glory and honor, Praise, adoration,
Now and for evermore be thine!

And the glorious crescendo and climax: the repetition of the last line, "Now and for evermore be thine!"

Martin walked the few blocks from the church to his apartment. Though it was nine thirty, he decided to stay up for a while, maybe even until midnight. He enjoyed the late evening hours, and he didn't have to teach on Wednesday. He knew that he could sleep in—or, since he wasn't very good at that, take a nap during the day.

In his study, he poured himself a short glass of Glenlivet, lit his pipe, and watched the smoke drift upwards. He decided to brainstorm ideas for a lecture he was to give in a few days in a large church on the other side of the country. His Saturday lectures were prepared, but he still needed to shape the Friday evening lecture. Brainstorming was one of his favorite things to do—he loved the focused freedom of thinking within the circumscribed framework provided by a lecture topic.

The group sponsoring the lecture had suggested a title: "Mysticism and the Christian Path." Martin had agreed immediately. He realized the topic would give him an opportunity to talk about

ered most to him—the reality of God and his under- what religion at its best was about. Now he wrote the top of a narrow-lined white tablet—to his mind, the only kind of tablet to use. He avoided yellow tablets, or white tablets with wide lines. He sat in silence for a few minutes and then began jotting down thoughts.

After about half an hour of brainstorming, he put together a preliminary outline:

> Begin with the gist of a quote from Karl Rahner (note that he was one of the most important Catholic theologians of the last half century): the Christianity of the future will be mystical, or it will not be at all.
>
> A broad and experiential definition of mysticism: a state of consciousness in which there is a vivid sense of the presence of God—of knowing God, the sacred, "what is," "the Real." Consistent with a definition from medieval Christianity: mysticism is the *cognitio experimentalis Dei*—"the experiential knowledge of God."
>
> As a state of consciousness, mysticism has two primary features (William James):
>
> - A sense of union, connection, with God, the sacred—with what James calls "a more," "the more."
>
> - A sense of illumination—of enlightenment. The language of mystics is full of images of light, seeing, and knowing and their opposites, darkness, blindness, and ignorance.
>
> Mysticism and the Christian path/life:

- Would affect our sense of what the word "God" points to: a reality that can be known and that is "all around us"—not a personlike being "out there," separate from the universe, a superpowerful authority figure whose existence can be argued about. (Note that the contemporary atheist critique of theism is directed against the latter notion of God.)

- Would affect our sense of the "inner" dimension of the Christian life: it's about opening ourselves to God, the sacred. The primary purpose of Christian spiritual practices: to open the heart, the self, to God by spending time in practices that can become "thin places" in which we sense the presence and reality of God.

Mysticism and the goal of the Christian life:

- A caution: mystical experience is *not* the goal. To focus on "having one" would be a form of grasping. Mystical experiences happen, or they don't.
- Rather, the goal of the Christian life is participating in the passion of God, as disclosed in the Bible and Jesus. God's passion is that we center more deeply in (1) God ("You shall love the Lord your God with all your heart, mind, soul, and strength") and (2) the world—a world of justice and peace. These are the inner and outer dimensions of the Christian life and of Christian mysticism—union with God's passion.

Martin looked at his outline and thought it worked. He could do the lecture with no additional preparation, but he also knew that he would return to it and fill in the details.

Setting his tablet aside, he poured himself another Glenlivet.

He moved from his desk, walked a few feet across a deep red and blue Turkish rug, and settled into one of his brown leather chairs. He relit his pipe, thought about God, and gently brought his attention into the moment. Looking around his room, he felt peaceful and grateful.

Martin had just arrived in San Diego, the closest airport to where his weekend lectures were to be given, and he felt foul—grumpy and snappish, ready to be a smart mouth. He didn't like the feeling, yet he was not ready to let go of it.

The cause was quite minor. His flights had been fine, but he was supposed to be met at the baggage claim by a local host, and nobody was there. He waited twenty minutes, then called the cell phone number he had been given, only to get an answering machine. He left a message, emphasizing that he had arrived twenty minutes ago; he said he would wait five minutes more and then catch a taxi to the hotel.

He fumed at the insensitivity of people. Why couldn't they arrange their lives so they could be on time? And why couldn't they imagine what it was like to fly all day, arrive in a strange city, eager to get to one's hotel, and find that the promised host is not there?

He strode to the taxi queue and within a few minutes was being driven into the city by a youngish black man. At first Martin thought the driver was sullen, disengaged to the point of rudeness. No word of greeting, no assistance putting Martin's luggage into the trunk. But Martin was wrong—halfway through the trip to the hotel, the man began to ask Martin about his life, and Martin began to ask him about his. Martin learned that he was Ethiopian and had left his country five years ago. Life in Ethiopia had been difficult, very hard. He had left with his brother, but the rest of his family was still there.

"Do you and your brother live together?" Martin asked.

"Yes," the driver said, enthusiasm and gratitude in his voice.

Martin hesitated, then asked, "Has it been a good move for you?"

"Yes," he said, "it's been a very good move."

And Martin was silent, thinking of this Ethiopian immigrant driving a cab at ten at night, no doubt struggling financially, perhaps having two jobs, and saying, "Yes, it's been a good move."

But even comparing his own privileged situation to that of the positive-minded young man didn't lift Martin's foul mood. When he arrived at the hotel, the bar was closing. When he tried to buy a diet cola from the vending machine, it wouldn't accept his dollar bills. He went down eight floors to reception, exchanged a ten-dollar bill for a bunch of quarters and crisp ones and went back to the vending machine, only to have it refuse both his dollars and his quarters.

Now in his room, he noted how small it was, even though luxuriously appointed. An expensive room in an expensive hotel, a king-size bed, yes, but little floor space. Bathroom barely the size of a semi-adequate closet. No place in the room to set his suitcase in an open position. Rather, he had to unpack it on the bed and then put it in the tiny closet.

Martin was aware enough to know that his mood was ridiculous. His life was exceedingly comfortable, and he was grateful for its ease and for his vocation. He had been very fortunate. But sometimes these edgy grumpy moods came upon him. Mostly when he was traveling, he realized. And he remembered how much he enjoyed being at home.

Still grumpy, he decided not to unpack his laptop and do some writing, as he had planned. He also decided not to watch TV, even though he sometimes did when he felt flat, or worse. Instead, he got ready for bed and then continued reading the novel he had brought with him, Richard Russo's *Bridge of Sighs*. He read for a long time and stayed awake later than he had imagined.

The next morning, his luck changed. The Episcopal priest who had been his contact person arranging the event met him for breakfast at his hotel. She had written him in her last e-mail, "Look for a tall blonde in a clerical collar."

As Martin walked into the hotel's restaurant, he saw her immediately. Tall blonde, oh yes. She was almost six feet tall, an inch more than Martin, and she was lovely. In her early thirties, and with a fine figure even her clergy shirt couldn't hide.

Her name was Kristina, and she was not only beautiful, but bright. At breakfast, Martin asked her questions about her life. He learned that she had attended an Ivy League college where she had been a religious studies major and even learned Tibetan. Then, some years later, she had graduated from one of New England's prestigious divinity schools.

Kristina told him that she had spent her early twenties in northern India teaching Hinduism and Buddhism to indigenous nonliterate Indians and Tibetans. Martin wondered what they made of this tall, young blonde American woman who was telling them about their own traditions.

There she had begun to feel a call to priesthood. Then she spent a year in Central America, where she became fluent not only in Spanish, but also with life among the impoverished. Returning to the States, she spent the second half of her twenties as a lay prison chaplain. Martin asked, "In a woman's prison?"

"Yes, but not only," she said. "I worked in both women's and men's prisons." Martin wondered again, this time about what prisoners, especially the men, made of this lovely young woman. No doubt they were happy to see her.

During the weekend, he and Kristina spent a lot of time together. She was his escort and driver (she drove a BMW with a stick shift—said she couldn't stand automatics). Being with Kristina and hearing her story made him think of Kate more than once. He wondered about the parts of Kate's life that he had missed, what had led her to pursue her doctorate in theology, what experiences had made her become more devout, as her writings led him to believe she was. Why hadn't he sought her out after she had left?

He realized that he had been at least partially embarrassed. The professor and his bright young student—what a cliché. And then he had come clean with his wife, and it had been so much easier trying to work through things with Kate gone. When they had finally divorced two years later, it had seemed much too late to look Kate up. Surely she was involved with someone else by now. And he couldn't help but question if the affair had meant much to her. What could be worse than seeking her out only to find that she barely remembered him or, maybe even worse, remembered him only in a chaste and vaguely fond way? It had been so much easier to move forward with his life. And now this lovely young woman was making him question whether his path could have taken a radically different turn.

These persistent and somewhat uncomfortable thoughts aside, Martin considered the weekend a success. He had large and appreciative audiences for his Friday evening lecture on mysticism and for his Saturday talks about living the Christian life today. On Sunday morning, he enjoyed preaching, the service enriched by a fine choir and a congregation that knew how to sing.

After church, a taxi picked him up for the hour-long drive to the airport. The driver was an African American, bulky and middle-aged—probably in his fifties, Martin thought. His appearance led Martin to make some assumptions about him, including that driving taxis had been his life and that he was probably just barely getting by. His name, Martin learned, was Otis.

But on the drive Martin learned that Otis had graduated from the University of Virginia, where he had been a football player, and then worked for the Drug Enforcement Agency for twenty-five years, much of the time as an undercover agent posing as a major drug broker. In one sting, his "cover" included living in a luxurious penthouse, driving a Ferrari, spending money lavishly, and being seen with beautiful women. This particular operation had lasted six years, involved many undercover agents, and cost the government $60 million, but had netted drugs and property worth $750 million as well as a number of convictions.

After Otis retired from the DEA, he went to seminary and then founded a church that had grown from twenty-five to forty-five hundred members in five years. He drove taxis two days a week as part of his ministry—he told Martin about the opportunities it gave him to help people.

Martin also learned about his family. His wife was a gynecologist and his children, now adults, included two medical doctors, a professor, and a lawyer. Ruefully, Martin realized how wrong his assumptions had been and wondered, not for the first time, how much his perceptions were still affected by race.

At the airport, Martin got upgraded to first-class. On the flight home, he finished reading Russo's *Bridge of Sighs* and admired Russo's ability to create so many characters you could care about.

Now in his study on Sunday evening, he decided to open up his e-mail. As a rule, he didn't do e-mail while he was on the road. He came upon a message to the faculty from the president's office. That was a bit unusual. Most messages to the faculty came from the dean's office, usually about routine matters that he didn't need to know about or respond to.

He opened it up. The date was three days ago.

To the Faculty:

I am calling a special faculty meeting at 4.30 Monday afternoon in the Faculty Seminar Room.

That's tomorrow, Martin realized. He continued reading:

At the meeting, I will inform you about a major gift that has been offered to Scudder to endow a chair in evangelical thought. The title of the chair is deliberately broad, thus permitting a range of specialized fields within that larger category.

It is a very generous endowment. It will produce an annual income adequate to cover a senior professor's salary, plus about $100,000 a year that can be used to support a broad range of faculty activity relevant to the purpose of the endowment.

The gift does come with a condition, however. The donor has specified that the holder of the chair must be an evangelical Christian. If we accept this gift, the person we appoint to the chair cannot simply be a scholar who knows evangelical thought and history, but must be an evangelical. In short, the donor's intention is to support a professor who will bring an evangelical perspective to the school.

Because of the condition, the seminary has not yet accepted the gift. Instead, the Regents and I want to solicit the advice and counsel of the faculty about this matter. I look forward to discussing it with all of you at the meeting. Copies of a draft of the proposed agreement between the donor and the seminary are in the attached file.

I hope you can all be there.

With best wishes,
Leitha Debnar, President

Interesting, Martin thought. He had heard a rumor fall term that the Development Office might be on to something big, and this was probably it. Martin did the numbers: if the annual income can support a chair's salary and benefits with $100,000 left over, the gift would need to be at least $5 million, maybe more.

And it was interesting that the seminary was involving the faculty in the decision whether to accept a major gift such as this.

That was a first. Obviously, the issue was the condition. He wondered for a moment what the other members of the faculty would think of it and how much contention there might be.

He scrolled through the rest of his messages and saw one from Kate. He exhaled; he hadn't quite realized how much he'd hoped to see a reply from her.

Dear Martin,

I met with my department a few days ago about applying to Scudder. They need to check with the dean of the college to see if it's okay for an untenured professor to go on leave to teach elsewhere for a year. I hope there's not a problem, as I do want to apply.

I've been thinking about the application, and I want to take you up on your offer to be of help. Specifically, I've been thinking about the question concerning the two courses I'd like to teach in addition to intro New Testament. Are there particular interests or needs at Scudder that it would be helpful for me to be aware of?

I hope I'm not cheating by seeking "insider" information.

How are you tonight? And where are you tonight? At home or "on the road"?

Best wishes,
Kate

Martin responded:

I'm just home from a weekend in California. Started out with me feeling foul, but ended up being very nice.

Pleased to learn that you're thinking about the application.

RE your question. Our question about what you would like to teach is a way of finding out what the applicants are interested in. So I encourage you to answer it not by guessing what Scudder might need, but by listing what you sincerely would like to do.

Hope that's helpful.

All the best,
Martin

13

On Monday Martin entered the faculty seminar room at Scudder and took a seat at the long table large enough for all of the two dozen faculty. With two hundred students, Scudder had a faculty that was small compared to that of other colleges and universities.

Martin looked around at familiar faces. About half were white and male, all in their sixties or soon to be. A few had slowed down as they neared retirement, but most were still engaged in their work, some because of duty and some because of vocation and pleasure.

The junior faculty looked very different. Mostly a generation younger, they had been hired after diversity became a goal. There were a couple of white males among them, but more than half of them were women, and some of them as well as most of the younger men were ethnically diverse as well: Asian, Latino, African American, Middle Eastern, and African.

Martin had come to Scudder as this new generation was being hired. They were first-rate, Martin thought, even though they did their theology quite differently than Martin's generation did. Martin liked the change, even as he was glad he wasn't a young white man looking for a seminary position today.

The diversity had fragmented the faculty as a social group, not because of acrimony but because of circumstance. In the "old days," Martin had been told, faculty members and their wives had monthly dinners together and their friendships were mostly with each other. But most of the new wave of faculty had spouses or partners who were professionals with their own network of social relationships, so the new faculty's primary friendships were outside of the divinity school.

President Leitha Debnar, who encouraged the faculty to call her by her first name in the chummy ethos of the seminary, walked to a place at the center of the table. Standing, she said, "The Lord be with you," the Episcopal way of silencing a chattering crowd. The faculty responded, "And also with you." Her "Let us pray" was followed by a prayer from Dag Hammarskjöld:

Give us pure hearts, that we may see you;
Humble hearts, that we may hear you;
Hearts of love, that we may serve you;
Hearts of faith, that we may abide in you.

She paused and then said, "Amen."

Leitha sat down, looked up and down the table, and said, "It's lovely to be here with all of you. As you know, my work takes me away from campus a lot, so I don't get to see everyone together very often. Thank you for managing to be here on short notice.

"As you know, the purpose of this meeting is to provide an opportunity for conversation about the gift we've been offered. You've seen the information in the e-mail, and I have only a bit more to tell you.

"The amount of the proposed gift is $6 million. It's the largest gift ever offered to Scudder, and its purpose is to endow a chair in evangelical theology. The donor wishes to be anonymous, so I can say nothing more about that. Indeed, I've never met the donor. All the negotiations were done through an intermediary, an attorney we know and trust. I don't even know if the donor is a man or a woman. I can tell you a bit more about the donor's purpose, though. The donor thinks our students and faculty should be exposed to a first-rate evangelical mind. Moreover, the donor thinks that a distinguished conservative scholar might attract some conservative students, thus further diversifying the divinity school community.

"Finally, I want to tell you that we are not the first school to whom this gift has been offered. It was offered to another divinity school, which turned it down.

"It is a generous offer. So far as I know, it would be the most richly endowed chair in theology in the country. Now, time to discuss this. And I suggest we structure our discussion into two parts. I am aware, of course, that the condition attached to the gift involves a question of principle or policy, but I suggest we save that for part two. So let's begin with some time for information questions and reserve the policy question for the second part."

After a brief pause, Hugh Alcott, a senior professor of New Testament, asked, "Do we know why the other divinity school turned it down?"

"No. The confidentiality surrounding this gift is extraordinary. I have not been told which school it was or why the gift was declined, but I know it was one of our peer schools. But, to say the obvious, I suspect the reason was the condition."

LeRoy Baldwin, an African American Old Testament professor, asked, "How broad is the category 'evangelical thought'? Is this a position in theology in the narrow sense of the word—you know, like systematic theology or historical theology? Or is evangelical thought broader than that?"

"Broader. As I understand the donor's intent, it could be a person in systematic or historical theology. But it could also be somebody in biblical studies or church history or contemporary evangelicalism or even religion and science. But it needs to be someone who would engage, from an evangelical perspective, the conflicts between modernity and Christianity."

"A conservative Christian apologist?" LeRoy asked.

"Well, that seems a bit strong. But if you mean a person with evangelical convictions, I suppose you could say that."

Carson Grant, a senior professor in church history, asked, "Will the donor exercise any role in the selection process?"

"No. The donor will not be consulted. Of course, as stewards of the gift, we will need to be faithful to the donor's intent. But other than that, the choice will be completely our own."

Paige Adams, an associate professor whose specialty was ethics, asked, "Could there be anything unseemly about the passion for absolute anonymity? Is that something we should be concerned about? Do we know where this money is coming from? Is it from a conservative foundation?"

"No—it's from an individual. And I've been concerned about that too. I don't think there's any reason to be worried about the source of the money. I mentioned that the intermediary is a lawyer we know and trust, and he assured me and the Board of Regents that this is good money—nothing tainted about it. Not Mafia money, or criminal money, and no connections to tobacco or alcohol or child labor or anything like that.

"When we asked if we couldn't at least know the name of the donor so that, if we were to accept the gift, we could express our thanks, the intermediary said that any communication would need to go through him. When we probed a bit farther, he said, and I quote, 'All I can tell you is that this is good money, and that the reason for anonymity has nothing to do with anything that might be an embarrassment to Scudder.' End of quote. Well, it's hard to know what that means. Not wanting a spouse to know about the gift? Not wanting heirs to know that a chunk of the estate is being given away? A deep religious division within the family? Not wanting to call attention to himself—or herself? Who knows?"

Leitha paused, looked around, and asked, "Other information questions?"

There were none, and so she said, "Let's go on to part two—the policy questions that might be involved. I know some of you have been thinking about this. Let's begin by naming our concerns without arguing them—and then after we have them before us, we can talk about them."

Martin looked around, curious about who would begin and what would be said. He had decided not to say anything until after he had heard what others thought. And maybe not then.

Winston Porter, a senior member of the faculty who taught twentieth-century theology, spoke first. "To say the obvious, the issue is the condition: the person must be an evangelical Christian. I'm bothered that that's an ideological requirement—or maybe I should say, ideological restriction. We've never had an ideological test."

Yes, Martin thought, *that is the issue.* Leitha said, "Okay, that's one important concern. Others?"

Rachel Ramirez, a Latina scholar, spoke up: "I know chairs

are often endowed in a specific area of study. If somebody wanted to endow a chair in liberation theology or feminist theology or Jewish studies, I don't think any of us would have an issue. On the other hand, if somebody wanted to endow a chair in White Aryan Nation theology, I don't think we would accept it. So there's a spectrum from acceptable to unacceptable designations, and the question is, where does a chair in evangelical thought fit on that spectrum?"

There was silence for a number of moments. Martin admired the way Leitha ran a meeting—let's name all the issues, and then see which ones we want to talk about. He knew that she had a Quaker background

Carson Grant said, "Another thing: I'm uneasy about the shape of Scudder being driven by a gift. I seriously doubt that we would consider creating such a position with our own resources. We have several priorities that would come before this. So, should we make this our next position just because somebody gives us a chunk of money?"

"And kind of a related point," said Hugh Alcott. "Do we need this chair? After all, most of us, and probably at least half of our students, maybe more, grew up with some form of evangelical theology. It was common in most mainline congregations until a generation or so ago.

"We already know what it is. Do we really need to be told about it? Do we really need to have it in our curriculum? This reminds me of evangelicals who complain that their point of view is not represented in academic settings—when in fact they're the most visible form of Christianity in our time. Not represented? My God, they own Christian television and radio."

Again there was silence. Then Ibrahim Costello, a Palestinian American Christian said, "I imagine an issue might be who decides who is an evangelical Christian. There are some progressive evangelicals, and I know some of them. They would fit into Scudder very nicely. But I also know that many evangelicals don't consider them real evangelicals. So who decides who's an evangelical? Us? Or do we need to accept the verdict of the majority of evangelicals as to who's evangelical?"

Leitha's assistant had been putting the comments in summary form on a flip chart. Leitha looked at it, looked back at the faculty, and asked, "Anything else we should name?"

Silence followed. She said, "So what do you think about our list, about what's been mentioned?"

Leah Stanley, an African American professor of worship, said, "I want to speak to the issue of an ideological test. I've only been here seven years, so I don't have personal experience of Scudder before that. But I think we have had an ideological requirement, even though it's never been formalized. I mean, look at us. Sure, we're a diverse group, but there's not a conservative Christian among us. We're all progressives—and I don't think that's accidental or coincidental. So I'm not convinced that an ideological requirement is a reason for saying no to this. I think Scudder has had one for a long time."

Laurie Goldschmidt, a Jewish scholar, said, "You know, I think I agree with Leah about the issue of an ideological test, but from a different angle. If somebody wanted to endow a chair in Jewish studies and specified that the person needed to be an orthodox Jew, I don't think we'd object. I think we'd conclude that having an orthodox Jewish perspective within the faculty would be a good idea."

The faculty was silent. After a few moments, Leitha spoke. "What else that hasn't been said?"

LeRoy Baldwin said, "Well, I want to second Ibrahim's point that the question of who is an evangelical is pretty important. Let me use N. T. Wright as an illustration—not because I think he

would be interested. He's bishop of Durham, a plum posi
the Church of England, in a beautiful city with a fine uni
and divinity school. The appointment even comes with a palace, and I can't imagine that he would consider leaving. So I'm using him only to make a point. He's very well known in the intellectual wing of evangelicalism. He's written thirty or forty books, maybe more. He's brilliant, thoroughly respectable, and rather charming. Indeed, he's an intellectual hero for many evangelicals.

"But some evangelicals are suspicious of him, because he interprets some of the sayings in the New Testament that seem to refer to the second coming of Jesus in the near future as in fact referring to the destruction of Jerusalem in 70 CE. So he saves the truth of the sayings by arguing that they refer to something that's already happened rather than being unfulfilled predictions of something still to happen in the future. But some evangelicals think he's on a slippery slope.

"And a couple other examples: Brian McLaren and Jim Wallis. I would love to have either of them on our faculty, though I don't imagine they'd be interested. They have their vocations. Both are committed evangelicals. Yet there are many evangelicals who reject their theology and politics. So who's an evangelical? If we accept this gift, we're going to have to wrestle with this."

"That's a good point," said Paige Adams. "It seems to me that there isn't a general sense of agreement about what makes an evangelical, and so exactly what criteria would such a candidate need to meet? For example, would it be enough if those under consideration identify themselves as evangelicals? Or does it mean that they have to meet certain standards, such as professing a belief in the inerrancy of Scripture, confessing Jesus Christ as the only way to salvation, having a personal relationship with Jesus Christ, or counting the Bible as the ultimate basis for their beliefs rather than experience or tradition?

"Would we ask the donor to be more specific or would we set our own criteria? And it seems to me that whether we have an unstated ideological test in place here at Scudder already, we've always looked at scholarship first and beliefs and practice second or third or last, if at all. What this gift is asking us to do is to choose someone primarily on the basis of personal beliefs or practices, and that to me is a problem."

"I'm not sure I agree with that," said Leah Stanley. "If someone meets whatever criteria for being evangelical that we or the donor came up with, that's only the first step. The most important criteria would still be his or her scholarship and how he or she would fit in here."

There was a half minute of silence. "Are there other comments?" Leitha asked. Martin sensed that the misgivings that were expressed did not suggest that the faculty as a whole would reject the gift. He thought they should accept it.

Then, almost having decided not to say anything, he said, "Just one more thing. You know, we can accept this, and then if we realize after three or four years, or ten years, that this is a bad idea, we can offer to return the endowment to the donor or the donor's heirs. We don't have to make a forever commitment—we can see how it goes."

"Could we really do that?" Rachel Ramirez asked.

Martin shrugged and looked at the president. She thought for a moment and then said, "I don't see why not. Though I expect we've never given a gift back." There were some chuckles.

Hugh Alcott said to the president, "Could you check on that and see if that's an actual possibility? It could affect the way I vote."

"I'll do that. Anything else?"

After a minute of Quakerlike silence, Leitha said, "No more

issues?" Pause. Then, "Let me suggest that we proceed in the following manner. It will be familiar to you. I would like to get a sense of the faculty. I don't know if we're quite divided or if we're more or less of one mind. So, by next Monday, I would like each of you to send your vote to the dean's office. We'll follow our usual procedure—a yes or no or undecided on a piece of paper in a sealed envelope placed inside another envelope with your name on it. If you wish, you can add 'strongly' or 'mildly' to your vote. And depending upon how the vote comes out, we'll know whether we have a consensus or whether we need to meet again."

Fair enough, Martin thought. He liked the way Leitha did things.

Back in his apartment, Martin made a grilled cheese sandwich for supper, ketchup and a sliced dill pickle on the side, and poured himself a glass of milk. He read the *Atlantic* while he ate. Now in his study, his pipe lit, he opened his e-mail and saw a message from Kate:

Dear Martin,

A quick note. I know that the deadline for applications is about a week away and I haven't applied yet.

As you know, I'm interested. But I still haven't had a decision from my college about whether a leave is possible. I've asked my chair a couple of times in the last week if he's heard anything from our dean. He hasn't. I'm surprised that it's taking so long.

I do want to apply, but I may need to wait until the last minute. So the question. Do you think I should send an e-mail to Scudder—presumably to the dean?—letting them know that I'm planning to apply, but want to wait as long as possible in order to see if I can get clarification here? Or should I just send my application at the last minute?

A bit confused.

And, as always, best wishes,
Kate

Martin had learned from a member of the search committee that they hadn't yet received an application from Kate. So this was why. He had started to wonder if she was having second thoughts about applying and even wondered if he was the reason, and if so, whether he should ask her about it or not. He was relieved to know that the reason was a pragmatic one. He thought about how to reply and decided that her question was actually very simple.

Dear Kate,

Sorry to hear about the lack of clarity from your department. But I don't think you need to worry about our reading anything into your not having applied yet. So long as we get it by the February 1 deadline, no problem.

He paused, and then added:

Of course, I (and we) hope you do apply. In case you need encouragement, here it is. I would love to see you here—you would be great for Scudder.

But I also know that you need to pay attention to your future at Wells. Staying in your college's good graces, especially with tenure coming up, matters. That should be your first consideration. Let's hope you don't have to choose.

Let me know if you need to know anything more.

All the best,
Martin

He considered having a short glass of Glenlivet, but decided to go to bed instead. Sometime in the middle of the night, he had a dream:

I am in my twenties and back in Oxford, leaving my flat in the large Victorian house where I live for an appointment with my thesis supervisor. I descend the staircase, and as I near the front entrance, I meet Kate. My surprise at seeing her in this unlikely locale is soon eclipsed by my appreciation of her appearance. No longer the shy coed hiding in her too-big clothes, Kate is a gorgeous and sensuous woman in blue jeans with almost impossibly long legs and a dark red lamb's wool sweater, its low neckline accentuating the rise of her full breasts. She smiles at me and says, "So, Martin, how are you today?" I am uncertain how much of an answer she wants, and so I say, "Fine." She looks at me for a moment and laughs.

Martin woke up, startled. *What's she doing in my dreams? And her laugh—what was that about?*

He looked at the glowing red numbers on his bedside clock: three twenty-five. He hoped he could get back to sleep.

14

Erin glanced at the clock over the classroom door. Kate was a couple of minutes late today, which was unlike her. When she finally arrived, looking a little distracted, she sat down on the table in the front of the room and said, "I heard on public radio today that the number two cause of death among people under thirty-five in our country is narcotic painkillers. Prescription drugs, not illegal drugs. I think that's an interesting and sobering comment about our time—what is it that leads young people to overdose on painkillers?"

I don't know, thought Erin. *I could think of a few reasons someone might want to dull their senses—confusion, disillusionment.* She looked up, hoping Kate wasn't watching her again, but Kate simply continued without missing a beat. "Well, that's not what we're going to talk about today, but I pass it on to you for what it's worth. Today we continue the section of this course on 'The Enlightenment and Genesis: Creation and the First Humans.'

"To review what we've done so far: we have focused on the challenges to the premodern worldview presented by Enlightenment astronomy and geology and responses among Christians. The new astronomy—Copernicus in the sixteenth century and Galileo in the seventeenth—countered the notion that the earth is the center of the universe. In the eighteenth century and continuing into our time, geology progressively extended the age of the earth—from six thousand years to a million years to five billion years. And the universe may be fifteen billion years old.

"Now we move from the impact of astronomy and geology to the impact of the Enlightenment on our understanding of human origins. Our focus is the stories of human beginnings in the first eleven chapters of Genesis—Adam and Eve in the Garden of Eden; their first sons, Cain and Abel, Cain's murder of Abel, and the descendants of Cain; Noah, the great flood, and his descendants; and the story of the tower of Babel. So let me start with a question. How many of you think Adam and Eve were real people?"

Erin glanced at Amy, who raised her hand immediately. No one else did. Amy shot Erin a questioning, almost accusatory, glance. Erin felt bad for deserting her friend, but the assigned reading had convinced her that Adam and Eve were symbolic, like many other cultures' creation stories, which help explain why the earth is the way it is.

Kate continued, "Let me change the question. How many of you remember thinking of Adam and Eve as real people when you were kids—you know, when you were rookies?"

After a few moments, about half the students raised their hands.

"But you don't now. What happened?"

They were silent for about half a minute. Erin looked around, wondering if she should raise her hand. Then a girl she didn't know said, "For me, it happened when I began to learn about prehistoric humans. Not just Neanderthals—I think there are still some of those around." A few students chuckled.

"But you know, the bones that Leakey found in Kenya—aren't they five million years old or something like that? And so I started thinking about who Adam and Eve were—were they just the first two people, no matter how long ago? But I had trouble thinking of Adam and Eve like we think of prehistoric humans. In Genesis, they seem a lot like us. But weren't Neanderthals kind of hulking brutes? And those bones from Kenya are millions of years older than Neanderthals."

Another student said, "I remember thinking about dinosaurs. I thought they were cool." Again a few chuckles. "And so I asked my folks how dinosaurs fit into the Genesis story of creation in six days. They said something like, 'Well, each day could have been a very long time—like millions of years.' That settled it for a while. It was only a lot later that I started thinking about how Adam and Eve fit into all of this—like maybe this week."

"What I remember about Adam and Eve," another student said, "was that they were naked. And when you're eight or nine, that's weird. Made me uncomfortable."

"And then there's that talking snake in the story," another said. "That's really weird."

"What I think," Andrew said, twisting his beret in his hands, "is that this story is a lot like other stories of what went wrong way back when. Like Icarus with his wings held together by wax flying too close to the sun and falling into the sea, or Prometheus having his liver eaten by birds because he tried to steal fire from the gods. Cultures all over the world tell stories like this."

"Other comments?" Kate asked.

"Yeah," Jonathan said. "I remember a guy asking me—I think it was in junior high—where Cain's wife came from. You know, it kind of makes sense—if Adam and Eve were the first people and everybody else is descended from them, where did Cain get his wife? Did he marry his sister? Or were there other people? But the guy who asked me was kind of a smart ass—sorry, Professor Riley. So I didn't take him too seriously."

"Well," Fiona said, "I grew up thinking it was because of Adam and Eve's sin that we need a savior. So for me, once I started wondering whether Adam and Eve were real, I started wondering what happened to the story of the fall and the Bible as a whole. I mean, if there wasn't a fall way back when, then what's original sin all about? And if there's no original sin, then why did Jesus have to be born of a virgin, and why did he have to die for our sins?" She paused. "It stopped making sense to me. But I think I'm beginning to get it."

Amy raised her hand. "That to me just shows what a slippery slope that kind of argument is. You decide that Adam and Eve are not real people, and all of a sudden Jesus isn't our Savior! You can't pick and choose what parts to believe; it's all or nothing. And I really don't understand how you can say there's no original sin, when it is so clear that we all do the wrong thing all the time. We hurt each other; we break God's laws; we act out of selfishness and greed. Everyone is imperfect—we're all sinners, and we were all born that way. It's true now, and it's been true since the time of Adam and Eve. That's why we need Jesus, so that we can be reconciled to God."

Amy's face was turning red as she spoke. Erin knew Amy felt alone, one person fighting a losing battle against a sea of liberals. She saw Andrew open his mouth to respond to Amy, and Erin jumped in before he could begin. "I think Amy has a good point.

Whether or not Adam and Eve actually ate from a tree in the Garden of Eden, it seems to me that people are pretty much universally messed up. What is that if not original sin?"

Another brief silence. Then a student said, "I have a friend, a guy I know, who says that if you can say that there never was an Adam and Eve, then the story isn't true, and then where do you stop? I don't mean you, Professor Riley, but you, like, you know, just anybody—I mean, how do you know which stories in the Bible are true?"

A longer silence. Kate said, "Okay, I need to call time on your responses, so we can move on. Good job. You've named some of the big issues that have surfaced because of the Enlightenment. And now I want to focus on a way of seeing theses stories that has emerged since the Enlightenment."

She nodded at the student who had made the last comment, "Let me begin with your friend who wonders what happens if the story of Adam and Eve isn't true. What's interesting is your friend's use of the word 'true.' It identifies truth with factuality. If the story of Adam and Eve isn't factual, if it didn't really happen, then it's not true—do you see what I mean? It seems to me that Amy used the word 'true' in a different way. She said, if I recall correctly, 'It—meaning our imperfection—is true now, and it's been true since the time of Adam.' "

Amy sat up very straight. Erin thought she was probably wondering if Kate was preparing to challenge her. Kate seemed to have the same idea, and she smiled at Amy before continuing. "Let me say a bit more. The identification of truth with factuality is a cultural product of the Enlightenment. The success of the scientific method led many people to think of truth as what can be verified, and what can be verified came to be identified with facts. Within this framework, if something isn't factual, then it's not true.

"So, in the minds of many people over the last few hundred years, truth and factuality became the same thing. This happened to religious people as well as to skeptics. A lot of Christians in our country—about half, according to a couple of polls—believe that the earth was created less than ten thousand years ago and that Adam and Eve were real people. And that's because they read these stories as factual stories, because in their minds truth and factuality are identical. So some insist on their factuality—and this is why we have a continuing public controversy about Genesis versus evolution. But to reiterate the main point. It's not just skeptics and rejecters of religion who often identify truth with factuality. Many religious people do too. That shows how widespread this identification is in modern Western culture, our culture."

Kate rose from her perch on the edge of her desk. "Now, take a breath," she said. "I want to use where we are to make the transition to what I want to emphasize today. And that is another way of understanding the Genesis stories that has emerged since the Enlightenment. It sees them as true even though not factual. Or, perhaps more precisely, it sees that their truth does not depend upon their factuality. Its foundation is the simple notion that stories can be important, meaningful, truth-filled, and truthful without being factual. So, Amy, when you said that it was true that people are imperfect now and always have been, I would agree with you. I would say that is the truth expressed by the Genesis stories. And that truth does not have to be connected to whether the stories are factual."

Amy relaxed into her chair, looking slightly confused. Erin thought she probably hadn't expected Kate to say that she agreed with her.

Kate continued, "The key to this understanding is the word 'myth' as used in religious studies and some other academic disciplines.

It means something quite different from its everyday common meaning. You know, when people say, 'Oh, that's just a myth,' they mean it's not true—that you don't need to take it seriously. This is the popular understanding of the word, and you really have to set it aside in order to understand the more scholarly meaning. It's too bad we don't have a different word.

"Scholars have offered lots of one-sentence definitions of myth. My favorite comes from Thomas Mann: a myth is a story about the way things never were, but always are. It's an elegant definition. A myth is a story, a narrative. And it's about the way things never were—it's not about something that happened, that's not its point. But it's about the way things always are. And his definition also provides a way of distinguishing true myths from false myths—a false myth is a story that's *not* about the way things are.

"So, within this framework, the Genesis stories of creation and of Adam and Eve in the Garden can be true, even though not factual. And that's what we'll talk about the rest of today's class period—the truths that have been seen in these stories as myths."

Kate took them through a handout that treated the story of Adam and Eve as the story of all people. It described how we begin our lives in a state of dreaming innocence in the presence of God. Then, with the birth of self-consciousness, we enter a world of separation and self-concern, hubris, exile and violence. We all begin our lives in Eden, but end up living our lives east of Eden.

Erin listened attentively, soaking up these new ideas. It all made so much sense to her. She'd always had trouble with the idea that just because some snake had talked a woman into eating an apple, they'd all been doomed to live a life of sin. Viewing the story as a metaphor, or a myth, seemed so much more helpful. Occasionally she sneaked a glance at Amy, who looked thoughtful. Maybe she was coming around to this point of view too.

Kate looked up from the handout and said, "Well, that's a lot to end with. But I'll start class on Thursday by giving us some interactive time to explore this further. See you then."

Erin slid her Bible and their small group's latest Bible study, "Jesus is *The Way*," into her backpack after they'd finished their closing prayer. The study they were doing this semester just seemed to be exacerbating her doubts about some of the group's beliefs. Talking about how Jesus saved them and how he was the only way was starting to feel uncomfortably exclusionary to her. *Could they limit God that way?*

Peter walked over. "Erin, how's everything going?"

"Fine," she said cautiously.

He sat on the arm of the couch next to her. "I've noticed that you've been really quiet in Bible study lately, and I wanted to check in with you. How's the religious studies class you're taking?"

Erin looked at Peter, who was gazing at her with obvious concern. Suddenly she felt a sense of appreciation for him. He really cared about her, and he was very intelligent. Maybe he could help her make sense of some of the things they'd learned in class.

"I'm enjoying it," she answered, "but some of the ideas are really challenging. Today we talked about seeing the creation story as a myth—that although it represents truth, it doesn't necessarily involve real people. I liked what Professor Riley said about truth not necessarily being the same as factuality, but I'm a little confused about how that interpretation would affect original sin."

Peter nodded. "I see the temptation of that kind of logic. There are many things in the Bible that are hard to believe, but just because we find them difficult or don't fully understand them doesn't mean that they aren't literally, factually true. It would be a lot easier to be a Christian in many ways, if we could go through the

Bible, pick out the stories and the lessons that spoke to us without challenging us, and throw out the rest.

"But we can't follow Jesus partway, believing only one-third of the things he said or one-eighth. It's pretty much all or nothing with following Jesus. And the problem with the kind of thinking you've just described is that it's a slippery slope. You start with thinking that Adam and Eve weren't real people—then original sin is out the window, and we're all just confused rather than sinful. And then it follows that we don't need Jesus. Then pretty soon Jesus wasn't actually born of a virgin, wasn't really the Son of God, and the resurrection was something his followers made up."

Erin listened in silence. Peter's argument made sense too, mostly. "I guess I'm just confused," she admitted.

"Pray about it. You can come to me anytime, and we can talk and pray together. I can give you some books to read too that can help dispel some of what you're hearing. But you might also want to consider whether it's worthwhile to stay in the class. It seems to me that Satan is using it to launch some pretty serious attacks on your faith. Maybe the best thing to do would be to drop it."

Erin frowned. "I don't think I'm ready to do that."

"Just think about it," Peter urged.

Erin nodded and went to meet Amy, who was waiting for her at the door. They were to walk to Fiona and Allison's together.

Erin was the first to talk that night at Fiona and Allison's. "I've been thinking a lot about Kate's class today. I don't have any problem with creation happening billions of years ago and that it's a process—I'm kind of relieved to know that you can interpret the creation stories that way. But I've been thinking about what happens if we see Adam and Eve as mythical figures in a story and not as real people. I agree that it would solve issues like the finding of human remains going back five million years.

"I was just talking to one of my friends about this, and I'm still puzzled by what happens to the notion of original sin. If there wasn't a fall, then why do we need redemption?" Erin stopped and looked around at the group.

"Well," Jonathan said, "what do you think original sin means—or maybe I should ask, what does your group think it means?"

Amy jumped in. "It means that we're born sinful."

Andrew asked, "So you mean a one-day-old baby is sinful?"

Amy said, "Actually, yes. I read somewhere that until recently babies were usually baptized when they were two or three days old because of the high infant-mortality rate—you know, in the Middle Ages and I guess even into the 1800s. They wanted to be sure babies were baptized before they died—and that's because of original sin—you know, they're born sinful."

"Sounds pretty ridiculous to me," Andrew said.

Erin said, "But isn't Amy right that most Christians have believed in original sin? And if so, can you set that notion aside and still be Christian?"

Fiona said, "I took a course from Kate last term—it was called 'Perspectives on the Human Condition,' and it was all about what ails us. You know, what philosophers and religious thinkers have said about the human predicament. We read a lot of books, and one of them was *Shantung Compound* by a theologian named Langdon Gilkey. It's a great read—it's about his experience with about fifteen hundred other Western civilians in a Japanese internment camp in China during World War II. I thought it was fascinating.

"Gilkey calls his book a case study of humans under pressure. And he concludes that what is meant by original sin is a universal human condition. He sees it as a primal anxiety that we all have that leads us to become self-centered, especially when the chips are down. So, he says, that's our problem and that's what we need deliverance from."

Then Jonathan said, "I was in that class too. Gilkey says that what Fiona's just been talking about is what Christian theologians like Augustine called pride—you know, in the sense of hubris. And that's what the stories of Icarus and Prometheus are about too. I think maybe you can even fit Buddhist grasping into this—sounds like the same thing to me."

Jonathan paused. "I was fascinated by Gilkey's stories of people rationalizing—you know, coming up with good-sounding reasons for doing things that were really very selfish. Then Kate asked us to think about our own experience of rationalizing. We all had stories. And then she asked, 'Do you think we always know when we're rationalizing?' I realized that many of the people in Gilkey's book didn't, and that sometimes I don't either. And I realized that means that I can deceive myself. That's pretty interesting, when you think about it—something in me can fool me. Seems important too. And it makes sense that it comes out of self-concern, which is usually pretty anxious."

"So," Erin asked, "self-concern is what original sin is?"

Fiona jumped back in. "Yeah, I think that's what he—Gilkey—is saying. In fact, I'm sure that's what he's saying."

"So original sin isn't inherited, but it happens to all of us—we've all got it?"

"Makes it sound like a disease," Andrew said.

"Actually," Allison said, "that's a word that Kate used—I was in that class too. Or maybe it was some author she was quoting. She said disease is a major image for the human condition, and to get the point we should put a hyphen in it—you know, we all suffer from dis-ease, and out of that dis-ease, that anxiety, comes self-preoccupation. And then she said a really cool thing: that the religions is to heal the dis-ease of existence. Isn't that get diagnosis and prescription in a single sentence."

was silence for a few moments. Then Erin said, "Diagnosis and prescription in a single sentence? I think if people in my group needed to put that in a single sentence, they'd say it differently—that our diagnosis is that we're sinful and the prescription is forgiveness. Or is that the same thing? It sounds different to me."

"Well," Josh said, "if the problem is dis-ease, I don't see how forgiveness relates to that. I mean, if we're dis-eased, what good does forgiveness do? Instead, we need healing. And you know Jesus was a healer."

Erin frowned. "I see what you're saying, but I have a hard time giving up the concept of sin and forgiveness. For me, forgiveness *is* healing. It seems like that is—" She hesitated. "Well, it has been at the center of my understanding of God—that we are sinful and that we need forgiveness for that. And it still makes sense to me. I mean, I do the wrong thing all the time. I make wrong choices, and I hurt other people and myself with them, so I have a hard time saying that this situation is not my fault.

"The idea of dis-ease sounds almost too easy—like we're foisting the blame off on someone or something else. I have no problem with the idea that we're all sick, all lost, but I think the difference between what you're talking about and what my understanding has been is whether we are at fault, and it seems to me that, at least part of the time, we are. I guess I can't quite let go of the idea of myself as a sinner."

She shook her head. "I need to think more about this. I'm still trying to see what the differences are between what I've learned before and what I'm learning now."

The conversation subsided. Allison, looking at her watch and realizing that they had only a few minutes left, said, "So what do you all think? Do we live east of Eden?"

"Life can be pretty sweet," Jonathan said. "But yeah, I think so."

"Me too," Andrew said. "I think we do live east of Eden—but I don't think religion is the solution. I'm not sure there is one—this is just the way life is. So I have no problem with the diagnosis. It's the solution that leaves me cold."

"But," Erin asked, "don't you wish there were a solution?"

"Wishing doesn't make it so," Andrew replied.

"Well," Allison said, looking at Fiona, "on that note, time to call it a night."

Erin and Amy left together. They walked in silence for a few moments, and then Amy said, "Well, what did you make of that?"

"Interesting. A lot to think about."

"Interesting?"

Hearing the tone in Amy's voice, Erin asked, "How was it for you?"

"It's really different—I mean *really* different from what I believe. I mean, I understand what they're saying, but it's just so different. I'd have to change so much to start thinking this way. I'd have to give up a lot, and I don't know if I'm ready to do that."

Amy fell silent. Then she added, "And I think you might be more ready for this than I am, and it worries me."

"Why's that?"

"Well, you know, it's because we became friends through The Way, and if you go far enough down this road so that you stop coming, I'm afraid that we'll lose a lot of what we have in common. Makes me sad."

As Fiona and Allison picked up dirty dishes and glasses after everyone left, Allison asked, "So, how are things going with Josh?"

"Good," Fiona said. She grinned. "Really good."

The phone rang in Allison's room, and she ran to get it. Fiona continued to clean up. She heard Allison's voice rising in anger or excitement, but she couldn't make out the words. Then Allison appeared back in the sitting room, her face pale.

"That was my mom," she said. "You won't believe what she just told me."

Fiona set down the glasses she was holding. "What?"

"It's about Kate."

"Our Kate?"

"Yeah. My mom says she got an e-mail today from another Wells parent, and it had a bunch of stuff about Kate in it, about how she was indoctrinating us with Christian beliefs. It had some quotes from her that were on the radio or something. And then—get this—it asked her to sign a petition to ask the school not to give Kate tenure next year."

"What? Are you kidding me? She's the best teacher we have!"

"I know. That's what I told my mom. She was all set to sign the petition. She wanted to know if Kate was forcing her beliefs on me, and I told her that whoever wrote that e-mail was crazy, that Kate was my favorite professor, and that she didn't tell me what to believe, just made me analyze it."

"Oh my God." Fiona sank into one of their chairs. "That must have been why she looked so distracted today when she got to class. And she was late. She's never late. We have to do something."

"Yes, we do."

15

Kate spent Wednesday at home working on a chapter-length comparison of C. S. Lewis's *Mere Christianity* with his later writing, but she was distracted by thoughts about the position at Scudder, the deadline now less than a week away. She had been waiting to hear the final result of the department's consultation with Dean Robinson. *Politically smart,* she thought, *not to go ahead until I have a green light, but time is passing.*

A week ago she had checked in with Vincent after he had spoken with the dean. He reported that she had told him there was no precedent in the college for an untenured professor to receive a leave in order to be a visiting professor elsewhere. Neither was there a policy prohibiting it. But, in part because this was only her second year at Wells, she didn't feel comfortable setting a policy on her own, but instead would consult with some of the senior faculty in the college to see what they thought. Kate had heard nothing since, and she had resisted the temptation to phone Vincent. But it was now the last Thursday in January, so after class that afternoon, she stopped by Vincent's office.

"Hello, Kate." He greeted her with what felt like a cautious smile.

"Hi, Vincent." She sat on the edge of the wooden chair across from his desk. "You probably know why I'm here. Have you heard anything more from the dean?"

"Ah, yes, your question about a leave. Well, I talked to the dean again, and she and the senior faculty with whom she is consulting are still in the process of deciding on a policy. Is there a time crunch?"

Kate couldn't quite hide her surprise. Vincent had a copy of the letter, and she'd talked to him about this matter more than once. She knew he knew about the February 1 deadline. But there was nothing to be gained by challenging him now. "Yes, actually, the deadline is next Tuesday. According to the letter, Scudder plans to interview in February and make its decision by the first week in March at the latest. And, I was hoping—am hoping—that I could get clarification before making the decision to apply." She added, "I don't want to do anything to jeopardize my position here at Wells," and then wondered if she should have said that.

"Well," Vincent said, ignoring her last sentence, "I doubt that we'll have a decision from the dean this week. This is Thursday, after all. And until we do, my hands are tied. I can't tell you anything, because I don't know anything. So you'll just have to decide what you want to do."

"Yeah, I can see that." Kate inclined her head. "Just one more thing. Do you mind that I keep asking you about this? I don't want to be a pest."

Vincent smiled. "No problem," he said. "Of course, I'll tell you as soon as I've heard something. But anytime you want to check with me, feel free."

Kate left his office, knocked on Geoff's partially open door, and put her head in. "I'm really glad we're having supper together tonight—but can we do it at Murphy's instead of at my house?" She thought he would agree—she had discovered that Geoff had unexpectedly developed a passion for Murphy's bacon cheeseburgers and would even put up with the smokers and the inferior white wine for the sake of indulging his passion.

"Sure," Geoff said. "When?"

"How about right now? I know it's only four thirty, but we could have an early supper. Or are you finishing something up?"

"Right now would be fine. Give me a minute to pull some stuff together."

At Murphy's Kate described her conversation with Vincent. "The college and the department are just being so inscrutable about all this. Maybe even obdurate. Makes me wonder if there's a subtext that I'm supposed to figure out."

Geoff asked, "What kind of subtext?"

"I don't know. I've thought about it a bit, but then I realize that I have no idea whether there's anything to what I come up with. How about you—do you have any ideas? What do you think?"

Geoff was thoughtful for a few seconds. "Well, there could be a subtext. I don't know anything firsthand—they know we're friends, and they don't talk very much about you when I'm around, except for remarks like, 'I see that Kate plans to write another book, and so soon.' But I could make some guesses.

"I think they feel ambivalent about you. I know they're proud of you—of how good you are at what you do, of your visibility in the college, of the fact that you've already written two books so early in your career, of your success with students. I think they feel good about the luster you add to the department—that the department has a young star, that it could attract somebody like you."

Geoff paused again. "But then there was so much attention for your last book, and of course not all of it was positive. Suddenly you're the public face of the Wells religious studies department, and I think that got them thinking about whether it was exactly the face they wanted to show. It seems to me, from what you told me about what Fred said to you over break, that he was already feeling that your scholarship was too overtly Christian, and then perhaps the Bob Bradley show and that petition got Vincent thinking along those same lines.

"I think there might also be some jealousy, both for your publishing success and your success in the classroom. Since you arrived here, our number of majors and minors has doubled, and many of them tell me it's because one of your courses turned them on. Vincent and Fred were the popular teachers in the department for a long time. But now, students are mostly excited about you—certainly more excited about you than about them. There may be some resentment of your popularity.

"But I think it might be more. They might be suspicious that you couldn't be so popular unless you were doing something questionable in the classroom—maybe you're too entertaining, or too inspiring, or too excited about this material, or you grade too easily. Though the records wouldn't support the last one."

Kate took a long pull from her Guinness. Geoff wasn't saying anything she hadn't wondered about already, but it was still hard to hear that her fellow professors might feel this way about her.

Geoff took another bite of his burger, chewed for a while, and continued, "Maybe they can't imagine that the serious and objective study of religion could generate that much excitement and enthusiasm. Their ideal student is one who sees all the problems with religion and finds the problems interesting, not somebody who gets excited by it.

"And then there's the fact that many of your students not only become majors or minors, but also get involved in religious organizations. I think our colleagues think you encourage it. Just the other day, I heard Fred say to Vincent, 'Apparently she suggests that they try out a religious community.' "

Kate nodded thoughtfully. "Well, I guess I do. But there's a context. I talk about religious practices in a couple of my courses, and students get interested in them. Some want to learn them and try them, so I suggest that they find a religious community that teaches practice and go there to learn about it. But I make it very clear that I'm not advocating Christian practice over Buddhist or Jewish or Muslim practice, but that I'm simply saying, 'Try a community of practice.' "

"Well, I think they wonder if you're a crypto-evangelist."

Kate frowned. "An evangelist? Really? I know some of the parents who signed that petition felt that way, but I didn't think my own colleagues would agree with them. After all, they know me."

"I don't mean a Christian evangelist in particular, but maybe they see you as an evangelist for religion in general—you know, a wolf in sheep's clothing—or would it be the other way around? You think that religion matters—not just for cultural and historical reasons, but that there's something to it. And that seems rather unsophisticated to them, even rather primitive."

"Or primordial," Kate said, thinking of Huston Smith's use of the word.

"You know," Geoff said, "you not only think religion matters, but you think God is real, and you communicate that to your students. That makes our senior colleagues uncomfortable. They've spent their lives giving good reasons for being skeptical and maintaining a critical distance from religion. I think that kind of thinking might be what's behind their continued questions about whether you belong in the seminary rather than the academy—rather than here."

"So—because I think there might be something to religion, I'm suspect? Would a music professor who thought music didn't matter be a more objective professor? Would it be better if I thought of myself as the curator of a museum displaying the religious relics of antiquity? I've sometimes wondered if our colleagues are more like curators." A sip of Guinness. "But you're scaring me here, Geoff. Do you really think they feel all of that?"

Geoff shrugged. "I'm just guessing, like I said. Could be none of it, could be all of it. Who knows?" He smiled at Kate. "I'm so helpful, aren't I?"

Kate made a face.

"And you're beautiful, my dear," Geoff said.

"Thanks." Kate sighed. "Well, if you're right that they're ambivalent about me, and if you're right about any of the things you've said, do you think they plan to vote against giving me tenure?"

"I don't know if they'd dare. Your record is awfully strong, and they'd have a difficult case to make for denying you tenure."

As Kate pondered, Geoff said, "Want to hear a really Machiavellian explanation of what's going on?

"Lay it on me."

"My hunch is that they hope you decide to apply to Scudder and that you get the appointment, so that you're gone from Wells before the tenure decision needs to be made. They might even be hoping that you'll not only get the visiting appointment at Scudder, but that Scudder will decide to offer you a permanent position. Or that some other school will snap you up because you're a bright rising star, or that you'll get impatient with your cool reception and uncertain situation here and apply elsewhere. You're a marketable commodity, you know."

"But why, then, are they dragging their heels about giving me permission to apply?"

"This is where the Machiavellian bit comes in. If you apply before receiving clarification from them about the policy here at Wells, they could use that as evidence of where your true interest lies. So if you go to Scudder and then come back to Wells and go through tenure, they could add that to a case against tenure. They've paved the way a bit in their conversations with you about this. Let me imagine how the case would go.

"They would cite your accomplishments, and then say something like this." He adopted a dead-on imitation of Vincent's deep, overly professorial tone: " 'Yet we have misgivings about granting tenure to Professor Riley. Her interests are broad and lack scholarly focus. We have questions about her objectivity in the classroom. She thinks primarily of her own career and requested an unprecedented leave of absence to be a visiting professor elsewhere, in spite of knowing the extra work and expense this would create for the department and the college. Her interests seem to be more in the church than in the academy.' And so they could question your 'appropriateness' for this secularized and pluralistic private college."

Kate couldn't even smile at Geoff's imitation. "But why should they care so much if I get tenure? They're almost ready for retirement. So they don't like me, so what? It's not as if we'll be colleagues for decades to come. They won't be here."

"But that's just it," Geoff said. "They *are* nearing retirement, and they want to leave the department in hands more like their own. You're young and gifted, full of energy and productive, and if you're tenured, you could very well become the shaping force in the department for a couple of decades. And I suspect that's not the legacy they want to leave. It would mean that their influence would simply disappear. I'm sure their egos are involved, but it's more. They believe strongly in how they see things, and they want their angle of vision to be preserved. They think it matters. It's their legacy. Tenuring you would threaten that.

"Think about it. If they tenure you, and if I get tenure in a few years, then you and I will basically be in charge of hiring their replacements. Paul's only a few years younger than they are, and they know that he is likely to go along with whomever we want—he'll simply transfer his conflict-avoidant compliance to us. Let me sketch a scenario. If Vincent and Fred decide to make a case against tenure, Paul will almost certainly vote with them. Of course, the department's recommendation has to be approved by the college promotion and tenure committee and the dean, but it's very rare for a department's recommendation to be overruled. So they can probably do it if they want to. If they do, you could make a stink, of course, appeal it, maybe even win. But it would be messy."

Geoff stopped, smiled, and said, "Keep in mind, this is all very speculative—subtext *in extremis.*"

"So, what do you think they'll decide about the leave of absence?"

"Oh, I think they'll find a way to let you do it. But my hunch is that the delay is deliberate rather than unavoidable. I doubt that Vincent is pushing the dean for a quick decision. I think he's happy to delay a decision as long as possible—might want to stretch it out until after you have to decide whether to accept a position at Scudder. But I think they'll approve it, and they'll emphasize how exceptional it is, how much work it will make for them, and they'll reiterate their misgivings. And I suspect that they will say that your year's leave does not count toward tenure consideration, and thus your tenure decision will be put off for an additional year.

"It won't be gracious or generous, and you'll be made to feel like a child who's being given an exceptional privilege by parents who think it's unwise. If they grant it, it will come with a not too subtle message that you really shouldn't do this."

Kate must have looked as somber as she felt, because Geoff reached across the table and grabbed her hand. "Darlin', I might not know what I'm talking about, and you look so serious. So let me lighten things up. I ran into a wonderful phrase in an Irish novel today. It's a Gaelic expression, and its spelling is strange, but it's pronounced 'a fuckle in your clewis.' And it's used in a sentence like, 'May I have a fuckle in your clewis?' "

Kate laughed. "Oh my," she said. "That sounds pretty intimate—or maybe I should say raunchy. What does it mean?"

"It means," Geoff said, lifting his wineglass, " 'May I have a word in your ear?' "

16

Early Friday, Kate concluded her morning devotions with a prayer from Padraigh Clancy, a contemporary Irish Celtic Christian:

Thanks to thee, O gentle Christ,
that you have raised me freely from the black
and from the darkness of last night
to the kindly light of day.
Thanks to thee, O God, that I have risen today,
to the rising of this life itself.
May it be to thine own glory, O God of every gift,
and to the glory of my soul likewise.

She looked at the words again. "From the darkness of last night to the kindly light of day. . . . I have risen this day to the rising of this life itself." She realized that she didn't feel that. Still felt distressed.

She prayed a prayer of her own. She began, "Lord, this is the rising of a new day and the rising of life itself." She searched for words. "I want to be present to it, present to You. I don't want to miss this day, miss You in this day. But I'm struggling, and I know I could spend this day in distraction." She thought of the difference between being distracted and being present. "So I want to be present to this day, and I want to be mindful of your presence in this day. So help me, dear Lord."

At mid-morning, Kate and a golden retriever named Bob walked to the college arboretum that stretched almost five miles along a stream. Kate was dog-sitting for a faculty friend who had gone away for the weekend to visit an aging parent. Kate reflected, not for the first time, that Bob was the only dog named Bob she had ever met—just as she had never met a dog named Bill or Jim or Ron or Ken or Dave. She wondered why.

Bob bounded down a snow-covered trail in the arboretum as Kate clamped on her skis. She loved the freedom that cross-country skiing provided—made it possible to hike in the woods even in the winter. She didn't understand snow-shoeing—there was never the payoff of a free ride.

A fresh fall of overnight snow had added four inches to the foot or so that had been on the ground since December. The day was sunny and bright. As Kate poled her way along the trail, Bob ahead of her, she admired the trees—birches interspersed with oaks and maples and fir. Though the arboretum was nice in summer, filled with the sounds of frogs and birds and insects, there were also mosquitoes and deer flies. She liked it best in winter, the riot of life mostly stilled, the spidery limbs of bare trees opening up to the sky, a tracery lit by the sun and casting shadows on the snow.

Bob continued to lead the way, making sure not to get too far ahead. Caught up in the rhythmic movement of poles and skis, Kate slipped into a reverie. The thought came to her that she was an "imagician," someone who thought in images, which made her quite different from many of her colleagues who thought in specifics and details. She rather liked the word "imagician," with its resonance of images and magic.

Right now the image was the earth as the body of Christ, a way of seeing that she had read about in an essay by Teilhard de Chardin. The landscape glowed in the pale light. Bob barked. There was no other sound, except the swooshing of her skis, her breath, and her heartbeat. For a few minutes, she lost herself in the moment and moments.

Then her thoughts turned to the day ahead, and the glory faded.

Early that evening, Kate walked from campus to meet Fredrika at a restaurant. The two usually went out for dinner once a month, but Fredrika's December had been so fully scheduled that they hadn't been able to do so since late November.

Wells was on the edge of Willow Falls, but also adjoined what the local folks somewhat grandly called the "business district." She passed the Dew Drop Inn Café, great for breakfast and okay for lunch, but closed in the evenings. She walked past a tavern where she and Geoff sometimes went to play pinball—not the video kind, but the kind with steel balls and flippers. Kate much preferred reality to virtual reality.

Then she passed a clothing store with a gigantic January sale sign in the window, a shoe store, another café, and the gray stone bank building at the town's main intersection. No chain stores in this town, except a Safeway grocery and a Napa auto parts store. Not even a Starbuck's, much to the chagrin of the Wells students.

Kate arrived at the restaurant, one of two in town that was somewhat upscale—which meant a dinner menu that had more than batter-fried chicken, meatloaf, Swiss steak, and chicken-fried steak with mashed potatoes and green beans.

Fredrika was already there, and Kate was ushered to her table by a young woman who smiled and said, "Good evening, Professor Riley. Nice to see you here." Kate looked at her, searching her mind for a name, and the young woman said, "Oh, you don't know me, but I go to Wells. I've never had a class from you, but I know who you are." Kate wondered if it was because of the Bradley show. The young woman continued, "My name's Abigail," and she reached out to shake hands with Kate.

As Kate arrived at the table, Fredrika looked up from her notepad, a glass of white wine to its side. She stood up, and they hugged. "Good to see you, Kate—it's been too long and I always look forward to time with you." Kate murmured mutual feelings.

They sat down. Kate noticed again how pretty Fredrika was. She was going through menopause and was a bit thicker and plumper than she had been a few years ago—but she was a fine-looking woman. Always smartly dressed—today a navy suit with a light blue blouse topped by a white clerical collar.

"Oh," Fredrika said, "almost forgot to take this off," as she removed her breakaway collar. "There; that's better. Friday evening is a time for civvies."

She leaned forward and confided, "I've already drunk a half a glass of wine—I thought of waiting for you but decided I wanted it now."

"Rough week?"

"Oh, not really. Just a lot of stuff. There always is. And by Friday afternoon, I'm ready for a break—well, I guess I mean I'm ready for a drink." She laughed. "So, want to get a bit tipsy tonight?"

Kate smiled. "Well, a glass or two of wine . . ." She leaned forward as well. "Or maybe three might be nice."

Abigail, still standing at the table, asked Kate, "So, would you like something to drink?" Kate looked at Fredrika's glass of white wine and decided she would like a red—went better with cold weather. "How about a glass of a full rich round red—do you have a good cabernet?"

Abigail nodded. "Absolutely."

As she headed off, Kate asked, "So how have you been?"

"Well," Fredrika said as she paused and sipped her wine, "pretty good. But, you know, I'm tired a lot of the time. It's hard to ever get two days off in a row—sometimes even hard to get a whole day off. I've barely recovered from Advent and Christmas, and Lent will soon be here—Easter is early this year.

"But you know I love being a priest, even though it's often a bit of a slog. There are some things about my job that I'm not all that excited about, but the other parts make it worthwhile. I get to be with people as they experience the most intimate and powerful times of their lives—not just baptisms and weddings and funerals, but all the searching that people do.

"And I get to interpret the tradition. It's rich living my days thinking about what all of this means, and then talking about it. So, yeah, I'm pretty good even though a bit weary." She smiled. "Just like Old Man River," she said and then sang *sotto voce,* " 'I gets weary, and I gets tired.' And sometimes I envy that lucky old sun that's got nothing to do but roll around heaven all day."

Abigail arrived bearing a glass of red wine. Kate thanked her.

"I've been doing all the talking. How are you? Better than the last time we chatted, I hope?" Fredrika asked.

"Hard question. I thought that controversy over my new book had all blown over, and I think the Bob Bradley part of it has. But now there's a petition on the Internet that some of the parents have signed. The title is—get this—'Deny Kate Riley Tenure.' "

Fredrika looked as shocked at Kate herself had felt when she first heard about the petition. "What in the world? Why would they want to deny you tenure?"

"Some of the people who saw the show or heard about my radio interviews apparently think that I'm trying to evangelize the students." Kate leaned back in her seat. Somehow talking about the petition made it feel less threatening. "Some of the people who signed are horrified at the idea of a Wells teacher having Christian beliefs and others are concerned that my beliefs are too progressive."

"But that's absurd. It's none of their business what your personal beliefs are, and I know you, Kate. I know you would never bring your faith into the classroom in a way that was inappropriate."

"Thank you, Fredrika. It's always good to be assured of that. Apparently my own department is not so sure. But that's another story. The other news in my life is that I've been invited to apply for a one-year position in New Testament at Scudder. And it sounds like, if I do apply, I might have a pretty good chance of getting it."

"Scudder? Good place. And?"

"Well, I'm in a bit of a muddle. Actually, a big muddle. I'm not sure that my senior colleagues in the department approve of my doing this. What they say is that there's no precedent in the college for an untenured professor to be given a leave of absence to be a visiting professor elsewhere, and so there's this conversation going on between the department and the dean and other senior faculty in the college, and it's not over yet. I don't know what the delay means—seems to me it's not a terribly hard decision to make.

"And to meet the application deadline at Scudder—it's next Tuesday—I have to apply without their go-ahead. I already went ahead and requested letters of recommendation, obviously not from anyone at Wells. But the deadline means I have to finish the application this weekend, if I'm going to. And without their permission—that makes me uncomfortable. I wonder if it could be used against me when I come up for tenure. And then I wonder if that stupid TV show and the petition have just made me paranoid."

Abigail returned for their food order. Fredrika chose the salmon with a maple syrup glaze crowned with bay shrimp. Kate wondered how many thousands of miles the salmon and shrimp had traveled to this town in Wisconsin and ordered a filet mignon in a red wine and peppercorn sauce, not allowing herself to visualize the slaughter of a year-old steer. She was fond of red meat, cooked rare.

"So what do you think? Are you being paranoid?"

"I don't know." Kate sighed.

"What are you going to do? Are you going to apply anyway?"

"Well," Kate said, "I've thought about that a lot. Yes, I think so. So I guess that's what I'll be doing this weekend."

"How do you feel about doing that?"

"Well, I would feel better if I thought my department was supportive. But I'm going to do it."

"It sounds like a good decision to me." They were silent for a moment. Then Fredrika said, "Change of subject?"

"Sure."

"Well, I ran into a marvelous line in a detective story this week—might be the funniest line I've ever read in a mystery novel. It's by Martha Grimes, and one of her main characters is walking across the room at a large cocktail party. As she passes one group, she hears a man in a very upper-class English accent say, 'I've never quite been able to see the point of Finland.' Isn't that hilarious?"

They both laughed, Kate so hard that tears began to form. "Oh my," she said, catching her breath. "I guess I needed that."

Their entrees arrived. They ate in relative silence for a few minutes, making brief comments about the food, guessing about the ingredients in the sauces and talking about Fredrika's favorite TV show, *Boston Legal.*

As they neared the end of their meal and slowed down, Kate gestured at the notepad still to the right of Fredrika's wineglass. "What were you working on when I got here?"

"Sunday's sermon. Jotting down a few thoughts. I'm early this week—I usually don't get started until Saturday."

"So what are you thinking of? What will your sermon be about?"

"Fourth Sunday after Epiphany. Rich texts—the gospel is the beatitudes in Matthew's Sermon on the Mount. And the Old Testament text is from Micah 6, that wonderful passage about what God wants from us—to do justice, love kindness, and walk humbly with God. I'm not sure yet where the sermon goes, but I know a couple things I want to include."

"Like?"

Fredrika paused. "Well, I'll begin by reminding people that we're in the season of Epiphany and that it means 'revelation' or 'disclosure.' Epiphany—the season—is about the revealing of who Jesus was and is and what he's about. Then I'll segue into the Sermon on the Mount as an Epiphany text—a revelation and disclosure of what mattered to Jesus. Matthew sets it up that way. It's the beginning of Jesus's inaugural address in Matthew. And then

I'll make some comments about some of the details in the text. It's stuff you already know.

"I for sure want to explain that Matthew's phrase the 'kingdom of heaven' doesn't refer to an afterlife, despite the use of the word 'heaven.' Rather, it's Matthew's version of Mark's phrase the 'kingdom of God.' Matthew substitutes the word 'heaven' for 'God' because, as a devout Christian Jew, he tries to avoid using the word 'God' out of reverence. But the kingdom of God, the kingdom of heaven, is about life on earth—what life on earth can and should be like. I'll remind them that it's in Matthew's version of the Lord's Prayer that Jesus prays, 'Your kingdom come, *on earth* as it is in heaven.' You know Dom Crossan's great line? 'Heaven's in great shape—earth is where the problems are.'

"And then I'll explain that the word 'righteousness' in the verse 'Blessed are those who hunger and thirst for righteousness' should be translated as 'justice,' because righteousness and justice are most often synonyms in the Bible. So the verse really says, 'Blessed are those who hunger and thirst *for justice.*' Sounds different, doesn't it?

"So in the first part of the sermon, I'll emphasize that Jesus's message wasn't really about heaven, an afterlife, but about life here on earth. I do that a lot, but I think it's important to remind ourselves again and again—I need to be reminded of that from time to time. That's as far as I've gotten—maybe that's the first half of the sermon. But I haven't decided where to take it from there."

Fredrika paused. "Well," she said, "I know you already know this stuff far better than I do. After all," she said, raising her glass and smiling mischievously, "you have a doctor's degree in biblical studies."

She continued, "I know that you're on at church this Sunday too—you're doing the adult education hour. Your topic, as I recall, is economic justice today. So how are you thinking of doing that?"

"Well," Kate said, "I'm going to try to do some consciousness-raising about the distribution of wealth in the United States today—which is what I think economic justice is about."

Now it was Fredrika's turn to ask. "And?"

Kate said, "I haven't figured out exactly how to do it. That's part of what I need to do tomorrow. But I think I'll make it largely interactive—I'll provide people with some basic information about incomes and the distribution of wealth in this country, and then invite them to talk about it."

"Sounds like some symmetry with my sermon."

Abigail cleared their plates and asked if they wanted dessert. They declined, but ordered decaf cappuccinos and glasses of Graham's twenty-year-old port.

As Abigail walked away, Kate asked, "Do you ever feel a disconnect between the comfort of our lives and what we're passionate about? I mean, here we are in a nice restaurant eating good food and drinking pretty good wine, including twenty-year-old port, and talking about the beatitudes, the kingdom of God, and God's passion for justice."

"Yeah," Fredrika said. "But that's kind of who we Episcopalians are. Most of us are pretty comfortable. But I've found a phrase I kind of like—we're called to become 'disenchanted elites.' You know, people whose lives have turned out pretty well as far as comfort goes, but who have become disenchanted with mainstream cultural values—people who have found a different vision of life. And that's a big part of what church is about—being resocialized, reformed, into that different way of seeing and living. Becoming reenchanted, I guess.

"I don't think being comfortable is morally reprehensible. What matters is what we do with whatever wealth and influence we have.

Do we use it to preserve the way things are? Or do we use it to make the world a better place? You know, 'From those to whom much has been given, much will be expected.' Anyway, that's what I preach and teach."

They sipped their port. Fredrika asked, "How's your book doing? I know they say any press is good press."

"That may be true," Kate said. "It's actually doing pretty well. That reminds me. I gave a lecture a couple of weeks ago about it and did a book signing afterward—I haven't done many of those. Anyway, it was a woman's turn, with about ten people in line behind her. As I was signing her book she said to me, in a very soft voice, 'I'm thinking of leaving my husband.' I looked up at her and said, 'Oh?' And she said, 'But my friends don't think I should.' I was sitting there, looking at the line behind her, trying to imagine where this conversation is going and thinking what to say, so I took a stab in the dark and asked her very quietly, 'Is there abuse?' I was imagining that maybe her friends thought her husband was a good guy, but he really wasn't. So then she leaned forward and whispered, 'No—but I'm afraid that I might kill him.' So I said, 'Really?' And I'm sure my voice sounded as astounded as I was. And then she said, in an even softer whisper, 'I killed my last husband, but nobody knows that.' I was still looking at the line of people and wondering what to say to her—I mean, good Lord."

Fredrika's eyes were wide. "So what did you say?"

"Well, I was tempted to say, 'Lady, this is a book signing!' But I didn't. So I just said, 'Sister, you need to talk to somebody about this.' And she said, 'Thank you,' and made room for the next person in line."

"Extraordinary," Fredrika said. "Was it somebody local?"

"Nobody I'd ever seen before."

"Your story reminds me of a friend of mine in my last parish who writes about spirituality. She's done a lot of book signings over the years, and she told me about some of the surprising things that people have said to her in the thirty seconds or so that it takes to sign a book."

"Why did she think that was?"

"Pretty simple, she thought. Once people think you know something about religion and the spiritual life, they'll tell you the most remarkable things. And, of course, it happens to us priests all the time. One of the reasons I love my job."

Abigail brought their checks to the table. Kate added a 25 percent tip, as she usually did.

As they were about to leave the table, Fredrika said, "I want to say again that I think applying to Scudder is the right thing for you to do. From all I know of you, I think you'd really like to be there for a year. Don't worry about what your department might think—you'll land on your feet. You don't need to be afraid."

"Fear not, right?"

Now with their coats on, Fredrika and Kate stood at the door to the restaurant.

Fredrika said, "So, home to the Sermon on the Mount."

Kate said, "Home to the Bible and justice."

"Aren't we something?" Fredrika said as they hugged.

17

On Sunday morning, the adult education class gathered at St. Columba's. Since the course had begun four weeks ago in early January, the number of participants had grown from twenty-five to about forty.

Kate recognized their faces and knew many of their names. Most were regulars in the adult education courses at St. Columba's, which Kate thought of as a progressive Episcopal church. Of course, there were some who regularly attended worship services but didn't take part in adult education, and so she wasn't sure what they thought. But the ethos of the congregation was progressive.

Kate noticed Fredrika at the back of the room. She often came when Kate was teaching, unless she had something pressing—like fine-tuning her sermon for the worship service that followed the education hour.

At nine o'clock, Kate stood up and said, "Nice to be with you again. And before I take you into today's topic, I want to begin with a prayer. It's from a Celtic Christian named Alcuin, who lived around the year 800. So we go back in time some twelve centuries:

Give us, O Lord, we pray:
Firm faith,
Unwavering hope,
A passion for justice.
Pour into our hearts:
The spirit of wisdom and understanding,
The spirit of counsel and spiritual strength,
The spirit of knowledge and true compassion,
And the spirit of wonder in all your works.
Light eternal, shine in our hearts;
Power eternal, deliver us from evil;
Wisdom eternal, scatter the darkness of our ignorance;
Might eternal, have mercy on us.
Grant that we may ever seek your face,
With all our heart and soul and strength;
And in your infinite mercy,
Bring us at last to the fullness of your presence
Where we shall behold your glory
And live your promised joys.
In your name O Christ,
Our body and our blood, our life and our nourishment.
Amen.

Kate was silent for a few moments and then said, "Today, we

move from the past to the present—from the Bible's passion for economic justice to thinking about economic justice today, from their then to our now.

"To remind you briefly, economic justice is about the just distribution of wealth, the just distribution of God's earth, grounded in the biblical affirmation that 'the earth is the Lord's and the fullness thereof.' Given that the earth and its fullness belong to God and not to us, what is fair, what is just?"

She paused as a few latecomers took seats. "We have already looked at the distribution of wealth in the ancient world of the Bible, and the protest of the Torah, the prophets, and Jesus against its unfairness. Now we turn to thinking about the distribution of wealth in our country today.

"What I've decided to do is to provide you with some statistical data and then invite your reflections about it. My purpose is not so much to convince you of something, but to equip you to talk about this with other people, especially Christians. It's a sensitive subject, especially for people whose lives have turned out well financially. How we approach it can make a real difference. We need to avoid making people feel guilty or attacked because they have more than enough. Rather, our purpose should be to raise consciousness about the effects of our economic system for the sake of treating a political question: What can be done about this?

"I don't want to overwhelm you with statistics, so I'm going to provide you with just a few. I begin with median household income. To explain, median is different from average. For example, Bill Gates and I have an average net worth of $35 billion." The class laughed. "Median income is not the same as average income. Rather, median household income means half of households are above this and half are below. And household means two or more people living together—could be a couple with no children, could be a single parent with one or more children, could be a couple with one or more children." She looked at the class to see if anyone looked puzzled.

"Okay," Kate said, "here's the figure. Median household income in this country last year was $50,000 a year. Half of households were above that, and half below. It doesn't mean that most households had $50,000 a year—half have less, many much less. Indeed, many households in the bottom 25 percent would think of $50,000 a year as a princely sum.

"Now, I want you to take a few minutes to imagine what it would be like to be a household living on $50,000 a year or less. Maybe that figure doesn't sound too bad if you imagine a retired couple whose house and car are paid for, who have Medicare, and who have no other major expenses. Or maybe it doesn't sound too bad if you imagine living in a rural area or small town like ours.

"So I want you to imagine what it would be like to live on that amount or less in a metropolitan area, where the majority of our population now live. Imagine further that there is at least one child in the household. To say the obvious, many households do include children.

"You might think about some of these questions. What kind of housing are you likely to have? Could you afford your own home? What size and quality rental housing could you afford? What kind of school would your child or children go to? Would you be able to afford a private school? What kind of car would you be able to afford? If you need child care because one or both parents are working, how much do you think that would cost? If your job doesn't provide health insurance—and remember, the less you make, the less likely you are to have benefits—could you afford health insurance? How much would you be able to save for retirement? How much anxiety would be in your life because of worries about money?

"Take about five minutes to do some thinking and jot down some ideas about this, and then I'll put you in small groups to share what you've come up with."

After the small groups had talked with each other, Kate regathered the class. "Soon I'll give you some time for questions and comments, but before that I want to provide you with a few more statistics about income distribution. I will do so with minimal commentary.

"First, median taxpayer income in this country last year—this includes all taxpayers, whether single or living as a household: $28,000 a year. Half of all taxpayers make more than that, half less. Now, if you're in your twenties and single or living with somebody else making $28,000 a year, that might not sound too bad. But suppose you're in your forties, fifties, or sixties and this is where you're topping out?

"Second, a formula for translating hourly wage into annual income. I mention this because many people, especially those of us who receive salaries, haven't thought about this. The formula is very simple. In round numbers, working full-time at forty hours a week means working 2,000 hours a year. So, annual income equals hourly wage times 2,000.

"To provide some examples, until very recently, the minimum hourly wage has been $5.50 an hour. Multiplied times 2,000, that results in $11,000 a year. Another example: because the minimum wage has been $5.50 an hour, many people think that an hourly wage of $12, $15, or $18 an hour sounds pretty good. Once again, do the math: those rates result in annual incomes of $24,000, $30,000, and $36,000—all well below median household income.

"Third, a statistic about the effects of present tax policy. Fifty percent of the total dollars of tax cuts since 2001 have gone to the wealthiest 1 percent of Americans—people with incomes of

$350,000 a year or more. One might perhaps ask if these are the people who need it most.

"Finally, among developed nations, the United States has the greatest differential between the top 10 percent of income earners and the bottom 10 percent of income earners. And the gap is growing."

Kate paused, looked around at the class, and said, "Well, I know that's a lot of stuff, but I hope not too much. So, any comments or questions?"

After a brief silence, a man spoke. "I have a friend who listens to right-wing radio talk shows a lot, and whenever we talk about politics, he regularly says things like even the poor people in this country live better than kings and the aristocracy did a couple centuries ago—they have indoor plumbing, a television, a car, maybe air conditioning, and might even take a plane trip once a year or so. What do you say to somebody like that?"

"Well," Kate said, "probably not anything that's going to change his mind." The class chuckled.

"More seriously, I suggest that he simply hasn't imagined what it would be like for him to live on $20,000 or $40,000 a year. And I suspect that he probably also thinks that if poor people only applied themselves more, they wouldn't be poor. That's the ideology that justifies huge differentials in wealth—the notion that people can become wealthy if they only work hard enough.

"Last term, in one of my classes, a student said his dad says that the great thing about this country is that anybody can become a millionaire. There's a grain of truth in that—someone born into a poor family can become a millionaire, and anybody could win the lottery. But unless we're careful about that kind of thinking, it carries a cruel corollary: if you don't become a millionaire, if you're among the poor, it's your own fault.

"And it's important to realize that there are some people whose minds you aren't going to be able to change, and your friend—

and most likely the talk-show host—may be a couple of them. If they're going to be changed, the Holy Spirit will have to do it."

Again a few chuckles. Kate continued, "But there is a large Christian *middle* who don't have strong opinions about this or who haven't thought much about this, and they may be more open to thinking this through. If we want to change things in this country, that middle is our primary audience."

A woman said, "When I talk about economic justice, I sometimes am told, 'Sounds like you're talking about socialism,' or 'Sounds like you're saying everybody should be paid the same.' And I don't really mean that, but I'm not sure what to say. Do you have a good response for that?"

"A couple of things," Kate said. "Sometimes I ask people if they've been to Europe recently and noticed how prosperous these countries are—nice cars, fine-looking cities and towns, well-dressed people, and so forth. Yet these countries have much less of a differential between rich and poor. And they have a much better safety net, including universal health care.

"So you can have a more economically just society without falling into our stereotypes about drab socialism or a society without incentives. A fair distribution of wealth doesn't mean that everybody needs to get the same.

"And then I invite people to think about what's fair. Probably the best people to judge are those in the bottom half of the population economically. Would it seem fair to them, for example, that a doctor would make four or six or even ten times as much as they do? I think to most of them it would. But twenty or thirty or more times as much? Or think of the obscenity of many CEO salaries. And extravagant salaries go pretty far down the chain of command in most companies.

"The issue is not whether some people have more than enough, but that everybody should have enough for the necessities of life—

and in the modern world that includes not just food and housing, but also education and health care."

Another woman said, "I have a comment, not a question. I'm a social worker, and I know quite a few families in which both parents are working full-time at a few dollars an hour above minimum wage. They're good people and they work hard, and yet money is a constant source of stress and worry. I think one of the problems is that those of us who are reasonably well-off usually don't know people like them. So I want to recommend a book, Barbara Ehrenreich's *Nickel and Dimed*. It's her story of working at a number of jobs that pay just over minimum wage, trying to live on it, and getting to know other people in that wage range. It's a real eye-opener—a glimpse into a world very different from the one most of us know."

"Thanks for the suggestion," Kate said. "I second it. And I want to add that the book is a great read." Kate looked at her watch. Five minutes left. "Anybody else? We've got time for one more question or comment."

A few seconds passed, and then a man said, "This is all pretty political, and I'm sympathetic to it. I think I'm beginning to see the connection between the Bible and economics. But what do you say to people who say that religion and politics should be kept separate—and they usually justify it by talking about separation between church and state?"

"Anybody want to piggyback on that?" Kate asked.

"I hear that too," a woman said.

"Anybody else?"

"I have friends who are upset about the Christian right, and they complain that they're mixing religion and politics. So they're opposed to bringing politics into Christianity, because they see what the Christian right has done."

"We might have to talk more about that next week. For now,

let me leave you with this. It's the Pharaohs of this world who would be happy to keep religion and politics separate. I mean, think about it. If Moses had simply said to Pharaoh, 'You know, all we want is to build a little synagogue down there in the ghetto where we can worship our God,' I think Pharaoh would have said, 'Fine.' But it's because Moses said, 'Let my people go,' that Pharaoh resisted with all his might. For the Bible, the issue isn't whether religion and politics are related—of course they are. The issue is what kind of politics. One that serves the interest of the wealthy and powerful, or one that embodies God's passion that everybody have enough."

Kate paused. "And with that, it's time to call it a day. See you next week. Take care of yourselves."

After church, Kate drove home, changed clothes, made herself a cup of tea, and turned to the task of writing her application letter. She had made some notes over the past week.

As she sat at her desk, she puzzled for a few minutes about how formal to make it. Like a business letter—cool, a bit reserved, and distant? Or more like just talking to them? She decided to just begin the letter and see what emerged.

I'm pleased to apply for your position as a visiting professor in New Testament. My curriculum vitae is attached, and I trust that you have already received the four letters of reference I have requested to be sent to you.

To respond to your question about why I would like to teach at Scudder, I will describe the passion that animates my work as a teacher and scholar.

About ten years ago, two events converged that account for my interest. After several years without a significant connection to a Christian community, I became a member of an Episcopal church. Soon thereafter I decided to begin graduate school. At the time, I was undecided between a priestly vocation and an academic vocation. Indeed, undecided is perhaps too weak a term; "torn" might be more accurate.

Then, in my first year of graduate study, I fell in love with the scholarly study of the Bible, especially the New Testament. And through my years of graduate study and into my first years of teaching, my involvement in the life of the church has deepened, including regularly teaching adult education courses in my congregation.

Though I value the historical study of the New Testament and early Christianity for academic reasons, and though I enjoy teaching undergraduates, my passion is what biblical scholarship can and should mean for the lives of Christians and the church today. Thus the opportunity to teach in an environment where that is the central emphasis is very attractive. I would value—indeed love—being part of a seminary faculty and teaching seminarians for a year.

Kate reflected on what she had just written and realized that that was the reason she felt so strongly about pursuing this opportunity. She wanted to be in a place where she could speak with candor and passion about the meaning of religion for people's lives, for the lives of Christians. She continued:

This passion is also reflected in my publishing. Though my book on the letter of James was a revision of my doctoral thesis and thus written primarily for an academic audience, I was drawn to study James because of the passion in the letter itself, including its passion for economic justice. In my thesis and in the book, I set the book of James within the historical context of a late first-century Christian community with a large gap between rich and poor in the Roman Empire, a method I learned from John Dominic Crossan's books on the historical Jesus and Paul.

Indeed, I thought of calling the book The Passion of James, but decided that it might be misunderstood as the martyrdom of James, which is not what I meant. Rather, I meant "what James was passionate about."

My second book, on the stories of the birth of Jesus, made the connection between then and now explicit. Though I am confident that the argument in the book meets rigorous scholarly standards, my central concern was to lead Christians to reflect on the meanings of the stories of Christmas for our now. As in my book on James, my emphasis in the Christmas book is both religious and political.

Currently I am working on a book-length study of C. S. Lewis that seeks to demonstrate the theological development between the early Lewis and the later Lewis in order to reclaim Lewis for more progressive Christians.

If I am appointed to the position at Scudder, I would bring this passion for the intersection between scholarship and contemporary Christian issues to my teaching of the introductory course in New Testament. In addition, I would be pleased to teach any of the following courses.

The first two are more specialized courses in the New Testament:

1. *A course on James, then and now—either a lecture course or a seminar.*

2. *A course on the kingdom of God, then and now. It would emphasize its meanings in the gospels, its roots within Judaism, its "counterimperial" meaning, and its significance for Christians today.*

The third and fourth move beyond the New Testament. Both reflect strong interests of mine:

3. *A course that could be called "Mysticism, Ethics, and Politics." To explain a bit, mysticism is often seen (wrongly in my judgment) as escapist and not very much connected to ethics and issues of justice. But I think the history of Christian mysticism suggests otherwise.*
4. *A course on notable Christian lives, in which the primary reading would be biographies and autobiographies, all suggesting that Christianity is about loving God and changing the world.*

Kate paused. What else should she add? Maybe, "Please, oh please, I really want this job"? Or maybe, "Perhaps I should tell you that I might not be able to accept it if you offer it to me, because my college might not guarantee that I can come back, and I don't want to be homeless"? No, probably not.

So she ended it with a conventional line:

If I can provide any further information that might be helpful to you as you make your decision, please let me know.
Dr. Katharine (Kate) Riley
Assistant Professor of Religious Studies
Wells College

Kate read the letter through and decided to look at it again on Monday morning. Then she would need to send it in order to meet the Tuesday deadline.

She realized that she should let Vincent know that she was applying. With a feeling she recognized as mild dread, she reluctantly wrote an e-mail:

Dear Vincent,
A quick note on a Sunday evening. Want you to know that I have just finished writing my application to Scudder,

and I'll be posting it tomorrow so that they will get it by the Tuesday deadline.

I would have preferred to wait until the college had clarified its policy about a leave of absence in my circumstances. But it became impossible to wait any longer.

I wanted you to know. Hope this is okay.

Yours truly,
Kate

She hit "Send," turned off her computer, and decided to call Geoff.

18

Promptly at the beginning of Kate's office hours on Tuesday, Erin Mattson tapped on her partially open door. "Professor Riley? I haven't made an appointment, so is this okay? Or are you already booked?"

"No—or yes and no. This is fine—nobody's signed up. Come in."

Kate rolled her swivel chair out from behind her desk and gestured to Erin to sit down in one of the three chairs clustered in the middle of the room. Kate watched as Erin took her coat off and placed her backpack on the floor. A beautiful young woman who seemed unaware of it and certainly didn't flaunt it. No makeup, or so little that you couldn't tell. No apparent effort to look glamorous. Fair skin, her hair a fall of flax. Kate wondered if most guys would be wary of approaching her—she combined "too beautiful" with an aura of inaccessibility.

Kate said, "It's nice to see you. I've thought it would be interesting to talk with you. I like the way your mind works—your essays are very good and your comments in class tell me that you're really chewing on what we're talking about."

Erin looked surprised. "Thank you." She smiled broadly, and Kate was reminded of Carly Simon or perhaps Julia Roberts. "I love your class—it's exciting. And I love the way you teach. But that's not the reason I'm here, though I'd love to talk about class stuff with you sometime." She paused.

"So, what do you want to talk about?"

"Well," Erin began, "I need to tell you some things first. I have a brother named Zach. He's three years younger than me and in his frosh year at another college. We're very close—always have been. And when we were both home at Christmas, he told me he was gay. I didn't know that, in spite of how close we are." Erin paused.

Kate said, "So you were surprised?"

Erin said, "I was. He's not obviously gay, if you know what I mean. I thought he had lots of girlfriends. He was just a sophomore when I went off to college, but I kept hearing from my folks that girls were calling him all the time. And he was always hanging out with one or another, sometimes more than one at a time. Now I'm realizing they were girls who were friends, not girlfriends. Have you ever known guys like that?"

"Oh yes," Kate said, thinking of Geoff and other gay men she had known. She asked, "Is he good looking?" and immediately wondered if she was indulging a stereotype.

Erin laughed. "Yes, he is. You know, when I look back on this"—she slapped herself jokingly on the forehead—"shoulda known.

"But," Erin continued, "that's only part of the reason I'm here—the background, I guess. Sure, I was surprised when Zach told me he's gay. But it doesn't really change my feelings toward him—I don't feel estranged or disapproving or anything like that. In fact, I feel closer to him—I mean, our conversation was very real.

"The problem is the Christian group I belong to here at Wells. It's called The Way—you've probably heard of it. Anyway, they're pretty conservative, and they're really down on homosexuality. They're not mean or nasty about it—they don't do gay-bashing or confront gay people or anything like that. But they think homosexuality is wrong because the Bible says it's wrong. They see it as a sin, and most would say that you can't be a practicing homosexual and a Christian—or at least they would say that you have to feel bad about it and try to change. We've done a couple of Bible studies about it. A few of the guys talk about the 'homosexual agenda' as something we need to oppose—I think it's a phrase they got from Christian television or radio.

"It's not that the subject comes up at every meeting. But it's part of the atmosphere, if you know what I mean—just like you're supposed to be against premarital sex and abortion if you're Christian. So," Erin continued, "that's what I want to talk about. I don't believe Zach is a bad person, but I'm in a group that thinks he is—or they would if they knew. It's not that I've told them. But it bothers me." She leaned down and picked up a bottle of water from her backpack.

"Do you think homosexuality is wrong?" Kate asked.

"Well, I don't think so. It's always seemed a bit strange to me ever since I learned what it was. But I had a couple of friends in high school who were lesbians, and it didn't bother me. At least I don't think it did. But now for the last couple years, I've been hearing that it's against God's will—that it's an abomination."

Kate leaned forward slightly. "So what would it be h
talk about? Your feelings? The group? What the Bible say

"Well," Erin said, "I think about what the Bible says. I've already read two books about the Bible and homosexuality that I found in the library. Do you know *Dirt, Greed and Sex* by William Countryman? Or *The New Testament and Homosexuality* by Robin Scroggs?" Erin smiled, "I guess they're both by what are called liberal Christians, but I'm learning to become open to liberal Christian thought in your class."

Kate said, "Good books. I would have mentioned them to you if you had asked me for something to read. And a third one I'd recommend is Jack Rogers, *Jesus, the Bible and Homosexuality.*"

Erin jotted down the title and then looked back up at Kate. "Yeah, I thought they were good too. And I get what they're saying. That the verse in the Old Testament that says that homosexuality is an abomination is in a context in Leviticus that also forbids lots of things that almost all Christians think are fine. Like planting two kinds of seed in the same field or wearing garments made of two kinds of cloth—I mean, that would rule out blends. We set those laws aside and say they don't apply to our time—so why should we think the verse about homosexuality applies to all times?

"And what they say about two of the three verses in the New Testament about homosexuality makes sense to me—that they probably refer to an older man having sex with a young boy." Erin shrugged. "You don't have to be a redneck to think that's wrong." She smiled slightly. "Well, maybe I shouldn't have used that word.

"But the part of the New Testament that I still have trouble with is that passage from Paul in Romans where he says—" Erin paused and took a well-thumbed NIV Student Bible out of her backpack and looked at Kate. "Can I read it to you? I know you probably know it by heart, but it will help me if I read it." Kate nodded.

Erin opened her Bible to the first chapter of Romans. "It comes right after Paul talks about the wrath of God and the fall and idolatry." Then she began to read:

> Therefore God gave them over in the sinful desires of their hearts to sexual impurity for the degrading of their bodies with one another. They exchanged the truth of God for a lie, and worshiped and served created things rather than the Creator—who is forever praised. Amen.
>
> Because of this, God gave them over to shameful lusts. Even their women exchanged natural relations for unnatural ones. In the same way the men also abandoned natural relations with women and were inflamed with lust for one another. Men committed indecent acts with other men, and received in themselves the due penalty for their perversion.

"That's really strong," Erin said. "Doesn't sound like it's on the same level as wearing blends, and it covers more than having sex with a young boy. So that's the passage I stumble over. I can imagine persuading some in my group about a different way of seeing the other passages, but probably not this one. Some of them even think that the last verse refers to AIDS. So that's what I wanted to ask you about."

Kate admired Erin's precision. She waited for a few moments and, when Erin didn't continue, asked, "Are you hoping for something that will be persuasive to your group? Or something that will give you an understanding that makes sense to you?"

"I suppose both. But maybe the second is more important—I'm not really looking for a way to argue with them."

Kate said, "I think that's smart—or perhaps I should say wise. I suspect that you probably couldn't change their minds. Of course, I don't know them. But from what I've heard, they believe in biblical inerrancy and infallibility, so I think they would reject any interpretation that says the text doesn't mean what it looks like it says. They have a lot at stake in their way of seeing the truth of the Bible."

She met Erin's eyes and smiled. "Ready for a little lecturette?"

"That's why I came to see you—I want to know what you think."

"Okay. And feel free to interrupt me anytime." Kate paused and thought about how to begin. "Well, there's more than one thing to say. Let me begin with the obvious. Paul was Jewish. He grew up as a Jew, and even after the experience in which Jesus appeared to him, he still thought of himself as Jewish. He might have described himself as a Christian Jew—he had been a Pharisaic Jew, and now he was a Jew who was a follower of Jesus.

"And when he was growing up, he would have heard standard Jewish synagogue rhetoric about what Gentiles are like—what they looked like through Jewish eyes. There was a standard Jewish indictment of Gentiles. They were, of course, idolaters. And another part of that standard rhetoric was that Gentiles were sexually deviant. And more. That passage in Romans is followed by a list of vices of Gentiles. Read me the rest of the passage—the part that follows what you already read to me."

Erin picked up her Bible again and read the rest of the first chapter of Romans:

> Furthermore, since they [the Gentiles] did not think it worthwhile to retain the knowledge of God, he gave them over to a depraved mind, to do what ought not to be done. They have become filled with every kind of wickedness, evil, greed and depravity. They are full of envy, murder, strife, deceit and malice. They are gossips, slanderers, God-haters, insolent, arrogant and boastful; they invent ways of doing evil; they disobey their parents; they are senseless, faithless, heartless, ruthless. Although they know God's righteous decree that those who do such things deserve death, they not only continue to do these very things but also approve of those who practice them.

Erin finished reading the passage and was quiet. Then she said, "So you're saying that this is just Jewish rhetoric about Gentiles?"

"Well, the long list of vices makes me suspect that. Whenever

Paul uses rapid-fire lists, scholars think he's probably saying something he's heard or said before. It's certainly possible, maybe even likely. This sounds like a standard Jewish perception of Gentiles.

"We need to be careful here. I'm not saying something negative about Jews or Judaism because they used harsh language about Gentiles. We need to remember that they had been oppressed and persecuted by one Gentile empire after another for a long time. So it's not surprising that they developed a negative attitude toward Gentiles and Gentile ways.

"And in this passage Paul may be reciting a typical list of Gentile vices as Jews perceived them in order to establish his credibility with the Christian Jews in Rome to whom he's writing. Paul had not been there, so they didn't know him in person, and he may have wanted to establish his 'credentials' "—Kate made quote marks in the air—"at the beginning of his letter."

Erin looked thoughtful. "So—if you're right, I'm not sure what that means. Are you suggesting that we don't need to take this seriously, because he's kind of reciting a list?"

"What I'm saying means at least this much—perhaps we shouldn't put a lot of weight on this passage, as if Paul has thought long and hard about homosexuality and then states his position on it. In its context in Romans, he's using this picture of the Gentile world as filled with vices as part of a larger argument—it's more like a building block than an authoritative conclusion that he's reached through prolonged reflection."

After a few moments, Erin spoke again. "Well, I think I understand what you're saying. But how can we know if that's the right way to read this passage? I think my friends would think it sounds a little fishy."

Kate said, "Ah, but there's one more thing to say. Suppose we knew that Paul was really, and strongly, against homosexuality—that he was convinced that it's sinful, and that it really mattered to him. Just suppose that for a moment. Now, a question: Would it be okay to say Paul was wrong about that? Would it be hard for you to do that?"

"Wow," Erin said. Her eyes moved away from Kate's face as she stared at the upper corner of the room for a few seconds, her lips pressed together. Then she spoke. "I must admit I hadn't thought of that. That's pretty wild. I guess I've thought that once we figure out what a Bible passage is saying, that pretty much settles it. But to say that Paul says something and he's wrong—that seems a lot different."

Kate was quiet as she continued to watch wheels turning in Erin's head. "Can you really do that?" Erin said. "You know, people in The Way would say this sounds like cafeteria Christianity—picking and choosing what you like and ignoring or rejecting the rest. I mean, how can you justify that?"

"Well," Kate said, "you have to have reasons—you can't just say, 'I like this' and 'I don't like this.' So you have to provide reasons—just as, I would think, people who interpret it as God's eternal will should have to provide reasons for seeing it that way.

"And it's important to realize that Paul was wrong about some things. For example, he thought the second coming of Jesus was near, and he was wrong about that." Kate leaned forward. "Or an example from a letter attributed to Paul, but almost certainly not written by him—that passage in the second chapter of First Timothy where, we are told, women should be silent and learn in full submission, that they are not to teach or have authority over men, and that they're responsible for sin coming into the world. That rules out, among other things, the ordination of women to be clergy. And, of course, for many centuries Christians understood it that way. But now mainline Protestant denominations ordain women. So they're really saying that this passage—whoever wrote it—no longer applies.

"And many of them—not all of them—are reaching the same conclusion about the Bible's passages about homosexuality. That they no longer apply. And one reason they give is that we now understand that for some people, same-sex behavior is natural, not unnatural. Paul's argument is that it's not natural—but he didn't know that homosexuality is a product of sexual orientation, not a choice that people freely make. We might say that it would be unnatural for a gay person to try to be heterosexual."

Kate wondered whether to say anything more, or whether to stop to see what Erin was making of this. She decided to give one more example. "You know, as recently as a hundred and fifty years ago, Christians in this country were deeply divided about whether the Bible permits slavery. Many thought it did—that the Bible's passages about masters and slaves meant that slavery was okay. Some even argued that slavery reflects the will of God. But I don't know anybody today who would argue that we should bring slavery back, because there are passages in the Bible that say it's okay.

"So Christians have often decided that passages in the Bible are wrong—or, if you wish, that they no longer apply. But that's just a gentle way of saying that maybe they've always been wrong—that the subordination of women and slavery were never right, but simply reflected the mores of the time."

Erin said, "Yeah, I can see that. And it's beginning to dawn on me that this is what follows from the way of seeing the Bible that we're exploring in class. But I hadn't thought until just now that a biblical writer might be wrong. I mean, they teach us in The Way that the Bible is inerrant. I guess I thought that God wouldn't let anything in the Bible be wrong. I thought it was all about knowing how to interpret the text—you know, if you interpret it rightly, you'll see that it's true—like the Genesis stories of creation and fall as myths rather than history. But this is new."

She took a sip from her water bottle. "Wow. I don't know

whether I'm near a breakthrough or about to fall off a cliff. You know, thinking this way would be a big change—a very big change—for me. If I started thinking this way, I wouldn't be able to tell my group. I can't imagine saying to them, 'You know, Paul was just wrong about this.' That's way beyond what they could accept. They would start praying for me—not that that's bad. But these prayers would be about helping me to stop becoming a backslider or an unbeliever."

She was thoughtful again. "If they knew I thought this way, I probably wouldn't be welcome there for very long. They wouldn't kick me out, at least not right away. But they would be concerned, and if I didn't return to the fold fairly quickly, I know I would start feeling a subtle form of ostracism—like 'Erin's not really one of us.' "

"How would that be for you?" Kate asked.

"Well, it would be hard. I like them, and most of us are really close. But I have to admit I've started to wonder if I'm maybe outgrowing them. I'm sorry—that sounds so elitist. But I do see some things differently than most of them do. Like I think the stories of creation and the Garden of Eden are myths—thanks to your class. Makes so much more sense." Erin smiled. "And I'm not into the Christian political right—not that you have to be in order to be part of the group, but most of them are. So, yeah, I've wondered if I'm still really at home there."

Erin stopped. She bit her lip and then said, "Can I ask you another question, kind of a personal one?"

"Sure," Kate said.

"Well, I have the impression that you think it's okay to be gay and Christian."

Kate nodded.

"And I have the impression that your view of the Bible is pretty liberal, or whatever word you would want to use. And that you don't think Christianity is the only true religion. And I also have the impression that you take Christianity very seriously. I mean, I know you can't talk about that in class, but I've heard that you go to church and teach classes there and that you start your days with prayer—there's a lot of stuff out there on the student grapevine."

Erin tucked her hair behind her ear and looked up at Kate. "So what I want to ask is, Is it hard to be Christian and to think like you do?"

Kate wondered what the most helpful response would be. Then she said, "No, it's not hard. In fact, it's made it easier for me to be wholeheartedly Christian. You know, there are some unnecessary intellectual stumbling blocks to being Christian—like needing to believe that the Bible is inerrant and that we are to interpret it literally and factually, or that really big miracles happened in biblical times, or that the earth is only ten thousand years old. The way I see things means that those obstacles are gone, and then the real meaning of Christianity emerges."

"And what's the real meaning?" Erin asked.

Kate shrugged. "It's pretty simple: it's about centering more and more deeply in God. And for Christians, that means centering in God as revealed decisively in Jesus. Of course, it's not simple *to do*—for most of us it takes a long time to become deeply centered in God. But I think that's what being Christian is about. It's not very much about believing things that are hard to believe."

Erin was silent and then said, "What do you mean by centering in God? I like the way it sounds, but I'm not sure what it means."

Kate thought for a moment. "Well, our relationship with God is somewhat like a human relationship. It grows and deepens to the extent that we pay attention to it—by taking time for it, spending time in it, attending to it. It's about longing and prayer and
at's how we center in God. To center in God and not
ıer things that we could center in. Actually, that's the
faith—faith isn't really about believing in God, but

centering in God. You know what St. Augustine said? 'Our hearts are restless until they find their home in God.' We find our home in God by centering in God."

Kate looked at Erin. "Does that make sense?" Then, looking at her watch, "Sorry to be a timekeeper. But I have about five minutes more before I need to pull some things together and go to my morning class. Anything we can talk about in that time?"

After a few moments, Erin said. "No, I don't think so. But I know I want to think about what you've said, and I'm pretty sure that I'll want to come and talk to you again. Would that be okay?"

Kate smiled at Erin. "Of course—I would enjoy that."

19

Kate returned to her office after her morning class and saw that the message light on her telephone was blinking. The voice mail was from Vincent, telling her that he had news and that she should see him. She phoned back and made an appointment to see him after her afternoon class.

At three thirty, Kate knocked on his door. "Come in, come in," Vincent said. He smiled and gestured to a chair. Kate sat down.

Remaining behind his desk as he usually did, he began, "Thanks for letting me know that you are applying to Scudder. Given their deadline, I understand that you couldn't wait any longer. And that's what I have news about. To get right down to it, Dean Robinson met with me this morning about the possibility of a leave for you. She and the senior faculty with whom she's been meeting have made their decision."

Kate noticed the formal and distant tone in his voice, at once peremptory and a bit nervous.

"The bottom line, to use that ugly phrase, is that there's good news and bad news—though I prefer not to think of it that way. Rather, it seems to me to be a rather ingenious and prudential solution to a problem.

"I begin with what could be seen as the bad news. The college will not give you a leave of absence to teach elsewhere. That may seem harsh, but it need not be seen that way. The overarching consideration is their unwillingness to set a precedent for granting an untenured professor a leave to teach somewhere else. They think it's a bad idea.

"Let me explain their rationale for not wanting to set a precedent." Vincent settled into his professorial tone, the pompous-sounding one that Geoff had skewered so mercilessly at Murphy's. "There are two reasons, and they're related. The first we've already talked about—the time and expense involved in finding a one-year replacement. The college is willing to do that for tenured faculty. And the college is willing to do that for untenured faculty for research or family reasons, like maternity leave or caring for a dying parent. The presumption is that, of course, they'll return to Wells. They're not considering going elsewhere.

"But when the purpose is to be a visiting professor at another school, a complication enters the picture. What if the other school is courting our professor, trying him or her out for a year, and we have to hunt for a replacement and guarantee our professor the right of return? And doing so at our expense?

"The dean and her committee told me to encourage you to look at this from our point of view. If you go to Scudder for a year, it means that we have to do a search for a one-year replacement. And then, if Scudder decides they want to keep you, then we'll have to do another search the next year for the tenure-track appointment you presently have. That's a lot for an untenured professor to put the college and the department through. It's both time and money."

Kate took a deep breath.

Vincent continued, "That's the bad news. Now the good news. The college—that is, the dean and her committee—has found a way of making it possible for you to do this. True, it's not without risk, but it's pretty safe. Here's what they propose. If you're offered the position at Scudder and accept it, the college will 'vacate' your position. That's a new term for us. It means that we will do a search this year for a one-year replacement. Then, next year, a search for a tenure-track position, namely, the one that you now hold.

"You would, of course, be eligible to apply—and if you are our choice, then you would get credit for your previous years of teaching here and would go up for tenure consideration in your first year back with us. I think it's quite a clever solution—you get to do what you want, and the college avoids setting a precedent that it doesn't want to."

Kate thought about it. "But I wouldn't be guaranteed a place to come back to?"

Vincent looked at Kate. "That's right—but we know you. Can you imagine somebody applying for your job whom we'd rather have than you?"

That's precisely the question, Kate thought, but didn't say so. She was silent for a few moments and then asked, "Do you know what they think of my doing this? I mean, what you've just told me could be heard as permission. But I wonder if I'm hearing something else—that perhaps they think I shouldn't?"

"Candidly," Vincent continued, "it's hard to know what they think. For what it's worth, my hunch—and I emphasize that it's a hunch—is that they'd rather you didn't. They might be afraid of losing you. But they don't want to forbid you to do this."

Kate thought about what she was hearing. "Can I ask you another question?"

"Of course," Vincent said, smiling slightly. "Goes without saying."

"Well, what do you think—or maybe I should ask, what do you and Fred and Paul think? You're the tenured members of the department."

Vincent pursed his lips. "Well, I've thought about what I would say if you asked. We want you to do what you want to do. So you have our permission. But if you're asking about our druthers, about what we would prefer, we'd rather that you stay here."

"Can I ask you why?"

"Well, a couple of things. One reason is that we wonder what makes teaching at Scudder for a year so attractive to you. I don't think we understand that."

Kate decided not to try to explain why she was attracted to Scudder, thinking it might muddy the water further.

Vincent continued, "And we do wonder if Scudder has long-term plans for you. I mean, think about it—their letter sounds as though they're courting you. Maybe they're thinking about offering you a permanent position, but want to see what you're like for a year, or just aren't ready yet to say that your position can become a permanent one. Of course, nobody can know if that's what they have in mind, but it's certainly possible, maybe even likely."

Vincent looked at Kate again. "So, the reasons we'd like you to stay are pragmatic and perhaps a bit selfish. It's extra work for us if you go, coupled with our uncertainty about whether you will come back. It would simplify our lives if you didn't do this."

Kate was silent. "So you're saying that I can do this, but without a guaranteed right of return, and that you don't think I should?"

Vincent lifted his hands in protest. "That's too strong," he said. "You asked why we'd rather you not do this. I'm simply trying to be honest and candid."

He pursed his lips again and looked thoughtful, as if deciding whether to say more. "You know—or I guess you don't know—we could have blocked this if we had wanted to. If I—if we—had recommended to the dean that she not give approval, I think she would have decided not to find a way to make what amounts to an exception. But I—we—didn't do that. We don't want to stand in your way. The important thing you need to hear is that we're willing to do what we can in order to make this possible for you."

Kate was puzzled by what she was hearing. Maybe the department was genuinely supportive of her, even making an unconventional leave possible. And also honest enough to say that they'd rather she didn't go. What Vincent was saying made a lot of sense. Maybe they hadn't been obstructionist and mean-spirited. Maybe they had been pretty good guys—cautious, thoughtful, honest, even afraid of losing her in a year to Scudder.

And yet she wasn't at all sure that that was it. How much should she trust the new perception opened up by what Vincent had said? Hadn't they been disapproving from the first? Had she imagined that or read too much into it?

Or was it that the permission didn't feel pure, didn't feel clean—you can go, but we wish you wouldn't. However honest it was from them, for her it created conflict.

Resolving not to let uncertainty into her voice, Kate said, "Thank you. I didn't want to do this without your—" She hesitated, looking for the right word. Blessing? No, she hadn't gotten that. Support? Not sure about that either. She settled on "go-ahead." Kate sat a moment longer, looked at Vincent to see if he had anything more to say, smiled slightly, got up, and left.

Back in her office, she stuffed a folder of student essays into her leather backpack, put on her coat, walked to her car, and got in. She sat for a few moments before starting it. Rather than turning on NPR as she usually did, she drove to Murphy's in silence.

She walked slowly into Murphy's. As she passed the bar, she put on a smile for Arthur, said, "The usual," and went to her booth by the window. She sat with her chin resting on her upturned hand and stared out the window.

"Everything okay, Professor?" Arthur asked as he placed a Guinness and a glass of water on her table.

She turned toward him, as if suddenly awake, and said, "Oh. Yeah." She smiled at him. "Things are fine."

Kate opened her journal, but felt too confused to write. Instead, she leaned against the back of the booth, aware of a tumble of thoughts. She was angry, she realized. Angry that this had become so complex when it could have been quite simple. She didn't know if it was fair to be angry with Vincent and the department—maybe they had done the best they could. But what was all this concern not to set a precedent really about? Couldn't they have decided on a policy of deciding on requests like this on a case-by-case basis? That would still give them the freedom to say no if something like this came up again. *Damn,* she thought.

She was angry about the choice she might have to make. She didn't like the thought of having to choose.

And angry about the anxiety she felt. What felt like a low charge of electricity filled her body. *Maybe this is what it is to be wired,* she thought. She hadn't felt this way since looking for her first teaching job.

It was the risk, she knew. She had a secure position here at Wells, a year away from tenure, which could hardly be denied to her if she stayed. To go to Scudder would jeopardize all that. She realized that her job at Wells represented safety and security to her. Or at least it had, until the senior faculty in her department had started making her feel that her future wasn't as safe as she had presumed. She was forty-two—what if she went to Scudder and wasn't rehired at Wells? She could hardly start over again in the academic world at this point, plus there would be the question that would hang over every interview: Why didn't you get tenure in your previous position?

Kate thought again of how alone she was. She had been responsible for her own security for a long time, ever since her parents' deaths—through college and her twenties and graduate school and still. Then, remembering her baby-sitting and dishwashing jobs in high school, she realized that her responsibility for herself had begun even earlier.

Was her anxiety keeping her from taking risks?

She felt stuck. Looking down at her journal, she wrote:

- *Need to talk to Geoff and Fredrika. Call them.*
- *E-mail to Martin? Need to think that through. Might be presumptuous. I'm not a finalist yet, so maybe it's premature to tell him about this.*

She leaned back once more and decided to have a cigarette and another Guinness.

Kate sat straight up in bed, suddenly awake. She had been dreaming:

I am with my mother shopping for new clothes at the beginning of my senior year of high school. We are having a good time—chatting and laughing and enjoying the day, especially because there is just a little bit more money this year. We are in a clothing store when, suddenly, as I watch, my mother vanishes.

Now awake, she still felt the absolute shock. The T-shirt in which she slept was damp.

20

At Scudder that same week, the faculty met again to discuss the gift to endow a chair in evangelical thought. On Tuesday, the dean had sent an e-mail to the faculty with the results of the poll. Eighteen had voted to accept the endowment, four said no, and two were undecided. Although three-fourths had voted yes, Leitha Debnar had called another meeting—she liked to have as much of a consensus as possible.

Because she was out of town when the faculty met, Dean Alberto Gomez presided. He began, "Before we discuss this matter today, I want to remind you of a suggestion made by Martin Erikson at our last meeting. Namely, that we could accept this gift and then if we discover after a time that it's not a good idea, we can offer to return the endowment to the donor or the donor's heirs.

"President Debnar has checked on that possibility with the Board of Regents. In their judgment, there is no impediment to our doing so, though this has never come up before. So accepting this gift doesn't involve a permanent commitment. We can see how it goes."

The faculty who had voted no or undecided had only mild misgivings—not strong objections, but reservations and hesitations. After these had been discussed (longer than necessary, Martin thought) and more or less resolved, Dean Gomez said, "Well, we seem to have a consensus that we should accept this. So let me ask." There was a solid yes from most of the faculty, a qualified yes from some, no objections, and the meeting ended.

On Friday morning, Martin was ushered into the president's office by her receptionist. "Martin, so nice of you to come by," Leitha Debnar said. "I always enjoy seeing you. Sit down, sit down."

She gestured to one of the leather armchairs grouped around a low oval table, sat down herself, and asked, "Coffee?" Martin declined and after a few pleasantries, she asked, "So, what's on your mind today? Of course, you don't need a reason for seeing me—but I suspect you do."

Martin returned her smile. Leitha was about Martin's age. Single for about twenty years—her former husband hadn't been able to handle her becoming an Episcopal priest and then, after a Ph.D., a professor, so they had divorced. Leitha was a handsome and lively woman. Martin had thought more than once about asking her out for dinner.

Back to business, though. He said, "I'm here to talk about the new endowed chair. First, I want to congratulate you for your role in securing the gift and for involving the faculty about whether to accept it. That was wise, and you did it well. I'm pleased there wasn't much contention, and you deserve a lot of credit for that.

"What I want to talk with you about is the donor's desire to remain anonymous. I understand that, and honor it. But given the size of the gift—I recall your saying that it's the largest Scudder has ever received—I've also been thinking that it would be too bad if nothing were known about the donor. I've got a strong historical interest, as you know, and I imagine somebody doing a history of the seminary fifty or a hundred years from now. For the seminary's archives to contain no information about the donor of such a large gift would be a pity. So I have a proposition. Would you consider asking the donor if he or she would be willing to be interviewed by somebody for the sake of the seminary's historical records?"

"She," Leitha said. "I'm pretty sure it's a woman—the intermediary slipped and used 'she' when he was talking with me last week. He immediately added, 'or he.' But I think he was covering up."

"Interesting. Well, you could tell her that the interview will be completely confidential—that none of the information would be disclosed to anybody until she gives permission or for any number of years after her death that she might specify. So her anonymity could be guaranteed, even as the memory of what she has done would be preserved in our archives."

Leitha looked thoughtful. After a few moments she said, "Do you have somebody in mind to do the interview?"

"I'd be happy to have anybody do it. But, to be candid, I would like to do it. I'm curious about people who give away large amounts of money, especially to a seminary. I suspect they have a story."

Leitha nodded. "I like the idea—makes sense to me. Of course, I have no way of asking her directly. But I can certainly send your suggestion through the intermediary. It can't hurt to ask." She paused and added, "And I like your suggestion that you do the interview. I have no idea whether she's heard of you, but you are our most famous professor. And you do have a fair amount of charm." She smiled again, and they both rose.

As Martin left her office, he saw Carson Grant waiting in the outer office. Carson was the chair of the search committee for the visiting appointment in New Testament, and Martin suspected he knew why Carson was here. Nevertheless, he said, "Carson, what are you doing here? Have you been bad?"

"No, of course not. And I think you probably know why I'm here. I have a meeting with the president and the dean to report the search committee's list of finalists for the temporary New Testament position."

"Can you tell me if Kate Riley is among them? Or is this all confidential until after your meeting?"

"No, I think it's all right to tell you that she is. She's a strong candidate—and your recommendation counted for a lot. You carry a lot of weight around here."

"Really? I thought I was pretty trim."

Carson grimaced. "Bad, Martin. You know what I mean."

"So what will happen next?"

"Well, assuming that the president and dean agree with our list of finalists, the invitations to come here for an interview will go out this afternoon."

"This afternoon? A Friday afternoon? That's impressive."

"We are on a tight schedule, you know."

Martin left Leitha's outer office and walked across the quadrangle. *So,* he thought, *Kate will be here for an interview.* Not that he was surprised.

He was looking forward to his weekend. Today, with no classes and his appointment with Leitha over with, he could be at home and do whatever he wanted. He planned to spend some of the day brainstorming ideas for a sermon for the first Sunday in Lent that he had agreed several months ago to preach in his own congregation. Then, tomorrow, a visit to his old friend Seamus, which involved a ninety-minute drive. He loved to drive his thirty-year-old Mercedes Benz two-seater convertible, and he loved seeing Seamus, shooting pool and playing chess with him. He planned his drive so that he could listen to Click and Clack, the Tappet Brothers, on NPR.

Back in his apartment, Martin changed into winter weekend wear—canvas slacks from Orvis, a bulky turtleneck sweater, and a pair of old loafers so worn and supple they were almost like slippers. Seated at his desk, mildly regretting that it was too early to have a glass of wine to go with his pipe and brainstorming, he reread the gospel text for the first Sunday in Lent, the story of Jesus being tempted by Satan in Matthew 4.1–11.

He jotted down some possible points to develop in his sermon. Later, he would decide what to keep and how to sequence them.

- *Locating this text in the season of Lent. Lent begins each year with Ash Wednesday, in which we are reminded of our mortality—"Dust you are, and to dust you shall return; ashes you are, and to ashes you shall return." And then, each year on the first Sunday in Lent, today, we face the question, "How then shall we live?" For that's what this Sunday is about—how shall we live? It's not just about the temptations of Jesus, but about the temptations that assail our lives—and the alternative.*
- *The story is about Jesus—but the fact that the church for centuries has put this text at the beginning of Lent suggests that it is also about us at the beginning of the most important season of the church year.*
- *Is there a devil? Is Satan real? Who knows? And if you pressed me, I would say, no, I don't think so. But there are*

temptations that are satanic, diabolical. This is what the story is about.

Martin got up from his chair and walked to his kitchen to make a cup of coffee. As he waited for the water to boil, he turned on the radio to hear a bit of NPR's *Fresh Air.* Today the guest, an author, was talking about the "grand ideas" that led the Bush administration to invade Iraq with the confidence that it would be quick and easy. The water boiled. Martin made a cup of instant coffee. When he was brainstorming, he didn't pay enough attention to taste to warrant taking the time to make coffee from freshly ground beans.

He returned to his desk:

- *The first temptation: "Turn these stones into bread." The material temptation—to satisfy our hunger with bread, the material basis of life. But life is not just about fulfilling our physical hunger; it is also about fulfilling our spiritual hunger. "One does not live by bread alone."*

- *The second temptation: Satan takes Jesus to the pinnacle of the Temple—throw yourself down, God will bear you up, protect you. The temptation to be stupid—go ahead and jump off high buildings, you won't get hurt. We live our lives like this a lot. But don't be stupid: "Do not put the Lord your God to the test."*

- *The third temptation: Satan takes Jesus to a very high mountain and shows him all the kingdoms of the earth—their splendor, wealth, and glory: "All these I will give you, if you will fall down and worship me." Both a personal and political meaning. Personal level: seeking wealth and power, what the kingdoms of this earth offer. Political level: the imperial temptation, to rule the kingdoms of this earth. This is the temptation we face as a nation—and it is sa-*

tanic, from the devil, from the pit. Rather, we are to worship the Lord our God, and serve God only.

Conclusion? Lent as a season of repentance. Two resonances of "repent" in the Bible: (1) to turn, return, to God; (2) to go beyond the mind that you have—to see anew and again. In short, to center more fully in God: "Worship the Lord your God, and serve only God."

Martin decided that was enough for now. He wanted to incubate the ideas for a few days. He put his notepad away and pondered what to do with the rest of his Friday.

On Saturday morning, up early as usual, Kate showered, made coffee, and did morning prayer. Then she checked her e-mail. She liked to get it out of the way, so she could forget about it for the rest of the day. Scrolling through, she saw one from the dean at Scudder and opened it.

Dear Professor Riley,

I am pleased to inform you that you are one of the finalists for our position as visiting professor in New Testament. The next step is an on-campus interview here at Scudder. We would like you to visit us for an evening and the following day. We see your visit not only as an opportunity for us to meet you, but for you to meet us.

We suggest the following schedule:

Evening of arrival:

6:30. Dinner with the search committee, the dean, and the president (if she is available); concludes by 9:00.

The next day (very full):

7:30–9:00. Breakfast with a small group of students (four or five).

9:00–9:30. Walking tour of campus and buildings, escorted by one or two students.

9:45–11:45. Two meetings, each an hour long, with a few of our faculty and students in small groups.

Noon–1:30. Lunch with the faculty. Most will be there. When you have finished eating (about 12:30?), an hour or so of Q & A.

2:00–3:30. Lecture (with at least half an hour for Q & A) to a group of faculty and students on a topic of your choice that you think would be interesting to our students. You should imagine yourself talking to them (and not to the faculty, as if you were presenting a paper to colleagues at a professional meeting). What we are interested in seeing is how you would teach seminary students.

3:45–4:30 or so. "Exit" session with the dean and the search committee. This is an opportunity for you to ask any questions that may have arisen for you during the day or that haven't been addressed.

You are then free to leave, so you could catch an evening flight back home. However, if you would like to stay for another day or two, we would be happy to provide accommodation.

Our preference would be for a Thursday evening and a Friday. Because we do not have classes on Fridays, more faculty and students will be free to be with you. However, if a Thursday-Friday combination is difficult for you, we would be willing to make arrangements for another day.

Let us know which days and dates will work best. We hope to complete our interviews in the next three weeks, before the end of the month.

Yours truly,
Alberto Gomez
Academic Dean

Oh my, Kate thought. *Maybe I will have to make a decision.* She had almost hoped that she wouldn't be on Scudder's short list. Almost, but not quite. But it sure would have made life simpler.

Kate walked to her kitchen and turned on the stove to boil water for a pot of tea. She paced through the house, back to the study and back to the kitchen.

Finally, she sent an e-mail to Dean Gomez, thanking him for the invitation and promising to get back to him on Monday or Tuesday with proposed dates. Then she wrote an e-mail to Martin.

Early in the evening, back in his apartment after a good afternoon with Seamus, Martin checked his e-mail. A message from Kate:

Dear Martin,

A pleasant surprise to begin my day—just got an e-mail from Dean Gomez telling me that I'm a finalist (as perhaps you already know).

I'm pleased, of course (I guess I've already said that). But I'm also conflicted, and I seek your counsel. Let me tell you why.

The big reason: I learned earlier this week that my college will not give me a regular leave of absence for this. Instead, they've come up with something they're calling "vacating" my position—which means if I'm away for a year, they'll replace me with a one-year appointment and then next year do a national search for the position I now hold, and they hope that I would be one of the applicants. If they choose me, I will get credit for my five years here and would be considered for tenure the first year after they rehire me.

It's confusing to me. From their point of view, they've come up with a way of letting me do this without setting a precedent for the future. And when I point out that their decision gives me no guarantee, they say things like, "Can you imagine our finding anybody else that we'd rather hire than you?"

But—and maybe this is the paranoid within me—I'm not sure that I trust all of that. I have no clue what they're really thinking.

Enough, enough. These are issues on my end.

But what I want to ask you is this. Because of my confusion about my status here, I'm not sure that I would accept a position at Scudder if it were offered to me. Given that, I wonder if I should come for an interview, or whether I should withdraw my candidacy? Your counsel?

Thank you again for whatever role you may have played in the invitation.

All the best,
Kate.

Damn, Martin thought. *Helluva position for Wells to put her in.* He wondered if he should call her—probably not tonight, but perhaps tomorrow. The thought of hearing her voice on the phone after so many years was both exciting and a little nerve-racking. He decided to stay with e-mail as it might provide a more focused and reflective way of thinking this through:

Dear Kate,

Good to hear from you—and, yes, I did know that you are one of our finalists.

And very sorry to hear about the decision your college has made. They may feel good about it, but they've put you in a difficult position, indeed a dilemma.

Regarding your question: should you come to an interview if you're not sure you would accept the position here? Let me suggest two scenarios:

You're almost certain that you wouldn't accept a job here

because of the risk of losing your position at Wells. If so—if you're almost certain—then perhaps an interview doesn't make sense.

You're conflicted—meaning that you don't know yet what you would do, but can imagine deciding either way. If this is where you are, then come to the interview. You'll have more information as a result, and that might be helpful for resolving the conflict.

And keep in mind: we don't assume that a candidate will of course accept an offer if we make one. Academic institutions are accustomed to candidates saying no as well as yes.

All the best,
Martin

Kate wrote back in a few minutes:

Dear Martin,

Thanks for your quick response and counsel.

No further thoughts on what I might do—haven't figured out which of your scenarios describes me best. Working on it—I'm seeing a woman friend tomorrow, who is also my priest.

And I note that you're checking e-mail on a Saturday night. As my students would say, "Get a life."

All the best to you.
Kate

Martin wrote back:

Dear Kate,

And to say the obvious, you also are checking e-mail on a Saturday night.

Physician, heal yourself.

Martin

21

Kate left her office to go to her Tuesday afternoon class. For three days—four, she realized, as she counted them out in her mind—her thoughts had been dominated by "the decision," as she had come to think of it, her waking moments preoccupied with turning its elements over and over, rotating them round and round, always returning to the stubborn fact: she could go to Scudder, but with no guarantee that she could return to Wells. What to do? Would she, should she, really be willing to risk her virtually guaranteed position here? Would that be really dumb?

Of course, she told herself she didn't have to know now—no job had been offered to her, so was she unduly obsessing about a decision that maybe wouldn't need to be made? But she did need to decide whether to go for an interview.

Long conversations with Geoff and Fredrika over the weekend. She prayed, "Dear Lord, I'm confused. I don't know what to do, and I'm more than a little bit scared. I don't want to be afraid, and I also don't want to be stupid. So help me, help me."

She tried silent prayer, but the silence was filled with unwilled thoughts about the decision. She could not become quiet inside.

Finally, she resolved this much: she fit Martin's second category. She was definitely conflicted, and yet not certain that she would decline an offer from Scudder if one were made. That much was clear to her, though she was aware that she had no idea what she would decide if she were offered the position. So not much was clear, but enough, Kate thought, to go ahead.

Martin's counsel had been helpful to her. Also, she realized that she was pleased about how easily they had slipped into a comfortable e-mail relationship. She had felt some lingering awkwardness over their affair and the confusing way it had ended and wondered if he might also. But their e-mail communication had been easy, sometimes even funny and warm. Felt like friendship. Maybe their long-ago affair didn't have to create awkwardness. She wondered how much her renewed friendship with Martin added to Scudder's appeal for her. The real appeal was Scudder, of course. But had Martin become a bonus? She was curious about him again.

On Monday evening she had sent an e-mail to Martin:

Dear Martin,

A long weekend. I've been spending a lot of time seeking to discern what to do. And without going into all the drearily repetitive reasons, I've decided that I'm in your category two. Thanks for your helpful suggestion that I might see it this way.

Tomorrow morning I'll let Dean Gomez know that I'll be coming for an interview. I'm going to suggest the third Friday of this month, arriving in time on Thursday for a dinner that evening.

Are you in town that weekend? Or on the road somewhere? Hope you're around.

Wearily,
Kate

Erin hesitated at the open door of Kate's classroom. She almost hadn't come at all. With three papers due in her other classes and midterm exams coming up, she hadn't had time to do the reading. She was still wondering if she should just skip class today and take a nap or get some more writing done. But Kate was already there, sitting on the edge of the desk as usual, and Erin didn't want Kate to see her leave, so she went in and found her seat in the second row of the double horseshoe.

When everyone else had straggled in, most of them looking as tired and stressed as Erin felt, Kate stood and distributed a handout. Returning to her perch on the desk, she said, "Today we start a new unit in the course. On the syllabus, it's called 'The Enlightenment and the Gospels: History, Fiction, or Parable?' We could call it in shorthand 'The Enlightenment and Jesus'—how the Enlightenment, with its emphasis on investigation as the path to knowledge, has affected perceptions of Jesus in Western culture.

"Let me start with a question. It's not meant to check up on you—it's just information for me so that I know how best to do class today. How many of you were not able to do today's readings?"

Erin slumped in her chair and glanced around the class. She hated to admit that she hadn't prepared, but she saw that about half of the other students raised their hands, so she joined them.

Kate said, "I understand. I know we're getting near midterm with its exams and papers, so I'm aware that some of you may be preoccupied by matters other than today's class." She smiled. "I appreciate your showing up at all.

"To be sure we can have a good conversation about our topic today, I've crystallized the main points of the readings on the handout I've just given you. And to inform those of you who didn't have time to do the reading, and to remind those of you who did, I'm going to go through it paragraph by paragraph, adding some comments as I do."

> 1. We have seen how Enlightenment knowledge collided with and changed understandings of the Genesis stories of creation and the first humans. To a large extent, the issue was scripture and science. Now we turn to the Enlightenment and Jesus. To a large extent, this issue is about scripture and history, though the new science of the Enlightenment also played a part. We will see how Enlightenment knowledge collided with and changed perceptions of Jesus.
>
> And of course, this is no small matter, given Jesus's importance for Christians and Western culture more generally. He is seen by Christians as the primary and decisive revelation of God. Given that he's that important, what was he like? This is the quest for the historical Jesus, and it began in the Enlightenment. Was he just like the gospels portray him? Or?

"Okay so far?" Kate looked out at the class. Erin nodded, and Kate continued:

> 2. The first skeptical books about the gospels by scholars in Christian countries were published in the first half of the 1700s. The skepticism was directed primarily at the stories of the miracles. Within an Enlightenment worldview, everything happens as the result of natural causation—there are no interventions or interruptions of the natural order. The denial of the miraculous was a continuation of the scripture-versus-science issue.

3. The book commonly named as the beginning of the quest for the historical Jesus was published in 1778, anonymously and posthumously ten years after the death of its author, Hermann Samuel Reimarus (1694–1768). Its German title is variously translated into English as *On the Intentions [or Aims or Purposes] of Jesus and His Disciples.*

In its title lies its central claim: the aims or purposes or intentions of Jesus and his followers were very different from each other. Jesus, Reimarus argued, proclaimed the kingdom of God as overthrowing the rule of the Roman Empire. Rome killed him, but his followers didn't want to return to the simple lives they had before they met Jesus. So they invented the story of the resurrection and began to proclaim a second coming of Jesus in the future. Their intention and his intention were very different: he proclaimed the kingdom of God, and they proclaimed Jesus. Thus, in Reimarus's eyes, Christianity was a fraud.

"Now," Kate said, "if you want to know more about that, it's in the readings. Or you can ask about it later in the period. What I want to do is to move on to the foundations of the quest for the historical Jesus, which are also found in the readings. So let me move to part two of the handout."

4. Reimarus's more sensational claims were generally not accepted by scholars. But the claim behind his work was: that there is an important distinction to be made between what Jesus was like as a figure of history and the way the gospels and the New Testament tell his story. The distinction has been variously named—the Jesus of history, or the historical Jesus, and the Christ of faith; the pre-Easter Jesus (what Jesus was like before his death) and the post-Easter Jesus (what Jesus became after his death).

5. The distinction is grounded in a historical realization: the gospels are a developing tradition. Jesus lived in the first third of the first century. The four gospels of the New Testament were written in the last third of the first century—Mark first, around the year 70, Matthew and Luke probably next, and John probably last, most likely in the 90s. Thus the gospels tell us how Jesus's followers talked about him forty or

> more years after his death. But they are not simply historical reporting about what he was like. Rather, they are a combination of memory and testimony, memory and witness: they tell us about what Jesus meant to his followers several decades after his life and death—the significance he had come to have in their lives, experience, and thought. They thus combine memories of the pre-Easter Jesus with post-Easter testimony.

Kate looked up from the handout again and asked, "How many of you have heard of the Jesus Seminar?"

Erin raised her hand hesitantly. She didn't know much about the Jesus Seminar, but Peter had mentioned it more than once as a bunch of liberal scholars who had the audacity to color-code the gospels, keeping the parts they liked the best and taking out the rest. Another example of cafeteria Christianity, he had said. About a third of the class raised their hands along with her.

"What do you know about it?" asked Kate.

Jonathan said, "They're a group of scholars—I think mostly guys—who started meeting about twenty years ago to vote on how much of what's in the gospels goes back to Jesus. Didn't they vote by using different colored balls—or beads? Like red if you think it goes back to Jesus, black if you're pretty sure it doesn't, and pink and gray if you're kind of in between? But I don't know much more than that."

Amy said, "Well, I've heard that they don't think the gospels are true—they think that early Christians made up a lot of stuff about Jesus. I don't think they take the Bible and the gospels very seriously. They sound pretty weird to me."

Erin nodded. Amy's take was the same one she had heard from Peter, but at the same time she was struck by how certain Amy sounded in her disparagement. Didn't she at least want to hear more?

"Okay," Kate said, nodding at Amy. "Some do see the Jesus Seminar that way." It seemed to Erin that Kate's eyes rested on her for an extra fraction of a second.

Josh said, "Well, what I get from the Jesus Seminar is that there are earlier and later layers of material in the gospels. The red and pink stuff is what they're pretty sure is early, and the rest is later—in descending order of gray and black."

"That's right—that's the way they see what they're doing," Kate said. "Now, whether they're right or wrong, the reason I brought up the Jesus Seminar is that their system of voting illustrates very clearly the understanding of the gospels that emerged in Enlightenment scholarship: namely, the gospels are a developing and thus layered tradition. And let me add, very importantly—even the later layers of the tradition, the material the Jesus Seminar puts in gray and black, are important. Every layer matters. The layers that don't go back to Jesus are nevertheless a testimony, witness, to how early Christians saw Jesus. Parts of them are also applications of Jesus's message to their time. So the later layers tell us a lot—they're not to be discarded.

"And now, back to the handout—we're almost done. Let's look at section six.

> 6. The result of the application of Enlightenment historical scholarship to the gospels and the New Testament: Jesus as a historical figure was not the same as the gospels portray him. This is especially the case in John's gospel. The gospel of John is a very developed layer of the tradition. To use the voting colors of the Jesus Seminar, John is mostly in black. Mark, Matthew, and Luke are closer to historical memory than John, even though they also reflect a post-Easter perspective and contain post-Easter convictions and applications.
>
> The difference between the historical Jesus and the Jesus of the gospels is considerable. Scholars disagree about how great the difference is. At one end is skepticism about whether we can know anything about Jesus. A centrist position affirms that we can know some important things about him with a reasonable degree of probability. At the other end of the spectrum is a continuing affirmation of the essential histori-

> cal factuality of the gospels. This end of the spectrum is found mainly in fundamentalist and much conservative Christian scholarship, but generally not in mainstream academic scholarship.
>
> To illustrate the difference between the historical Jesus and the Jesus of the gospels, virtually all mainstream scholars of the gospels agree on two matters that are important to many people.
>
> First, "exalted" language about who Jesus was does not go back to Jesus himself. Familiar words and phrases like "Son of God," "Messiah," "Lord," "Light of the World," "Bread of Life," and so forth are the testimony and witness of early Christians—this is who Jesus was for them. But this language does not go back to Jesus; he didn't talk about himself this way. It follows that his message was not about himself, but about something else. And what was that?
>
> Second, the saving significance of Jesus's death is a post-Easter development. Though the New Testament affirms in a variety of ways that the death of Jesus served the saving purposes of God, Enlightenment historical scholarship sees these as retrospective post-Easter interpretations. Within this framework, Jesus did not see his own purpose to be his death. Rather, he was executed for what he was doing. And what was that? Why did he end up being killed by the authorities who ruled his world?"

Erin frowned at her handout. This last paragraph sounded like the mainstream scholars didn't believe that Jesus died for humanity's sins. And what did they think about the resurrection? The handout didn't say anything about it. She could handle the idea of Adam and Eve as myth, and she was working through the idea that Paul might have been wrong about homosexuality, but to say that Jesus's purpose was not to die for the sins of the world—and, who knows, maybe that the resurrection hadn't really happened? That was the cornerstone of the faith she had learned in The Way. What would be left of her faith without that?

Kate continued:

> These realizations—that the gospels combine memory and testimony, that there is a difference between the historical Jesus and the Jesus of the New Testament, and that Jesus's message was neither about himself nor the saving significance of his death—are the foundations of the quest for the historical Jesus. In the rest of this unit of the course, we will look at a number of scholarly portraits of Jesus, their cultural reception, and their cultural conditioning.

Kate set the handout down on her desk. "Okay, that's the introduction to this unit and an overview of where we'll be going. It's a lot, I know, and I look forward to exploring the details with you in the next several classes. But let's start with the 'so what' question. In other words, why does this matter? So what if Jesus was different from how the gospels portray him? What's at stake? Why does this matter to people? Does it matter to you?"

Jonathan said, "Well, I did the readings for today," and then turned slightly red. "Sorry. Didn't mean to sound like I'm bragging about being a good student or whatever. Anyway, I was struck by how controversial this stuff was. I mean, Reimarus deliberately didn't publish his manuscript during his lifetime, and when it was published ten years after his death, it was done anonymously because of fears about his family's well-being. And some reviewer—I can't remember if it was about Reimarus's book or somebody else's—called the book something like the most pestilential volume ever vomited from the bowels of hell."

Jonathan shifted in his chair. His large body made it seem comically small. "And then there's Strauss, what, fifty years later? He wrote his fourteen-hundred-page life of Jesus in the 1830s—and he was only twenty-seven, not much older than us. A reviewer called it something like the Iscariotism of his time, and he was never again able to get a teaching position in a university."

"Well," Andrew said, "no wonder. Reimarus and Strauss were challenging the foundations of the European world—not just whether the world was created in six days, but Jesus and the Bible. I mean, think about it—Christianity had been the foundation of Western culture for centuries and now its foundations were being questioned. And if the foundational story of a culture is up for grabs, then everything is."

Fiona joined in. "Didn't the French Revolution happen soon after Reimarus's book? In 1789, I think, so like about ten years later. And it really scared a lot of people in Europe—especially the rulers—you know, the aristocracy and the upper classes. They saw what happened in France. I'd have been scared if I was one of them."

"Do you mean that Reimarus's book helped cause the French Revolution?" another student asked. Erin thought his name was Justin.

"No, I wouldn't go that far," Fiona responded. "Or better, I have no idea. The point I'm making is that the questioning of the Bible and the gospels was happening at the same time that all these other changes in Europe were happening. You know, the world was kind of falling apart, and I think authors like Reimarus and Strauss were attacked because they were seen as aiding and abetting the collapse of that world."

"So," Andrew said, "you're saying that the historical study of Jesus is subversive?"

Fiona cocked her head and thought for a moment. "Well, maybe. Yeah, I guess so. It all seems pretty radical to me. At least when you think back a century or two." Then she added, "And I suspect it's still kind of alarming to a lot of people today—I'm thinking of Christians. I mean, it seems to me that they have the most at stake in all of this."

Josh chimed in. "I grew up Christian—well, I still am, but not quite in the same way that I was then. Anyway, when I learned a couple years ago that Jesus might have been a lot different from how Christians talk about him, it was a big deal. Kind of scary. But also kind of exciting. For me, it was like a sacred cow was being challenged. And I realized that if this sacred cow could be challenged, then all the sacred cows could be challenged—you know, everything we think we know."

Erin regarded Josh with new interest. That sounded a lot like how she felt. Maybe she could talk to him about his experience.

Josh continued, "I think that's when I began to become an adult in my thinking—you know, somebody who steps back and looks at what they think and why. And it happened because of what we're talking about today."

"The beginning of epistemological anxiety," Allison said. Andrew shot her an impressed look.

Josh said, "Yeah, that's about right."

Justin said, "I know quite a few members of the class are Christians, so I'd like to hear from more of you about how this sounds to you."

The class became quiet. After several moments, Erin spoke up. "Well, when I signed up for this course, I knew this would come up. I saw the syllabus online, and that's one of the reasons I took this class."

Out of the corner of her eye, she saw Amy shoot her a quick glance, but she soldiered on. "I've been a Christian for a while now, but I got curious about whether there was a different way of looking at things—you know, the Bible and Jesus and religion. So what we're talking about right now is why I'm here. But I keep thinking about what Kate said about whether it matters if Jesus was different than he is portrayed in the gospels. And for me right now, I feel like it does. I've based my faith on the Jesus presented in the gospels, so if that Jesus isn't the real Jesus, then what is my faith about? I don't fully know what I make of it yet. I'm puzzling it through."

After a few beats of silence, Kate said, "Let's think back to our earlier discussion of myth and metaphor. Recall that myths and metaphors can be true even though they're not factual. Now let's think about how that might apply to the gospels. If Jesus didn't say he was the Son of God or the Light of the World, does that make it any less true? And if the saving interpretations of his death are post-Easter and originate in Christian communities, does that make them any less true?" Kate paused. "I don't mean that seeing things this way settles the issue—I'm simply suggesting a connection between earlier in term and where we are now."

The class was quiet. Erin wanted to ask about the resurrection, but she didn't know if she was ready to hear the answer.

Kate asked, "Anybody else want to say anything about why this matters?"

No one said anything.

Kate looked around. "So what else do you want to talk about—either in response to the readings or to my summary of the readings?"

A woman Erin didn't know raised her hand. "Just one more thing before we move on—are there churches that teach this?"

Kate nodded. "Yes, there are—and more than there used to be. It's still true that the majority of Christians see the gospels as essentially historical reports that they're supposed to believe in. But there are more and more Christians, mostly mainline Protestants and Catholics, who are becoming aware of the different viewpoint. So, yes, but it's by no means a settled question."

"Tonight we're going to focus on Jesus's famous statement in John 14.6: 'I am the way, the truth, and the life. No one comes to the Father except through me.'" Peter looked around at all the members of The Way's Tuesday night Bible study. It seemed to Erin that his gaze lingered on her a little too long.

He continued, "For a lot of people this statement is the ultimate in snobbishness and exclusivity. Yet that's not the purpose at all. Jesus came to earth to save us; his salvation is freely available to everyone. There's no membership requirement other than faith.

"We live in a time when people preach tolerance. We hear a lot about tolerance here at Wells, don't we? The siren song of our culture might be characterized as 'Believe what you want, and let others do the same.' But how can we justify doing that? To just let others believe what they want, when we know—because Jesus made it abundantly clear—exactly what the truth is, is morally reprehensible. The stakes are terribly high. We are talking about nothing less than our eternal lives with God. There is no ambiguity in the statement, 'No one comes to the Father except through me.' We're not talking about tolerating a different hairstyle or a weird way of dressing; we're talking about tolerating a way of thinking that leads to death.

"And I have to say, I hear over and over again from liberal Christians that we aren't tolerant enough, but where is their tolerance of our point of view? Tolerance is not the point. There are many things that we don't tolerate in our society, because it is clear that they are wrong—murder, incest, rape—and may I point out that all of these are clearly outlawed in the Bible as well. So 'tolerance' "—he made air quotes—"seems to be prized only when it's convenient, when those preaching tolerance are practicing something they think others should accept unconditionally."

He leaned back in the chair. "I'm trying to give you some answers that you can offer to others when they say relativist things to you such as, 'Why do you care what I believe?' I'm sure you've heard comments like that frequently, especially in an academic environment like this one. Here's something else I'd like you to think about. What does it mean for the death of our Lord and Savior to say that it didn't cover everyone? Doesn't it demean his sacrifice, even make a mockery of it?"

Erin looked around at the other members of the small group. They were nodding in agreement; several were jotting down notes in the margins of their study guides. Was she the only one who was troubled by what he was saying? Hesitantly, she raised her hand. "But what if Jesus didn't really say that?"

Peter cocked his head. "Say what?"

"Well, that line from John about being the way, the truth, and the life. Today in class, we—" She looked to Amy for support, and Amy looked away. "Well, Professor Riley was talking about how most scholars think that the entire book of John was written way after Jesus lived. Post-Easter, she called it. So I guess most of them don't think he actually said those words."

"Okay," Peter said. "And how did they draw this conclusion?"

"Well, I don't know exactly, but I was impressed by the fact that there seems to be a general consensus about it." She looked around again, but no one would meet her eyes. She saw Amy raise her eyebrows at Peter, a look that said, *See what I'm dealing with?* With a shock, she realized that Amy must have talked to Peter about her. "I'm not saying that I believe it; I'm just trying to talk it through. What do you think?"

Peter's tone was firm. "That's what faith is about. We believe that the Bible is true. We believe that Jesus was the Son of God, that he died for our sins, and that he is the way to God because the Bible tells us, and in more than one place. I would say that faith is what's lacking among these scholars who vote, actually vote, on what Jesus said or didn't say. I believe that faith in Jesus is rational and logical, but at some point you have to stop parsing and just believe. Where's their faith?"

Erin bit her lip. Kate had said she had faith. She had also said that Christianity didn't have to be about things that seemed impossible to believe. But she didn't want to argue anymore tonight, to distance herself any farther from the group, so she just nodded.

Peter held Erin's gaze. "I suggest that you pray about it. See what God tells you about this."

"Okay," she said. "I will."

At their Tuesday evening discussion group, Fiona noticed that although Erin and Amy arrived together, they didn't sit next to each other like they usually did. Andrew came in next, drawing Allison aside and chatting with her. The rest—Jonathan, Josh, and a recent addition, Justin—arrived a few minutes later. What was it, Fiona wondered, about guys whose names begin with J that attracts them to Jesus?

Gathered around the low table, they helped themselves to the nachos, chips and dip, and red wine. Fiona said, "So we're all in Kate's class—what do you think about today's discussion?"

"Well," Josh said, "I've been thinking about this memory and testimony bit, and that Jesus as Son of God and Lord and Messiah is all post-Easter testimony, not how Jesus spoke about himself. So, I thought, all of this language is testimony—this is what other people thought about him. And I started thinking: Was he the Son of God because that's who he was from the beginning? You know, the way we learned the stories about him, it's like being the Son of God was a status he had from his birth—from his conception, I guess. Or maybe even earlier—you know, he's the Word who was in the beginning with God.

"But—and this is what I've been thinking about today—would he have been the Son of God if nobody thought so? You know, what if his being the Son of God is the language of testimony, of—I'm looking for a word here—acclamation? That his followers acclaimed him as the Son of God, even though he didn't say that about himself? That's real different. So, would he have been the Son of God if nobody thought so? Or is he the Son of God because his followers thought so?"

Josh stopped. Silence. Then Amy said, frowning, "I think I understand what you're saying. But doesn't that mean he wasn't really the Son of God, but people only said so? I don't think I could accept that."

"Well," Josh said. "I don't know if it means that. Maybe it's like our talking about Lincoln as the Great Emancipator—he didn't talk about himself that way, but that's who he was—or who he became, I guess. So people can be more than how they see themselves or talk about themselves."

Erin said, "I'm still working this through. Ever since my conversion experience, I've thought that Jesus was always the Son of God—you know, even when he was a baby and a kid. So for me to think that his being the Son of God is an acclamation and conviction proclaimed by his followers only after his life is a stretch. I might be able to get my mind around that at some point—but for now, I'm not sure."

She sighed. "This is starting to get really hard for me. Now that I've accepted that a few things about the Bible might not be the way that I thought they were, it does seem like my whole belief system is questionable. Do you ever wonder if, after all the historical sifting, you might not end up with anything left?"

Andrew said, "That's what I think. It's all shifting sand. Think about it—the clear implication of what Kate said today is that it's very hard to know what Jesus was like because of the mixture of memory and testimony in the gospels. And the rest of our readings indicate that scholars are all over the place on what Jesus was really like. So why not just give up on it? Why not say that Jesus is a protean figure who can be seen in all kinds of ways, and that the ways that people choose to see him have very little to do with historical considerations? He's just what people want him to be. Seems clear to me."

Fiona saw Allison look at Andrew, her forehead furrowed. Clearly she wasn't fully on board with his argument either. But before she could speak, Jonathan did.

"I don't think we should give up on it," he said. "It's pretty interesting to me, and I think we probably *can* know some things about Jesus. And in response to what Erin said, I think that it's not about your whole belief system being open to question so much as that it's important to think critically about what we believe, since if you're a Christian, it affects so much about you and the way you see the world. For example, if we take uncritically every word of the Bible, we would say that women should be silent in the church and that they shouldn't wear gold jewelry or even braid their hair. And I think most of us in this room would disagree with those ideas. So I think it's important to think about what you believe and why you believe it.

"But let me get back to what Josh was saying—that all of these titles of Jesus are the language of acclamation and testimony. Now, I think there must have been something really remarkable about Jesus to lead his followers to talk about him this way. I mean, think about it: What would a person have to be like for you to start calling him *the* Son of God and Lord? For me, it's even more impressive, more significant, that his followers called him that than if he had said all of this stuff about himself. I mean, we've all heard of people who thought they were messiahs—but none of them were.

"One of my profs told me that he's known two people who

thought they were the Messiah. So what matters is not whether you think you're the Messiah, the anointed one and all that stuff, but whether other people do. Doesn't that make sense? Or am I missing something?"

Erin nodded. "So the fact that Jesus's followers thought he was the Messiah might be even more convincing testimony than if he himself had proclaimed it? I like that. Thanks, Jonathan. That helps me."

The conversation ranged on until Fiona checked her watch and saw it was ten thirty. "The hour grows late," she said. "It's time to disperse." A few in the group groaned, but then they all got up to get their coats.

She heard Amy say to Erin as they walked out, "Now I think I know what you feel like at Bible study. I don't know if I'm ready for this."

The same evening, Martin checked his e-mail before going to bed and read Kate's message about deciding to come to Scudder for an interview. He wrote back:

> *Dear Kate,*
>
> *Very pleased to hear that you'll be coming for an interview. I appreciate that your situation at Wells makes all of this difficult. No wonder you're feeling conflicted. But I'm glad you've decided to give us a chance.*
>
> *I will be at Scudder that weekend—gone the weekend before and the weekend after, but that weekend I'm here. I'm looking forward to seeing you again.*

Martin paused and then continued:

> *I know that your interview finishes late Friday afternoon and that you could catch a flight home that evening. But if you don't need to do that, what would you think of staying*

over Friday night so that we could have dinner together? We could process your day—and I would enjoy seeing you.

All the best,
Martin

At home, also checking her e-mail before going to bed, Kate read Martin's message and wrote back:

Dear Martin,

Good to know that you'll be around that weekend. And I am planning to stay over Friday night and then catch a flight home late Saturday afternoon.

Dinner Friday evening would be great.

Best wishes and good night.
Kate

22

Martin stood at the door of the donor's downtown condominium. He had been impressed as he entered the building—a concierge, an atrium lobby three stories tall with a waterfall, an unusually swift elevator to the fourteenth floor. He paused at the door. Her lawyer had told him very little, just that her name was Margaret Bardwell; that she was in her early eighties, still sharp and healthy; that she was a widow, lived alone, and was a bit of a character. He knocked.

She opened the door. Martin—unsure of whether to call her "Mrs. Bardwell" or "Ms. Bardwell" or "Margaret"—had decided to use first and last names. "Margaret Bardwell, I'm Martin Erikson." Pausing a beat, he added, "Thank you for agreeing to see me."

Margaret Bardwell was tall, with white hair that was swept neatly back into a French twist. She was wearing a two-piece cranberry knit suit and expensive-looking high-heeled shoes.

"Nice to meet you," she said, "and please call me Margaret. But only if I can call you Martin."

"That would be fine."

She led him into her living room, and Martin looked at the fine vista of the city through the tall windows. "Nice view," he said.

"Yes, I enjoy it, though living here seems a bit of an extravagance. But I bought it ten years ago, soon after my husband died, and prices weren't so high then. It looks like a bargain now."

She paused. "Would you like some tea? Or perhaps a glass of sherry? Or both? I often have both this time of day."

"If you're having both, both would be fine," Martin said.

She disappeared into the kitchen. Martin looked around the room. On the wall opposite the tall windows, about ten oil paintings—Martin didn't count them—of pastoral and city scenes, their colors harmonizing with each other and the ochre wall. On another wall, a fireplace faced with black marble and, on both sides, floor-to-ceiling shelves filled with books. On window ledges and end tables, an assortment of artifacts, mostly Middle Eastern, and in a glass-fronted case, a collection of ceramic dogs.

A dog wandered into the room. Gray and shaggy, built long and low like a Welsh corgi with a large head like an Irish wolfhound, he was short and large at the same time. He walked up to Martin, stared at him, and then turned in a circle before lying down between Martin's chair and the one Margaret would soon occupy.

Margaret returned from the kitchen carrying a tray with two pots of tea, a plate of scones, and bowls of clotted cream and strawberry preserves. Setting the tray down on the coffee table, she said, "I see you've met Henry. He's a very good dog."

"I've never seen a dog quite like him. Is he a mix or a breed?"

"Henry is from Ireland—he's a Glen of Imaal terrier. He comes from a place in the Wicklow Mountains south of Dublin. Beautiful place."

"He's certainly an interesting-looking dog." Henry, with his head on his paws, looked up at Martin.

"One of the reasons I got him is that the dog books said his breed is very spiritual. I couldn't imagine what that could mean, so I decided to see for myself."

"So, is he—is Henry—spiritual?"

"Oh, most definitely. Henry is quite contemplative. He likes to observe. And I take him to a small Anglican monastery just outside the city where I go for evening prayer once or twice a week. Do you know the place?"

Martin shook his head.

Margaret continued, "I asked if I could bring him, and the guest master smiled and said, 'Let's try it once and see how it goes.' Well, Henry was very quiet and attentive, so now he does evening prayer with monks. We're quite alike."

She gestured to a cabinet holding a small assortment of bottles. "I have sweet sherry and dry sherry. Which would you like?"

"Dry," Martin said, "unless you would recommend the sweet."

"No, no," she said. "I prefer dry. You've made a good choice."

She poured two glasses, put them on the table next to the tea tray, and sat down opposite Martin. "Cheers." They both sipped.

Martin said, "Mmm—very good." He sniffed the glass, sipped again. "Possibly a Domeq Fino?"

"Nice to meet somebody who knows something about sherry. Not many people do—at least not in this country."

She smiled. "Well, should we get down to it. I understand you want to ask me some questions."

Martin took another sip of sherry and looked at Margaret. "As President Debnar told your attorney, I'm here on behalf of the seminary. We're interested in knowing as much of your story as you would like to share. And we're interested in knowing what led you to give this very generous endowment to Scudder. I'm sure there's a reason for that."

"Where would you like to start?"

"Well, tell me something about your life."

"What a terrible request," she said. "Reminds me of dating days—'So tell me about yourself.' What does one say? But I understand the question. Let me give you some basics. I'm eighty-three, soon to be eighty-four. My husband died twelve years ago. He was a history professor. In the academic world, he was a 'prickly'—one of those detail people who like to take things apart and resist putting them back together. I'm more of a 'gooey' myself—I like to put things together. But we were a good pair—we had a sweet life together. He was ten years older than I, and I knew when we married that I would most likely be a widow someday. And though I miss him deeply, I wouldn't trade our thirty-six years together for anything.

"We married late—I was thirty-five, and he was forty-five. We met when I got a job at the college where he taught. I was an English professor—literature, not composition—and my love was nineteenth-century British women novelists. What a glorious time. Jane Austen, the Brontë sisters, George Eliot—who of course was really Mary Ann Evans. Other than Dickens, can you think of a nineteenth-century British male novelist who is still so widely read as these women are?"

Before Martin could respond, Margaret said, "We—my husband and I—wanted a family. So I—we, of course—had two children rather quickly, a boy and a girl, though it seems odd to call them that now—they're in their forties and quite remarkable. They've turned out rather well.

"But back to my life. I kept teaching while they were young—

didn't want to give that up. I retired when I was sixty—by then my husband was seventy, and I wanted to make sure that I could share some years of his retirement with him." Margaret paused, as if lost in thought. Henry looked up at her.

She continued. "And we did—ten years." She looked at Martin. "Are you thinking of retiring soon? I guess you're a little young for that."

Again before Martin could respond, she said, "Well, that's none of my business, and I guess this conversation is supposed to be about me."

"Tell me about your children."

"Well, Julian is forty-six and a psychologist—and a very good one. He's in private practice. He's married to a fine woman named Clare, and they have two boys. And my daughter, Ariel, is two years younger. She's a professor like her parents—she teaches Russian literature and philosophy in a small college in Ohio. I didn't even know there were any Russian philosophers—do you know of any?"

She didn't skip a beat, but continued, "Ariel isn't married—I never quite understood why. She's quite lovely, and I know she's had opportunities. But she seems to prefer being alone."

"And your grandchildren?" Martin asked.

Margaret frowned slightly. "Well, I'm quite willing to talk about them—they're wonderful, of course. But we might have things to talk about that would be more interesting to you—I don't think that praising my grandchildren will tell you much about me." She sipped her sherry.

"Fair enough," Martin said. "So, if you'd like to move on, let me ask you about what led you to make this gift."

Putting down her sherry glass, Margaret said, "Well, there's more than one thing to say. Let me begin with the amount. I'm worth about $9 million, which is far more than I need. I couldn't spend it all if I tried. And my children don't really need it—oh, maybe Ariel could use a half million or so. But that's all. So I met with my financial adviser—everybody should have one, you know—and asked him how much I could give away and still be secure. He told me he needed some time to do an analysis. When we met again a week later, he said I could comfortably give away $3 million.

"That would have left me $6 million—and you know how much income that generates a year without even touching the principal, about a quarter of a million. What am I going to do with that? My condo is paid for, and I have my pension and my husband's pension and Social Security. So I told him that was ridiculous, that he was being too conservative—financial advisers and accountants always are—and that I wanted to give away $6 million.

"That still leaves me $3 million. He tried to persuade me to reconsider, and I finally said, 'Walter'—that's his name—'this is my money and I'll do with it as I wish.' Goodness, sometimes he acts as if I'm a minor needing protection. But he is good at what he does, and I like him. So that's the reason for the amount."

"It's a very generous gift," Martin said, "and we're grateful. And you said there is more to say."

"Well," Margaret said, "it's really David Friedrich Strauss who brought us together." She smiled and took another sip of sherry. "I know you've written a book about him," she added, as if speaking a confidence. "And to explain how Strauss brought us together, I need to tell you a bit about my grandfather. The money is really his—an inheritance from him that came down to me through my parents. But he made the money. I've been thinking about what he might like me to do with it and decided that this sounds right. So what I really want to do today is to tell you about him."

She looked thoughtful. In the pause, Martin sipped his sherry.

"My grandfather's name was Fergus MacDonald, and he was born in 1853. He grew up in New York City. His father was a banker—not rich, but definitely middle-class. Fergus went to Yale—the family lore is a bit vague, so I don't know what he studied. He graduated in 1875 and got a job on Wall Street. But then there was the financial crisis in 1876, and so he moved to Montana and became a rancher."

Martin interrupted, "To Montana in 1876? Custer's Last Stand happened in Montana that year. I'm impressed—he must have had a lot of courage. Or maybe he was foolhardy?"

"I know what you mean. I've wondered myself. Let me tell you the story. After a year in New York, he moved west to become a sheep rancher. He wasn't married yet, so he did this on his own. In the summer of 1876 he traveled by train to Toronto, where he bought a special breed of sheep known for the quality of their wool—twelve of them. Then he got back on a train with his sheep and traveled to a town in Iowa on the Missouri River—I think it was Sioux City, but I'm not sure. It was as far as the railway went. So he caught a boat going up the Missouri as far as he could to somewhere near Great Falls. Then he led his sheep overland the last seventy miles to his land. He got there in late September, and managed to build a cabin for himself and a shelter for his sheep before winter came.

"Think of that. And keep in mind that he was only twenty-three, a city boy, and alone. What must that have been like? I marvel at our ancestors, don't you?" She paused.

"Yes, I know what you mean." Martin thought of his own grandparents. All four had left Scandinavia in their late teens, half from Sweden and half from Norway. Each left alone, knowing they would probably never see parents and family again, walked to the nearest port where they could catch a boat to America, and then made their way to the Midwest, where they became farmers. Martin had often wondered what they had felt walking away from their homes and families.

"And then what happened?" he asked.

"After a few years, my grandfather decided to switch to cattle, and he ended up becoming quite wealthy. So that's where the money comes from."

Margaret took another sip of sherry, smeared jam on a scone, and spread clotted cream on top. Martin followed her lead, took a bite, and said, "Mmmm—very nice. Where do you get these?"

"Oh," Margaret said, "I made them. I don't do a lot of cooking, but I've always thought scones should be homemade—don't you? It's a family recipe. Fergus was a Scot, as you might have guessed." She lapsed into silence and seemed content nibbling on her scone.

Martin asked, "So, how do we get from David Friedrich Strauss to a successful Montana rancher to an endowed chair at Scudder?"

"Oh," she said, as if being reminded of why they were talking, "I've left out the important part. Fergus took only one trunk with him to Montana, and I know what was in it—he made a list of what to take, and I have it—like an inventory. He must have been a meticulous man.

"And even though he took only a single trunk, he included a number of books—ten, to be precise. A Bible—I suppose there's nothing surprising about that. People did that in those days. But I found the other books very interesting. I don't remember all of them—I could check if you like. But among them were Darwin's *Origin of Species,* a book about Indian tribes of the Great Plains, a volume of Shakespeare's plays, a collection of Henry Ward Beecher's essays—have you read the new book about him, *The Most Famous Man in America*?"

Again, she did not pause for a response. "And a book by Ralph Waldo Emerson and another by Walt Whitman. But what caught my attention most of all was *The Life of Jesus Critically Examined* by David Friedrich Strauss, in two volumes. Think of it—ten books taken into the wilds of Montana, and two of them by a radical German theologian."

Martin was intrigued. "Really? That's remarkable."

"I read my grandfather's copy of Strauss about sixty years ago shortly after he died. It took me a long time to get through it—fourteen hundred pages, as I recall. Or was it eleven hundred? I found it quite fascinating, even if occasionally tedious. I was intrigued by his argument that so many of the gospel stories are symbolic rather than historical. It was a very radical book for its day—but then you know that. And I wondered why my grandfather found Strauss so interesting. He—my grandfather—must have been a bit of a freethinker, even a radical."

"Did you know that about him when he was still alive?"

Margaret thought. "A bit, perhaps, but I was only twenty-one when he died, so most of my memories of him are from childhood and my teen years. And he was in his seventies and eighties then. I mean, he was a retired rancher, and I knew he read a lot. But our times together weren't about that, about ideas and books—I was too young for that. I remember him as being rather stately, even as an old man, and gentle. It was nice being with him. But we didn't talk about the contents of his trunk. So when I learned that he had brought Strauss—and Darwin and Emerson and Beecher—with him to Montana, I got curious.

"To get back to Strauss. After reading him and knowing that he was important to my grandfather, I started reading books about Strauss. I've kept doing that, and so about twenty years ago, I read your book on Strauss. I thought it was quite good," her voice rising on "quite."

"That's part of the reason I offered this gift to Scudder—I knew they had a Strauss scholar. And it's the reason I agreed to this conversation. When my attorney brought me President Debnar's message that you would be the one to interview me, I thought what fun it would be to spend time talking with you about Strauss. So tell me, what do you find most remarkable about him?"

Martin set down his pen. He hadn't expected to be the one talking, but he didn't mind. "Well, you may know as much or more about him as I do. Most of what I know is in the book of mine that you've read. What I would say to anybody who asked that question is that his *Life of Jesus* is probably the most influential academic book on Jesus and the gospels written in the nineteenth century. And it's remarkable that he was only twenty-seven when it was published in 1835, so he must have finished writing it when he was twenty-six. Think of that. Precocious, to put it mildly. He must have been a genius."

Margaret interrupted, "And Albert Schweitzer was only twenty-five when he finished his first book on Jesus and the kingdom of God, and only thirty when he finished his *The Quest of the Historical Jesus.* I've always thought it remarkable that such important books about Jesus have been written by young men."

Martin was surprised that she knew these details about Schweitzer.

Margaret continued, "I really enjoyed how your book set Strauss's work in the context of his life and time. You know, how the book cost him a university career. Dismissed from his position at Tübingen, and then, when he was offered a position at the University of Zurich, there was so much public protest that it was cancelled. He never again had a teaching appointment."

"Yes," Martin said, "but it's hard to know if we should feel sorry for him. We probably shouldn't think of him as an intellectual martyr—Zurich gave him a pension for life, and he was only thirty-one when he started receiving it. Plus he was left an inheritance, so he never had to work again."

Margaret said, "I remember learning from your book that he

married a beautiful opera star and traveled around Europe with her. I rather like the thought. As I recall, they had two boys, but the marriage didn't last long?"

"That's right—about five years. For the rest of his life he was a freelance journalist, dabbled a bit in politics, and wrote a number of books, including a later and rather banal book about Jesus for a popular audience in 1864. He died in 1874 when he was sixty-six. He was buried without Christian ceremony, as he had requested."

"Do you know what happened to his boys?"

"Not much. I know that one of them became a medical doctor and took care of Strauss in his final illness. Rather touching. Suggests they had a decent relationship, in spite of Strauss's marriage ending when his boys were not yet five."

Martin concluded, "You know, none of his later books had the significance of his first one. I've often wondered what it would be like to have done your most important work in your twenties."

"So what made that first book so important?"

"Well, it's what you mentioned—his claim that many of the stories about Jesus are to be interpreted symbolically rather than historically. He attacked the two dominant understandings of the miracle stories in his time, the naturalist and supernaturalist interpretations. Proponents of the former—rationalists, as they were called—argued that there were natural explanations for the miracles of Jesus, and the other group insisted that they were what they look like—supernatural interventions. Both agreed that they happened—the issue was the cause.

"Strauss argued for a third way of interpreting miracles stories: that they weren't stories about something that had happened, and so the debate about natural or supernatural causation was foolish as well as sterile. Rather, they were 'myths,' as he called them. We might prefer to say 'symbolic,' given that 'myth' is a negative word to so many people today.

"It was a radical idea when he wrote his book, and yet now it's become one of the foundations of modern scholarship. So Strauss has become more than he expected. Largely rejected in his own time, he's now one of the pillars of modern scholarship."

Margaret gazed slightly above Martin's head and smiled. "I loved the way he wrote about the story of Jesus feeding five thousand people with a few loaves and fishes, making fun of both rationalists and supernaturalists. He could be quite wicked."

She was silent again. "Do you remember how he did it? I've forgotten the details."

"I love his treatment of that story too. It's found in all four gospels, but only John's gospel mentions that a young boy contributed the five loaves and two fish. The rationalists fastened on this detail and argued that the boy's example inspired others in the crowd to share the food they had brought with them, and so five thousand people were unexpectedly fed. Thus, though the rationalists affirmed that the event really happened, the miracle disappears. It becomes instead a story about the importance of sharing. Strauss argues that the rationalist approach violates the clear meaning of the text: it purports to be a story about a divine act, about something Jesus did through the power of God. So far, the supernaturalists would agree with Strauss. But then Strauss turns his critical guns on them. They also believed, of course, that the event really happened—that Jesus really did feed five thousand people with five loaves and two fish, and that the explanation was divine intervention.

"So Strauss says, in effect, all right, let's imagine for a moment that you're right—that it really happened. Then he invites us to enter into the scene by asking us to imagine what we might have seen if we had been there, especially *when* the multiplication of food might have occurred.

"He suggests three possibilities. Jesus could have multiplied the loaves and fishes all at once, so that if we had been there, we would have seen an enormous pile of bread and fish suddenly appearing. Or the multiplication could have occurred as Jesus handed the loaves and fishes to the disciples, or as the disciples distributed the food to the crowd—and so we would have seen loaves and fishes miraculously being replaced either in his hands or in their hands. Strauss is very clever—it's hard to think of other possibilities.

"Strauss argues that all three possibilities are impossible to imagine as actual events. His conclusion was that as soon as we seriously try to imagine that the story of the feeding of the five thousand really happened, it disappears as a historical story."

"I remember that," Margaret said. "I remember smiling as I read that section. And as I recall, then Strauss made his move to mythical interpretation. He didn't dismiss the story as untrue, as a mistaken report or as early Christian exaggeration or propaganda, but argued that it's true as myth, as symbol. I think that's fascinating."

"You're right," Martin replied. "He said that the purpose of the story was never to report something that happened. Rather, it uses the imagery of the Jewish Bible, which was the sacred scripture of early Christians, to make a statement about the significance of Jesus. It echoes the story of God feeding the people of Israel in the wilderness after the exodus from Egypt. And so it presents Jesus as the new Moses leading a new exodus, even as it also presents Jesus as the spiritual food that nourishes his followers. Jesus is the bread of life, as John's gospel puts it. It's really quite brilliant."

"What I've never been able to understand," Margaret said, "is why it's so hard for many Christians to see that. It seems so obvious. And what's lost? Nothing, so far as I can see. I don't get it."

Margaret continued, "And there's one more thing. Strauss's book was translated into English by George Eliot, my favorite of the great women novelists. Of course, you already know this. She was still Mary Ann Evans then and was only twenty-four when she translated this difficult book of German theology. And, can you believe it, she taught herself German in order to do so."

"You know that she grew up as an evangelical Christian?"

"Yes," Margaret said, "I do know that. But she gave it up in her late teens and early twenties, flirted with Unitarianism, and, I think, was some kind of mystic the rest of her life."

Margaret sipped the last of her sherry. "And now Strauss and Mary Ann Evans and my grandfather have brought you and me together. Remarkable, don't you think? We wouldn't be here this afternoon sipping sherry together except for events of over a century ago."

Martin looked at his watch. It was almost six o'clock. "Well," he said, "want to talk about Strauss some more?"

Margaret looked at her watch. "No, I guess not. Or if we do, we'll have to do dinner together."

Martin was silent, willing to have dinner if she wished. But Margaret said, "I'm not really serious. But I've really enjoyed this, and so maybe we could talk again sometime."

Martin responded, "That would be fine. I've enjoyed this too. But before we end today, do you have time for another question?"

"Certainly."

"To return to your grandfather. Because Strauss was in his trunk, you concluded that a gift to a progressive Protestant seminary would be what he would wish?"

"Well, I certainly wouldn't want to endow a chair at a conservative seminary."

"But why a chair in evangelical thought at a progressive seminary?"

"You know, I think the issue that Strauss addressed is still with us. I have a number of Christian friends who are shocked by the suggestion that the miracle stories are symbolic rather than factual. And I think those of us who are progressive Christians need to understand why this matters to most conservative Christians. So I want that conversation to continue—but in a way that might create more understanding than division. I think it's important for progressive seminarians to encounter a sophisticated form of conservative Christianity.

"I suppose I could have done it the other way around—endowed a chair in progressive Christian thought in a conservative seminary. That would have served a similar purpose. But I must admit that I'm skeptical that a conservative seminary would have accepted it. Or maybe one would have accepted it and then looked for a way to get around its purpose. I just don't trust people who are convinced that they know the truth. You know what Yeats said, 'The best lack all conviction, while the worst are full of passionate intensity.' I think that's a pretty good description of our century—I still think of the twentieth century as my century."

Then she looked at Martin. "You seem to be among the best—but I suspect you have convictions?"

Martin paused. He considered that the endowment was already a done deal and decided he didn't need to be political.

"Well," he said, "I do have convictions. And they're both relative and absolute. I know that anything I say about them, what I can put into words, is relative—we are products of our time and place, and we can only see as much as we've seen. In another sense, they're absolute. For example, I can't imagine being shaken from my conviction that 'the way,' the way to live, is to center in God—and for me as a Christian that means to center in God as known especially in Jesus. So that's my conviction—even as I know that there are only culturally specific ways of talking about that."

Margaret smiled. "I think we understand each other." Then, turning to Henry the dog, she said, "Well, are you ready to go for a walk? We need to let Professor Erikson go home."

23

Kate stood in the entryway of the Italian restaurant Martin had suggested. Although she had seen Martin briefly at the faculty lunch and presentation earlier that day, they hadn't had a chance to exchange more than brief hellos. She was looking forward to their dinner together, and if she were honest with herself, she was a little bit nervous too. She wore what she had worn all day—a black pencil skirt, heels, and white blouse.

There he was, bringing a cold wind from outside into the foyer with him. *Twenty years,* she thought. *How do you greet a former lover and now potential colleague whom you haven't seen in twenty years?*

Mutually, they moved forward for a brief hug. She was

glad he seemed to be of the same mind. Somehow a handshake might have been even more awkward.

"Kate, very nice to see you again," Martin said, "and especially to see you by yourself apart from the crowds you've been with most of the day."

Kate stepped back, looked at Martin, and said, "Nice to see you again too. You've aged a bit." Then hastily she added, "But you look good."

Martin raised an eyebrow. "Thanks. And so do you."

The hostess, who was tall and striking in a slim black dress, looked eastern European. She took their coats, smiled, and said, "Nice to see you again, Professor Erikson. Booth as usual?"

Martin said, "Yes, Nadya, that would be good."

Comes here often, Kate thought.

Nadya ushered them through a dimly lit, long narrow room, the tables and booths almost filled with couples and occasional foursomes. *No children in this place,* Kate observed. *Not a family restaurant.*

After they had settled in a booth in the back corner, Martin said, "Would you like to share a bottle of wine?"

"That would be fine."

"Red or white?"

"Whatever you'd like."

Kate sat back and regarded Martin as he scanned the wine list. As she had noticed with other academics, his appearance seemed to have improved with age. His silver hair, glasses, and even the lines on his face gave him a distinguished look that she found attractive.

He glanced up from the wine list, and she dropped her eyes back down to the menu. "How about a red?" he asked. "I enjoy whites—but I think reds can be more complex and interesting. I've never seen the point in spending fifty dollars or so for a white, but for a red—yes."

He ordered an Oregon pinot noir from Stephanie, the pretty young server, then turned to Kate. "It's one of my favorites, and I think you'll like it. So how was your day? Are you exhausted?"

"No, not really. But I feel pretty full—all these people and experiences, and I haven't had a chance to process it all. But I enjoyed it."

"Impressions?"

"Well, yes. But I haven't sorted them yet."

"Don't worry about sorting them—just go ahead and blurt them out. Doesn't matter what order they come in."

She smiled. "I don't usually do things that way—I hear that extroverts process their lives by talking about them, but I usually have to think things through before I say anything. I'll try, though."

She thought for a few moments. "There were a lot of things I liked. I liked the people I met. I thought the questions after my lecture, from both faculty and students, were good. They weren't arcane, but mattered. And people have been very hospitable—I've really felt welcome. Maybe the only thing that surprised me were the questions the faculty asked when I met with them at lunch—pretty softball."

"Well, nobody's trying to trip you up. We're courting you, Kate."

"Really?"

Stephanie arrived with the wine. Martin performed the ritual dutifully: checked the label, touched the cork for moistness, solemnly tasted the wine, looked thoughtful, and said, "That's good—that's fine. Thanks, Stephanie."

Martin said, "How about a toast? To you and the person you've become."

Kate said, "And to you—and the person you've become."

"To resume—yes, we're courting you. We want you here. Of

course, I need to say that the search process isn't over, and that we are courting all the finalists, and I can't say that you're our choice. But my vote will be for you, and I think the faculty will vote the same way. We're not simply looking for a placeholder for a year. We could easily find a new Ph.D. who would be pleased to have a one-year appointment. But we want somebody with at least a few years of teaching experience. That's the reason we sweetened the appointment by offering a pretty good salary plus free housing.

"We need you here, Kate. Or somebody very much like you," he added. "On a very practical level, we need somebody who can teach the introductory New Testament course well. Your predecessor—the fellow who is retiring—is so uncertain about anything that matters. His passion—if you could call it that—is keeping up with scholarship and then reporting in his classes all the possible options for interpreting a New Testament text. You know, 'Here are all the things it could mean.' There's a place for that—but not as the primary content of an introduction to the New Testament for future clergy. I think he is a frustrated academic. He really wanted to be at a first-rate graduate school teaching doctoral students. And he never stopped trying to prove that that's where he really belonged. But we need you—or somebody like you—for another reason."

Kate wondered why he kept saying "or somebody like you." Was it because there was another finalist who might be offered the position? Or just because he had to make it clear that, even though she was the favorite, it wasn't decided yet?

Kate returned her attention to what Martian was saying. "We have so many specialized points of view here—Asian, African, feminist, womanist, gay, lesbian, plus, of course, older white male. We need some faculty who see the larger picture.

"Don't get me wrong—I've learned a lot from feminist theology and African theology and Asian theology and gay theology, and I'm grateful. But we need some faculty who can speak from a perspective that is broader than particular vantage points—or maybe from underneath them. We need somebody who can speak the gospel with power—and I think you can, in a way that our students will be able to hear and use. My sense of you, Kate, is that you've got passion—and we need your passion."

Stephanie returned. "Sorry to interrupt—but are you ready to order yet? Or would you like more time? No rush." She smiled at Martin.

"Well," Martin said, "I usually order the same thing. But Kate, you haven't had a chance to look at the menu yet."

Kate said, "What do you usually have?"

"I usually get the saltimbocca. They do it very nicely here."

Kate smiled. "Sounds good to me. Did you know that saltimbocca means 'jumps into your mouth'?"

"I didn't know that, but that's perfect. And a starter or a salad?"

"What are you having?"

"Well, I think tonight I'll have the mixed greens with pear, currants, pancetta, and gorgonzola."

Kate said, "Let's do it. Makes things simple."

"Got it," said the server with a smile.

"So," Kate said, "you think there's a pretty good chance that I'll be offered this job?"

"Well, I can't say anything official or certain. It hasn't been decided yet. But yes, I think there's a very good chance that you will be our choice. Certainly better than even."

Martin paused. "So I think you will be the one who has to make a decision about coming here. And from what you've told me about your situation at Wells, I imagine that will be hard for you."

"Yeah," Kate said. "It will be hard. There's all this uncertainty. You know, I'm hearing that of course they'll want to hire me back—but I do wonder if they'd just as soon get rid of me. I also think they're trying to discourage me from doing this, even as they're also being quite nice, well, at least sort of nice. It's very hard to read them."

"Do you think they're worried about losing you? That we'd bring you here for a one-year appointment and then decide that we want to offer you a permanent position?"

"My friend Geoff suggested that possibility. So did Vincent, my chair. I don't know. But if that's what they're afraid of, what they've done isn't the most attractive way to make me want to stay there. All the hemming and hawing and then coming up with the idea of 'vacating' my position. And I've wondered if applying here, and coming here if I'm offered the job, might be used against me, or even as a way of getting rid of me. It's complicated."

"Will they give you any clarity about whether they really want you back?"

"I don't think so. Maybe I should ask them straight out, but it feels like it would be breaking the rules to do so. Almost as if my decision whether to come here has become a loyalty test."

Martin frowned. "Well," he said, "I need to tell you there's been no serious conversation about whether we would ask you to stay beyond the one year. So I think you need—will need—to make this decision on the assumption that you want to keep your position at Wells. I don't—we don't—want to lure you here if it might be against your best interest. You really need to think about that."

Kate sighed. "I do. If they're looking for an excuse not to give me tenure . . ." She hesitated, wondering whether she should share with him or whether it might hurt her chances of getting the Scudder position and finally decided she didn't care. "It's been a difficult couple of months. I don't know if you heard, but I had kind of a disastrous radio interview about my new book. Somehow my publicist set up an interview with a conservative Christian radio station. We had quite a discussion, and that discussion led to some other press."

A sudden spark of recognition in Martin's eyes caused Kate to stop. She asked him, "Did you know about it?"

"Now that you mention it, I did think I heard your name mentioned on a Christian talk show I was listening to in the car. I turn on the right-wing talk radio every once in a while just to test my blood pressure. I just barely caught your name, and when I didn't hear anything further, I assumed I'd just imagined it, but it must have been related to your interview."

"Do other people at Scudder know?"

"I doubt it. I've never heard a peep about such a thing, but at Scudder, as you surely know, being vilified on the right-wing Christian talk-show circuit could only serve to make you more attractive."

Kate smiled. "I'm glad to hear it. I don't mind too much being the object of scorn among evangelical Christians, although I do wish I'd been offered a few more chances to dialogue with them, rather than just being excoriated in absentia."

Her smile faded. "Truthfully, I'd thought that had all blown over after Christmas, but my department head told me that a few of the parents at Wells were circulating a petition to deny me tenure next year. The worst part was that the parents' chief complaint wasn't that I was too liberal, but that I was proselytizing in the classroom. Just because I've been honest about being a person of faith.

"I can't help but think that if I come here, the senior members of my department might use it as further ammunition to deny me tenure and destroy all that I've worked for these last years." As she talked, she was horrified to realize that tears were coming to her eyes.

Martin reached across the table and placed his hand on hers. "Kate, I'm so sorry you're having to deal with all of this. It seems to me that they're treating you very badly. You have to make the decision that's best for you, but I do hope that you are able to come to Scudder next year. I can promise you that we see talking about your faith in the classroom as an asset."

Stephanie arrived at their table with the salads, and Martin hastily withdrew his hand. Kate dabbed quickly at her eyes. "I'm sorry. It seems that this situation is bringing up a lot of baggage for me. Baggage I wasn't even aware I had." It had always been so easy to talk to Martin. It certainly hadn't taken her long to open up to him again. She also wondered how the young server saw the pair she was serving. A professional dinner? A date? Father and daughter? Probably not that one.

Martin asked gently, "Would you like to talk about something else?"

Kate smiled gratefully. "Good idea." She took a bite of salad.

Martin regarded her thoughtfully. "It's been twenty years since we—since I saw you last. So I don't really know much about your life since then. Of course, I know some things from your application and recommendations—that you were a superb graduate student, landed a job at a fine private college, got your thesis published, and then a second book—but otherwise I don't know much. So how about that awful question, 'Tell me about yourself.' I mean, bring me up to date on your last twenty years."

Kate said, "Well, you probably remember that I left for a job as a journalist for a weekly in a Chicago suburb." *And that was the end of our relationship,* she thought, and wondered again how he felt about the suddenness of the ending.

"It didn't pay much, but I had always kind of fancied being a journalist, and I knew reporting jobs were scarce. So I thought I should take it. I started off with some low-level local politics, but soon they also let me do an occasional feature. I ended up doing about half a dozen a year. They let me write about whatever I wanted to. That was fun. I did pretty well as a journalist. Three years later, a Chicago daily offered me a job, and I took it. Now I was doing mostly features, and I was only in my late twenties. I loved it. And I got to do some public radio as well.

"About the same time, I went back to church—a progressive Episcopal church. Small but not tiny—a couple hundred members. They did the worship beautifully. And they had great programs in education and Christian formation. Before long, I became a member and got really involved. After about a year, people in the congregation started saying to me, 'Have you ever thought of being a priest?' Or, 'Do you think you might have a call to ordained ministry?'

"It made me stop and think. Did I? Or was I supposed to stay with journalism? I was pretty sure I had a future in it. But I started thinking about going back to school as a way of figuring out whether I wanted to remain a journalist or shift paths. I was thirty-one, and thought I still had time to make a change. I even thought of coming to Scudder. But I decided to enroll in an academic master's program and then decide whether to shift to an ordination degree. And in my first year of graduate school, I fell in love with the intellectual side of it—I realized teaching was what I wanted to do. So I stayed on the academic track and got the blessed Ph.D. And you know a bit about the rest, even if only from my application. I revised my thesis on James and got it published, got a job teaching at Wells, where I've been almost five years. So that's the executive summary."

Martin smiled. "Well, there's a lot more, I know. Let me ask you something else about the last twenty years. Your two books sound quite passionate about Christianity, and your application does too. That's a bit different from how I remember you from when you were in college. You were serious about religion, I knew that—I could tell it mattered to you. But you also seemed quite skeptical. You were looking and seeking, but I didn't sense that you had found. So is something different?"

Kate was silent for a few moments. "Well, yeah, it is. It's really about God. When I was a kid, God was no problem for me, even though I grew up with parents who didn't go to church. From as early as I can remember, God seemed real. I had a sense of something 'more' all around me.

"But as I got older, God kind of faded away. I suppose it happened gradually, but I really became aware of it when I was a teenager. I started wondering if God was real—you know, if there was anything to the whole notion. I realize now that this happens to a lot of people. I know that part of the problem, probably the biggest problem, was language—the way I heard God being talked about by my Christian friends didn't make sense to me. You know, 'Our father who art in heaven' and all of that."

"Was the problem male language, father language?"

"Not really, not when I was a teenager. Though the notion that male language for God is the standard is strange when you think about it. You know, those Christians who are bothered by the move to inclusive language. What are they thinking? That God is really male?

"But back then the problem was the 'in heaven' part of it—that God is out there, somewhere else, separate from the universe. I knew—or at least was pretty sure—that God is right here, all around us. That's how I knew God. God wasn't somewhere else, up in heaven. But I didn't hear people talking about God this way. So I got pretty skeptical—I thought maybe what I meant by God wasn't what the word meant. And thinking of God as a personlike there' who watches over us and sometimes intervenes ...aking less and less sense to me. All of that was going on when I was at Concord and you were my professor."

Martin took a long sip of his wine. "So what changed?"

Kate was thoughtful for a moment. "Well, two things, I think. My understanding of language and culture changed. You had a big part in that. Do you remember that you made us read Peter Berger's *The Sacred Canopy* in your intro class? I remember—you made us write a paper on it, and then it was half of the midterm take-home exam. God, it was almost too much. Berger's not easy, you know. I remember slogging through that book twice—but it ended up being really important in my life.

"There's his big idea—what culture is and how it affects us. His great triad—that culture is a human product, a human construction, the sum total of what we add to nature; then, having created culture, we objectify it and treat it as a road map of the way things are; and growing up in a culture means internalizing it within our minds. It took me a while to figure that out, but when I did, it seemed really persuasive.

"And I saw what Berger meant by saying that this applies to religions too. Even the ones that claim to be based on revelation are human constructions. Berger convinced me—what else could they be? It doesn't mean they're wrong, but it does mean that we made them up. You know, we erect a canopy under which we then live and religions are sacred canopies."

Martin nodded. "I remember the essay you wrote about that in my class. I thought, 'By golly, she's got it.' "

She smiled. "You probably don't know how much that book you assigned way back then affected me. But I'm talking so much. You still interested in hearing more about my journey?"

"I'd love to," Martin said quietly.

"Well, it took a while for it to settle in—years actually. The really mind-stretching part of Berger for me went beyond seeing religions as human constructions. It was the realization that all ways of seeing reality are human constructions. Even science. As I sometimes say to my students, 'If you doubt this, study the history of science.'

"And here's the big part: if all ways of seeing reality are human constructions, so is mine. I learned it from other people, and even when I go my own way, it's still a human product, namely, mine."

Kate paused. "You know, when I really saw that, it was almost a religious experience." She leaned forward. "If everything we say about reality, about 'isness,' is a human construction, a grid that we lay over 'what is,' a lens through which we see 'this,' " she said, gesturing at the table and the room, "I realized that, in a very fundamental sense, we don't know what 'this' is—that 'what is' is beyond our words and categories and labels. I said it was almost a religious experience—I guess I would say it was a dumbfounding experience with tinge of wonder in it."

She paused again. "I remember walking around for several days saying to myself, 'We don't know what this is.' And I still say it to myself every once in a while. Do you know what I mean? Am I making sense?"

"Oh, yes," Martin said.

Stephanie arrived, cleared away the salad plates, and set the saltimbocca before them.

"Mm," Kate said, "this is delicious."

"I'm glad you like it," Martin said.

She took another bite of saltimbocca. "All of that was the first thing that brought about a change in how I thought about God. I realized that a big part of the reason that I had become skeptical about God was itself a human construction—pretty much the product of the modern world. That was kind of an intellectual conversion, but it was important. Berger undermined my intellectual objections to the notion of God.

"And then a second thing happened that changed how I think about God. In my late twenties, I had several—well, about four or five—mystical experiences. A couple of them lasted a few minutes and were pretty intense, and the others were briefer but seemed like glimpses or glimmerings of the same thing.

"The two most intense ones happened when I was driving alone in my car. Funny, I had never thought about that before—no wonder I love cars." She smiled. "So I had my Damascus road experience in an old Honda Civic—and a pretty battered one at that. Basically, what happened is that for a minute or two, all the words and labels and categories that I had learned fell away, and I simply experienced what was right in front of me—no extra beings or visions or voices.

"But what I was seeing looked very different—as if the landscape and the road signs were suffused with light, and my sense of being 'in here' "—she pointed at her chest—"and the world as being 'out there' vanished. I was far more aware of my connectedness to everything. I could almost see the connectedness—I remember seeing one of those yellow signs with a black arrow indicating a curve ahead, and what was remarkable is that I could also see—what to call it?—like a stream of energy connecting me to the sign. And these experiences were utterly wondrous. I had never experienced anything like them before. I loved—love—them. I would have been happy to live in that state of consciousness forever.

"And one more really big thing: I felt like I was seeing more clearly than I ever have. It felt like a knowing—you know, that I was seeing for the first time the way things really are."

Kate cut off another piece of saltimbocca and forked it to her mouth.

Martin said, "Had you read William James by then—body else who has written about mystical experiences?"

"No," she said, her mouth still full of food. She quickly swallowed and then continued. "I remember that you told us about James in class, but I hadn't read him. I did try to read a couple of books about mysticism in my early twenties, but they just seemed like gobbledygook—that's a technical term." She smiled.

"But after these experiences, I started reading about mysticism, and I found experiences like mine being named as experiences of God—you know, the whole earth filled with the glory of God, the transfiguration of 'ordinary' reality, experiences of 'radical amazement,' to use Abraham Heschel's phrase. Ever since, 'this' "—she again gestured at the room—"has seemed to me to be 'glory.' I don't know how else to say it. Only most of the time we don't experience it that way. But that's what it is. You know Sallie McFague's way of putting it—the universe as the body of God? Well, I feel like I've experienced it that way."

"I know what you mean," Martin said. "I remember reading Teilhard de Chardin's essay about celebrating Mass at dawn on a mountain in China and his speaking of the earth as the body of Christ. I think it's the same thing."

"I think so too. But to bring this to a close: these experiences made God real to me. It wasn't any longer about believing or trying to believe."

Then she added apologetically, "Well, that got much longer than I imagined. But," she pointed her fork at him with a playful smile, "you asked. And this is where my passion for God and religion comes from. I guess I'm a bit of an intellectual mystic."

"My story too," Martin said.

Kate said, "So I started attending church again. And one of the reasons I became an Episcopalian is the language of the prayer book. I love its beauty and the way it sounds—and in its beauty and humility it points beyond itself. Of course, it stammers and stumbles, as all language about God must. But it works wonderfully for me. I've found a home."

"Me too," Martin said. "I became an Episcopalian almost twenty years ago, just after"—he paused—"the time we knew each other. Soon after"—he paused again—"you moved, I went into therapy. Saw a Jungian therapist weekly for about three years. And one of the results was that I realized that I wanted to become part of a community that took symbol and ritual seriously. Given where I lived, that meant Episcopalian. It's become a home for me too. Did you know that nationally, only about 40 percent of Episcopalians were raised as Episcopalians? We're a church of refugees."

Kate said, "And of natives who can't believe what's happening to 'their church.' "

"Well, maybe. But I've found that many 'cradle' Episcopalians are also on the progressive side. It's had a liberal stream for a long time."

Kate nodded. "I've often wondered why there aren't more of us—that is, more Episcopalians. It seems to me that we combine the best of the Catholic tradition with the best of the Protestant tradition—an ancient liturgy with Protestant freedom of thought. But instead, we're on the edge of becoming the best-dressed sect in America."

Stephanie cleared away their empty plates and asked if they would like dessert or coffee. After conferring with their eyes, they declined dessert. Martin ordered a decaf and a glass of port, Kate a regular coffee.

"You can still drink regular at this time of night?" Martin asked. "About fifteen years ago—about the age you are now—I had to give up drinking regular after about two o'clock. Kept me awake."

Kate said, "Not yet. Maybe when I grow up I'll have to."

"Can I ask you something a bit more personal?" Martin asked.

"More personal than my beliefs and mystical experiences and that I still drink regular coffee?" Kate laughed. "Sure, I guess so."

"Are you married? Or have you been married? Or single all this time? I confess I don't know."

Kate smiled. "Yeah—basically I've been single. I've had a few relationships, one of which lasted a couple of years." She looked down at the table. "I thought for a while it would be permanent, but it didn't turn out that way.

"And once I got to graduate school, I decided not to be distracted by short-term relationships—you know, that rush at the start of a relationship that becomes all-consuming? I haven't been very much interested in rushes for the past ten years or so." She thought about whether to mention Peter and decided not to.

"And being single is okay—I don't pine anymore, even though sometimes I think a mate would be nice. But I'm not interested in dating—life is simpler without that. So I have friends instead. It works pretty well—I'm fairly content, not lonely."

She brushed back her hair with her hands, feeling self-conscious all of a sudden. "Okay, let's turn the tables. We've talked about me all evening. But what about you?"

Martin said, "That's fine. This is your time, Kate, and I've enjoyed it."

"Well," Kate said, sipping the last of her wine, "at least one question. Your last one was pretty personal, so let me ask you one. I heard that you got divorced?"

Martin nodded. "About fifteen years ago."

Not long after their relationship had ended, then. Until this point, both had studiously avoided any mention of their affair, but all of a sudden Kate felt she wanted to lay it out on the table. "I'm very sorry for that. I've wondered, a lot, about whether our relationship was part of the reason, maybe the reason. I mean, did your wife leave you because she found out? Sometimes I feel really guilty. I never wanted to hurt you, or her."

Martin met her eyes. She saw surprise and, she thought, relief that she had brought the subject up.

"I—I've prayed a lot about that over the years," she said.

Martin shook his head. "Any fault was mine. I broke my marriage vows, and I did hurt her, which I very much regret. But you know, you didn't create our problems. We would have gotten divorced eventually anyway. But all of that is in the past, and you and I have both moved on." Martin looked at his decaf, took a sip, and then said, "I don't regret—I've never regretted—being with you."

Startled, Kate held his gaze for a moment, and then Stephanie came by with the check, and the moment was broken. Kate found she was relieved; for a minute the years had rolled back, and she'd been just as enamored with Martin as she had been as a young woman.

"Any relationships since then?" Kate asked, trying to make her tone as light as possible.

"Well, I've had a couple. Each was for just over a year." Martin looked down at the table, and then up again. "They were good relationships, but they didn't last. I've avoided short-term sexual relationships—not that I've had that many opportunities. I avoided them when I was a young man too. But the reason feels different now. Then, I think it was because I was afraid. Now, it's more that I would feel foolish, or embarrassed, or, I don't know—maybe trivial."

He looked at his watch and shook his head. "Ten thirty already. What's your day look like tomorrow?"

"Well," Kate said as she wondered where Martin's question might be going, "I'm having breakfast with one of your colleagues, Leah Stanley. My flight leaves late in the afternoon—around four thirty."

"How about having lunch together? We could do more catch-up. Then I could drive you to the airport." He hastily added, "That is, if you don't have other plans."

Leaning back in her chair a bit, Kate looked at Martin appraisingly. "That would be nice. Thank you."

"Do you like shellfish—like mussels or clams?"

"Sure," she said, trying to remember the last time she had eaten them.

"How about if you come to my apartment about eleven thirty? It's right on campus. Or is that too early for lunch?"

"Sounds fine."

Martin paid for the meal, over Kate's protests, and then walked her to the door and to a waiting taxi he had asked the hostess to call for her. They hugged good-bye, and she kissed him quickly on the cheek. "See you tomorrow."

24

Early Saturday morning, Kate sat at the desk in the guest suite at Scudder and opened her prayer book. She was already dressed. At home, she usually did morning prayer in her robe, but had not packed one in her carry-on bag for this brief trip.

Earlier, as she was waking up, she realized she had been thinking about what to wear for lunch with Martin and then remembered she didn't have much choice. In addition to her interview outfit, she had brought only a dress that was probably not suitable for a casual lunch and the outfit she'd planned to wear today, denim jeans with a navy sweater. So sweater and jeans it was.

Finishing her devotional time, she ended with a prayer from *Prayers for a Planetary Pilgrim* for a Saturday in winter:

> How quickly, O creator of wintry ice and snow, has this week passed. May any chill within my heart be melted by your Spirit, as a summer sun would melt a field of snow. As this winter day begins, may I see your glory in the heavens and in all the earth. Grant, O Blessed One, that I may look with love upon every person, object, and event that I will encounter this Saturday.
>
> Long ago you called Moses to spend this day in restful pleasure in your presence. May I use whatever this day holds for me to refresh my body and rest my soul, and so give great pleasure to you. I pray for all who must work this day as well as those who have no work and must struggle for the bare essentials of life. May this day lead me to trust more fully in your great care for all the earth and her children. And may I grow in the capacity to care as you do. Blessed and beautiful are you, my God. May your light be my sun this winter day. Amen.

She got up from the desk, went to the kitchen, tiny but adequate for a guest suite, and poured herself another cup of coffee. Returning to the desk, she lit a cigarette. She had faced the smoker's dilemma when she arrived Thursday evening: Is it okay to smoke here? When she chose where to stay, she always made sure that the hotel or motel had smoking rooms and reserved one. But when somebody else made the accommodation arrangements, that was different.

She thought it probably wasn't okay, so she hadn't asked. Instead, she decided that if she opened the windows fairly wide and left them open, even though the weather was cold, and rationed herself to three cigarettes a day, nobody need know.

She knew for sure that she didn't want to go outside to smoke—didn't want to stand in the quad at Scudder, staring into the distance with a cigarette in her hand, looking like a femme fatale in a French movie, or worse. She closed her eyes and inhaled.

She had enjoyed yesterday—the meetings with students and faculty, the question-and-answer period at lunch. Her lecture in the afternoon had gone well. She had spoken about the meanings of sacrificial language in the Bible, that it was not about substitution, and that seeing the death of Jesus as a substitutionary sacrifice for sins is not only anachronistic, but also blasphemous in what it implies about God. The students and faculty who attended seemed thoughtful, receptive, appreciative. There had been no red flags, nothing that had signaled to her that Scudder would be anything less than a fine fit for her.

In an hour, she was to have breakfast with Leah Stanley, who had been in one of the small groups of faculty and students with whom she had met yesterday morning. At the end of the session, Leah had come up to her, extended her hand, smiled, indeed laughed, and said, "I like you. Want to have breakfast tomorrow? I hear you're staying over. We could talk about what it's like being here at Scudder—or whatever you like."

Taken by surprise, Kate's first reaction was to groan inwardly, wondering if Leah was suggesting yet another interview, but seeing her open and friendly face, she reconsidered and said, "Sure—I'd like that."

Then lunch with Martin. Kate found herself anticipating that. Last night at dinner she had talked about herself nonstop, and it felt as though he had hung on every word. Quite the opposite of their previous relationship when she had hung on his every word. She also realized she felt incalculably better after saying what she had about his wife. There was perhaps more to be said, about why she had left when she did with hardly a good-bye, but there would be another time for that. For now it had felt good to clear the air.

Was there any chance they could have a relationship now? She caught herself and smiled. *Kate, you don't have to figure anything out about that,* she thought. *At least not now, not yet.*

As Kate neared the café where she was to meet Leah, she walked by a pipe and tobacco shop, already open though it was not yet eight thirty. She checked her watch, saw that she had five minutes, and went in. She bought a pack of American Spirit Blues for herself and on impulse also a handsome pipe lighter. She liked the way it looked and felt in her hand—and it was designed especially for pipes. "It draws down wonderfully," the middle-aged male clerk said as she struck it. It would make a nice thank-you gift for Martin.

She walked into the café next door and immediately saw Leah, the only African American in the breakfast place, which was less than half filled with casually dressed Saturday morning patrons. *Lots of people sleeping in,* Kate thought, *or having breakfast together at home. Or maybe alone.*

As Kate approached Leah's table, Leah stood up and smiled. "Good morning. It's good to see you, Kate. When I heard how you interacted with our students yesterday morning, I knew I liked you right away and that I'd love to have some time with you. And so I thought, why not breakfast? And I thought it might serve a very practical purpose—I'm happy to have you ask me anything you want about what it's like being here at Scudder."

As she had yesterday, Kate looked at Leah's open face and liked what she saw. "Thank you. I'd like to do that." They sat down.

Immediately a waiter was there for their order. Knowing she would be having an early lunch with Martin, Kate ordered light—a toasted bagel with cream cheese, a fruit cup, and coffee.

Kate leaned forward, her elbows on the table, hands clasped just beneath her chin. "Actually, I'd like to learn about you first. How did you get here?"

Leah rolled her eyes. "How did I get here? Here this morning,

I walked. Here, as in how did I get to Scudder? Here, as in what's my story?"

"Whatever you'd like."

"Long version or short version?"

Kate was silent for a couple of beats.

"Okay, short version," Leah said. "I'm an African American lesbian in a straight white male world." She laughed. "That's too short and kind of misleading—it hasn't all been hard. In fact, it's been pretty good."

Kate tried to hide her surprise. She hadn't guessed Leah was lesbian.

Leah's hands fluttered from her lap to the table. "Let me give you kind of a telegram version—do you think our younger students even know what telegrams are? Anyway, born in Chicago in the early 1960s. Grew up there in a middle-class family, my father a lawyer and my mother a teacher. When I was a child, we lived in an all-black neighborhood—the city still had racial restrictions on neighborhoods. Martin Luther King's Chicago campaign didn't happen until I was four or five. When I was eight, we—my family—moved to a neighborhood that was beginning to be integrated. My parents could afford it, and they thought it would be better if we kids grew up mixing not just with black folks, but with white folks too. But my parents stayed connected to the black community—they were members of a black church and active in projects like Operation Breadbasket—we even had Jesse Jackson over to the house once."

Kate nodded. "I lived in Chicago for several years. I wrote for the *Weekly Reader* and then the *Herald*."

"Small world," Leah said. "I loved Chicago. I had a great childhood, really. I think I began my story with my parents, because they have a lot to do with me being here. I got a lot from them, including my religion and my politics. I haven't had to reject very much of what I learned as a child. It's nice—there's a lot of continuity in my family."

The server brought their food, the bagel for Kate and an egg-white omelet with spinach and whole-wheat toast for Leah. "Trying to avoid cholesterol," Leah said, nodding at her food. "And trying to be the first one in my family without diabetes. Now, let's see. I need to start condensing. I went to college at Oberlin to study music and fell in love with religious studies too, and so I decided to go to seminary. In my third year in seminary, when I was twenty-five, I fell in love with Jackie. We've been partners ever since. We're even married—did it in Canada."

Leah leaned forward and smiled. "And Jackie's white—so I'm even in an interracial marriage." She laughed. "A school like Scudder gets a lot of diversity points for me. Anyway, after seminary, I went to graduate school to get a Ph.D.—I did it on the relationship between liturgy and social justice—kind of combined my interest in music with my interest in religion and politics. Then I began to feel a call to ordained ministry, and the United Church of Christ was happy to have me even though they knew I was a lesbian in a partnered relationship. I was a college chaplain for a couple of years, and then Scudder advertised a position in liturgy and life, and I've been here ever since. I was surprised that they'd hire somebody other than an Episcopalian for a liturgy position."

She smiled. "I guess I convinced them that I really am pretty high-church, even though I'm a black lesbian from the United Church of Christ. Not exactly known as high-church people. But I'm a good fit for Scudder, and Scudder's a good fit for me."

"That's enough about me," Leah said. "I want to be helpful to you. What do you want to know about Scudder?"

Her bagel almost eaten, Kate said, "Well, let me ask you about the older faculty. I mean, the visual difference is really strong. I noticed at lunch yesterday—all the older faculty are white males, and you younger faculty are all over the place. It's like looking at uniformity and diversity. So is that a big difference? What's that like? Or maybe I mean, what are they like—the older faculty?"

Leah paused. "They're basically all right—they're good guys, at least most of them. I don't know that any are bad—like reactionary. They're on the right side of the important issues, even though I think a few of them are a bit bewildered and working hard to stay current. Let me give you an example. They're all against racism and sexism—that's a given here. And they're basically in favor of full rights for gay and lesbian people—but when they talk about what the problem is, they name it as homophobia. But you know," Leah continued, looking at her almost untouched breakfast, "a lot of gays and lesbians don't call the problem homophobia anymore. It's not that people are afraid of us—the problem is heterosexism. You know, that the norms of our culture and the church are heterosexist. That's the problem—not homophobia."

Leah stopped long enough to take a mouthful of her omelet. "So," she continued, "that's not a big issue, but it's indicative of a generational difference. I suppose the difference is on the edge of political correctness, but it seems a bit more important than that."

Leah smiled. "We're so politically correct here that it sometimes makes me laugh. About twenty years ago—that was before I got here, so this is all secondhand—the administration announced that they were reconsidering the policy prohibiting pets in seminary housing. Scudder was starting to have more and more second-career students who not only had children but also pets, and many single students also wanted to have pets, so the dean of students said that they were seeking input about their pet policy."

Leah laughed. "Well, there was a brouhaha. The issue was that the word 'pet' was condescending, patronizing, and anthropocentric—that the right term was 'animal companion.' So don't talk about pets here."

She looked at Kate. "Don't misunderstand. I think that what some people call political correctness comes from convictions that matter. But I must admit I wouldn't get very passionate about 'pets' versus 'animal companions.' "

Kate smiled. "What's it like to teach here?"

Leah looked thoughtful. "It's good. We've got good students. I think the faculty are all basically on the same page. There's no pressure to conform or to pull punches. We can tell it the way we see it. We ruffle some feathers in the church, but it's good.

"Maybe the only downside is that we perhaps leave our students with fragments of a theology rather than a larger vision. We cover a lot of issues and points of view, and I wonder sometimes if students are able to integrate it very well. Most of them are excited about what they're learning, but I'm not sure how well we prepare them for parish ministry. We struggle with what it means to be a cutting-edge academic institution and what it means to do formation for parish ministry. We're working on it, but I don't think we've got it figured out yet."

Kate watched Leah finish her last bite of egg. Kate asked, "What do you think of Martin Erikson? What's he like? Full disclosure: he was one of my professors when I was an undergraduate twenty years ago."

"Yeah, I knew that. He mentioned it to me when the search committee had decided on you as one of the finalists. Martin's a good guy. I mean, what's not to like? I like what he does, and I think his books are great. Students—well, most students—love him."

"And," Leah paused as if looking for the right phrase, "he's kind of—oh, I don't know—courtly. He's really nice—you know, warm and pleasant, but also sort of formal. When he's talking to me, I can feel that he's pretty present, even as there's also a bit of distance. Does that make any sense?"

She hesitated again and then added, "He almost always wears a tie to class. But for an older guy, he's reasonably well evolved. What more can you ask?"

Kate said, "We had dinner together last night. And we're having lunch today before I go to the airport."

"Really?" Leah's eyebrows rose slightly. "Well, maybe I should ask you about him."

Kate laughed. "He's a good guy."

While shaving that morning, Martin fussed about what to make for lunch with Kate. Clams rather than mussels, he decided. Milder. But how to serve them? In a reduced white wine sauce over pasta—perhaps linguini? Or maybe not pasta? Maybe in chicken stock with white wine, chopped shallots, minced garlic, some Mediterranean spices, and a bit of anise?

And maybe a salad that he had recently learned about on a cooking show on television—he thought he recalled the ingredients: black-eyed peas, corn, red peppers, scallions, a light oil, and a splash of cider vinegar. And of course a crusty baguette.

He went to Whole Foods to shop. As he wheeled his cart through the vegetable section, he thought about Kate. It was hard to get her out of his mind—not that he really wanted to. He had enjoyed last evening, very much. She was bright, lovely, animated, every bit as beautiful and sexy as she had been in his dream. He loved watching her face and the way she moved her hands while she talked, often leaning forward, her animation calling forth his. He hadn't allowed himself to think about it for some time, but after seeing her, embracing her, he couldn't help but remember their lovemaking. What would it be like now? The somewhat awkward undergraduate had grown into a beautiful woman. Her slouch was gone, and she seemed at home in her body. *Whoa there. Don't get ahead of yourself, Martin.*

Back to lunch planning. He wondered whether to serve a white wine or whether that would be odd at an early lunch. Then he realized he could ask her. It was a Saturday, after all.

Finished with shopping, he was back in his apartment by nine o'clock. Too early to start cooking, so he spent some time straightening up—a little dusting in his living room, polishing the dining room table, picking up magazines and books that were scattered around his study, checking the guest bathroom, which was seldom used.

Turning on the radio in the kitchen, he recalled what Kate had said about her experience on the Christian talk show and decided on NPR instead. He chopped the red pepper and scallions for the salad. Then he began to simmer the broth for the clams, adding a cup of white wine to the chicken stock. Good for it to cook for an hour or more. Then, after Kate arrived, he could add the clams, and they would be done in about ten minutes.

Still an hour before she was to come. Martin considered what to wear. Perhaps his fawn-colored corduroy slacks with a burgundy cashmere turtleneck? Or maybe with an open-collar shirt and his navy sweater vest? He thought of some words from T. S. Eliot's "The Love Song of J. Alfred Prufrock." 'Shall I wear the bottoms of my trousers rolled? Shall I part my hair behind?' He smiled at himself. *Martin, you're thinking of this as a date.*

He dressed, having decided on the open-collar shirt with his navy vest. He looked at himself in the mirror and thought, *Good enough.* With nothing left to do before Kate came, he settled into a chair in his study, lit his pipe, and resumed reading a book he had begun a week before, Taylor Branch's thousand-page third volume of the Martin Luther King years. Soon he was back in the world of the mid-1960s.

25

Kate arrived at Martin's apartment promptly at eleven thirty. He took her coat and ushered her into his kitchen. She admired it—bright and sunny with plenty of long counters. Like Geoff's, it was the kitchen of someone who liked to cook. As someone who didn't particularly like to cook, Kate always admired this quality in others.

She perched on a stool while Martin watched the stove and offered her something to drink. "A glass of white wine or orange juice? Sparkling water? Or maybe a V8?"

Kate laughed. "It's been a long time since I've been offered a V8. Hmm—well, I might have a glass of wine with lunch, but right now some sparkling water would be nice—I like to call it *Sprudel.*" She pushed her lips forward to say the word. "I like the way it sounds. So make mine a *Sprudel*."

Martin poured a glass of sparkling water, put the baguette in the oven, and stirred the broth on the stove. "Ten minutes more, and then I'll put the clams in. Another ten minutes and we'll be ready to eat."

Martin poured himself half a glass of V8 and topped the glass up with sparkling water. "It's called a V8 Virgin," he said. "Not quite as nice as a Bloody Mary, but more virtuous. Cheers."

He took a healthy sip and continued, "How was breakfast with Leah?"

"Good," Kate said. "I like Leah. It was fun. And Scudder basically got a clean report." She looked at Martin. "You did too," she said, smiling. "Glad I did it. But I want to go back to last night, okay?"

"Sure," Martin said, looking over his shoulder at the pot on the stove.

Kate waited until she was sure he wasn't distracted. "I enjoyed it. But we talked only about me. So today is about you."

"Might not be that interesting."

"You're too modest—and you probably know that. Which might mean it's not really modesty?"

Martin raised his eyebrows and then grinned. "We'll see. Ask away."

"Okay," Kate said. "How about if we start with what it's like to be famous, to be a big shot."

Martin's shoulders seemed to slump a bit. "You know, I don't think of myself that way—sounds more than a bit inflated. If I'm remembered at all twenty or thirty years from now, it will be as a minor turn-of-the-century theological intellectual mentioned in a footnote.

"This week I've been reading a book about the history of Anglicanism. It described somebody as one of the most famous Anglican theologians of the nineteenth century—and I hadn't even heard of him. So famous doesn't seem right—or maybe the point is that fame is fleeting. You know, what the author of Ecclesiastes calls vanity—I love the fact that the Hebrew word means fog or mist. You can't hold on to it, it makes it hard to see, it's easy to get lost in it. So I don't what to be seduced by fame."

"Really?"

"Yeah. But I admit that when I was in graduate school looking for a book in the card catalog in the library, I sometimes noticed that an author had several inches of entries and I thought how great that would be. But now I know there's no fame or immortality in being in a card catalog—really doesn't matter much. For that matter, do card catalogs even exist anymore?" He shrugged. "So I don't spend any time thinking of myself as famous."

"But," Kate said, "you know what I mean. When I knew you twenty years ago, you weren't really known outside of our college and perhaps professional meetings. Now lots of people know about you. You've written best-sellers, and you lecture all over the country. I hear about you from people a lot—you know, 'Have you read Martin Erikson's newest book? It's really good.' And when I tell them that I was once your student, they're impressed. So what's that like?"

"Well," Martin said, looking at Kate, "in some ways it's very nice to be a little bit known. People buy my books and ask me to sign them, and they're grateful—sometimes embarrassingly so. Some even apologize for asking. They say things like, 'You must get so tired of signing books.' And I want to say to them, 'Think about it—get tired of people wanting my autograph, get tired of people buying my books and coming to my lectures?' This is not a hard life.

"And I do get treated as a minor celebrity when I'm on the road.

It's a treat for somebody like me who grew up as a shy introvert and spent the first forty years of his life trying to figure out how to strike up conversations with interesting people. Now I just show up, and people come up to me and start talking about interesting things. I just have to be there.

"So, I admit, it's nice, even as I want to set aside the notion of being famous. But it does have a downside. I remember a line from one of Mary McCarthy's letters that I read a couple years ago. Do you remember her? She wrote the best-seller *The Group* about fifty years ago. Anyway, she wrote to a friend that she had never known that being a success would be so time-consuming. And she wasn't referring to the time it took her to become a success, but to all the demands that came with it—lots of correspondence, lecture tours, interviews, requests for blurbs for books, more writing. And that's really been true for me. I'm often not sure whether I have more of a life now or less of a life."

Kate slid her fingers along the smooth granite countertop. "Are you glad your life turned out this way?"

Martin said, "Oh yes—I'm very grateful. I love what I do."

He looked at the kitchen timer. "Time to put in the clams."

She waited until he had emptied the clams into the large pot on the stove. He sat back down, and she asked, "How long do you think you'll keep teaching?"

"I guess I could retire anytime—I don't need my salary. Or I could keep teaching here until I'm seventy or so, by which time it would be decorous to retire, to say the least. But I don't think retiring from Scudder will mean much change in my life. Most of what I do now doesn't depend on teaching here. My writing and lecturing can go on as long as I have health and energy and interest. My role model is Huston Smith—you know, he's in his late eighties and still doing it."

"It?"

Martin smiled. "Writing and being on the lecture circuit."

He looked at the timer again. "Time to move to the dining room. Go ahead and sit down, and I'll bring in the food."

Kate sat at an old square oak table with massive round legs, narrowing at the ankle and then rounding out into what looked like rhino feet. She looked at a serving spoon and noticed that it was also old.

Martin put a broad shallow bowl of clams in broth in front of her, a tiny fork above the bowl, and what looked like a black-eyed pea and corn salad with some red stuff in it to the side. He returned to the kitchen and came back with a bottle of white wine and a basket of sliced baguette.

"Martin, this looks great. Smells great too."

"Well, hope it's as good as it looks. How about if I say grace?"

"Of course."

"Want to take hands?"

"Sure."

Martin prayed, "Blessed are you, creator of the universe. You bring forth the bread from the earth and the fruit from the vine. For all the blessings of this life, known and unknown, remembered and forgotten, we give you thanks. In the name of Jesus, our body and our blood, our life and our nourishment. Amen."

"Do you always say grace?" Kate asked as she speared a clam with the small seafood fork.

"Not out loud when I'm alone, which I often am. And when I'm at home alone, I eat pretty simply, and usually while I'm reading. Not a great example of mindfulness, I suppose. But when I have somebody over, yes. Seems both right and, I guess, communal."

"Mmm—these are good," Kate said as she speared another clam. "I'll want your recipe—but not right now. Right now I want you to catch me up with what happened to you during the last twenty years."

"Well, there's more than one thing to say. How much do you want to know? I've got a short version and a longer version."

"How about the longer version?"

"I think I need to begin way back, and then I'll jump ahead. The second half of my thirties—when you and I knew each other—was the most difficult time in my life. I had a lot of ambition as a young man, probably from my teens onward. Who knows, maybe it was even there when I was a child. I wanted to amount to something.

"And here I was approaching forty without much happening in my professional life. Sure, I had a doctorate from Oxford, and I was teaching in a fine private college—but did you know it was a temporary appointment? A fixed-term appointment with a maximum of five years and no possibility of tenure. And I hadn't published much yet—it was hard to find the time with young children and, truth be told, a marriage in which neither my wife nor I was very happy. So I wondered and worried whether my career and life were going anywhere. Even worried about not being able to get another teaching job, and what I would do if I couldn't. What do you do with a Ph.D. in theology other than teach?"

Martin stopped in order to eat a couple of clams, discarding the shells in a blue Chinese bowl in the middle of the table. "So," he continued, "I started seeing a therapist—a Jungian, because by then I was reading about Freud and Jung and depth psychology." He stopped again and ate a forkful of salad.

"How was that?" Kate asked.

Still chewing, Martin said, "Well, it was slow. And also fascinating. He made me work with dreams. And I couldn't remember recalling one for over ten years—the last one I remembered was when I was in my doctoral program at Oxford. I had a repeating dream of driving a car—a red Vauxhall like the one I drove at the time—up a hill that got steeper and steeper until it was nearly vertical, and then the car would fall backward. Not too hard to figure that out when you're working on a doctor's degree at Oxford.

"But after that, I didn't recall any dreams except for an erotic one or two for a decade. When my therapist told me he wanted to work with dreams, I told him I didn't remember my dreams, and he said, 'Well, time that you start—you know, we dream every night.' So he told me how to start a dream journal. I was to put a notepad or journal on a table next to my bed, ask for a dream as I went to sleep, and, if I became aware of having one, write it down immediately."

"Did it work?" Kate asked, tossing a clamshell into the Chinese bowl.

"It did. Pretty quickly. A lot of them were very hard to figure out—and when we talked about them, I would think, 'Yes, could be, that's possible.' But there were a few that were pretty unmistakable."

Martin paused to eat a few more clams and to take a sip of wine.

"Such as?" Kate asked.

"Okay—an example. I had a series of dreams in which the same man appeared. He was very tall, had a normal body but a huge head—imagine a man about eight feet tall with a head the size of a twenty-pound pumpkin. And his big head had scratches and cuts and Band-Aids all over it, as if he kept bumping into things. In one dream, he kept bumping his head on the underside of the doorframes he walked through. In another dream, he was fishing, casting into a lake. And here's the weird thing—he wasn't standing on the shore or in the water, but on the water. He wanted to catch something. He was curious about what was down there, even as he was fearful of the snapping jaws he saw just beneath the surface."

"Wow," Kate said. "So what did you make of them?"

"Well," Martin said, "I think they were pretty transparent—

indeed, frightfully so. They suggested that I had an overdeveloped head—a big head, to use the vernacular. Some of that was about ambition. But it wasn't just about hubris, as if I thought too much of myself. It was more about living in my head and being fearful of whatever I couldn't analyze with my head. Do you know what I mean?"

"I think I do," Kate said. "So what happened then?"

"Well," Martin said, "I worked hard on letting go of ambition, learning to enjoy what I was doing, and becoming content with who I was—a pretty good college teacher who, with luck, would get another teaching job, but who wouldn't amount to more than a teacher beloved by his students. Now that I've said that, I wonder if that's really a modest goal—still sounds a bit inflated.

"Anyway, all of this was happening after we knew each other back then. And it led to my divorce—a large bump. Otherwise, the last two decades have been pretty nice. Oh, there were some difficulties. Ending the marriage brought some financial anxieties—it's almost like starting over when you divide everything in two, especially since we didn't have all that much. No inheritances in our families. But I've been able to maintain good and affectionate relationships with my kids, and I'm grateful for that."

Martin stopped again, took a few bites of food and another sip of wine. "I just turned fifty-eight, and I've been feeling the onset of sixty. Turning fifty was no big deal—I was becoming established at Scudder, writing books that were being noticed, and receiving more and more speaking invitations. But the approach of sixty is different, When I was growing up, sixty was old—it really was.

"I think I've lived much of my life in the future—that goes with ambition, you know. Fulfillment is in the future—life will be good when I've made a name for myself, when I'm honored, when I'm financially secure, and all of that. But what's the future when you're getting close to sixty? It seems to me that sixty and older is about decline." Martin paused. "I've even thought that the next car I buy might be my last. Who knows how long you can keep driving after sixty? Puts a lot of pressure on deciding what kind of car you want—and everything else.

"You know what it feels like when you're in water up to your neck and trying to walk? Everything is so effortful. Well, I've felt that a lot." Martin ate another clam.

"So," Kate said, setting her fork aside, "is that still how you feel?"

"Not sure. It feels like it's passing. I think it began to pass last Christmas. I spent Advent feeling like Mary, heavy with child. And sometime between Christmas and New Year's, the heaviness seemed to lift. It felt like an answer to prayer—or maybe prayer isn't the right word. Maybe it was about the efficacy of the liturgical calendar—I remember really paying attention to Advent as a time of waiting for birth."

Kate smiled. "So you've been pregnant?"

Martin smiled back. "Yeah, I guess so. And you?"

"Like that, more than once," Kate said. "But tell me about what changed."

"Well," Martin said, "I shifted from thinking about the future to appreciating the present. It wasn't easy—but I moved from worrying about how many years I might have left to living more in the present. I thought, well, I can spend the next decade lamenting the loss of an indefinitely long future, or I can be grateful that my life has turned out well and that I'm still here and healthy."

Martin paused. "When I think about it, these last few years have been the best time of my life. I live more in the present that I ever have. I still have to remind myself a lot to do so. I slip in and out of it—but when I realize I've slipped out of it, I can usually slip back in pretty easily.

"The old drive to prove myself, to amount to something just

isn't there. My friend Seamus said to me a couple weeks ago, 'You know, Martin, you could just tie a ribbon around what you've done and call it good enough. And then do whatever you want to do.' It was very helpful—I realized he was right. The need to prove myself isn't there anymore. That driver is gone. That's very nice—ambition is a hard taskmaster."

Martin noticed that his wineglass was empty and Kate's almost was. He asked if she would like her glass topped up, and she said, "Well, this is early in the day for me. But I don't have to do anything the rest of today except get on an airplane. So, sure, I can have one more."

Martin poured wine for each of them and then said, "I'm grateful to be out from under that need to amount to something. But I don't know that I can claim much credit for it going away. It's like there are two ways to stop worrying about money. One is the way of saintliness—you know, absolutely trusting God to provide. 'Why are you anxious? Consider the birds of the air—they neither sow nor reap nor gather into barns, but God feeds them.' The other way is to have enough money so you don't have to worry about it. But doing it that way doesn't count as virtue."

Martin noticed that Kate had finished her clams and that his bowl was still half full. He said, "I've been talking too much—you're almost done eating, and I'm not. Sorry."

Kate smiled. "Don't worry—I wanted you to do most of the talking today. Remember last night."

"I do," Martin said, looking at Kate.

He checked his watch. "We've got about an hour before we need to leave for the airport. How about if we move to my study for dessert and coffee? That way I can smoke my pipe—unless smoke bothers you."

Kate smiled. "I have a dirty little secret—I smoke cigarettes.

Well, only six a day. So if cigarette smoke doesn't bother you, I would love that."

"Deal," Martin said. "I'll make some coffee. And if you'd like dessert, what I can offer is vanilla ice cream with or without chocolate sauce—I can warm it up. I'm not much of a dessert guy except for ice cream."

"Sounds good to me," Kate said, "and put some warm chocolate on it."

Moving to Martin's study, they sat in compact leather easy chairs at right angles to each other. Kate gestured at a glass case that contained a dozen or so hand puppets. "What are those?" she asked. "Do you collect hand puppets?"

Martin smiled. "Don't you recognize them? There's Socrates and Plato and Aristotle, and Augustine and Thomas Aquinas, and moderns like William Blake and Kierkegaard and Nietzsche and even one of Paul Tillich. My children—well, they're in their early thirties now—gave them to me for Christmas."

Kate smiled. "Do you ever take them out of the case?"

Martin laughed. "I did think about taking them to my history of theology class—I thought I might ask them questions and then have them respond."

"So, did you?"

"No," Martin said. "I practiced a bit here in my study and decided it might be a bit too silly. But it was tempting."

Kate finished her ice cream and lit a cigarette. "Want one?" she asked.

"No, I guess not. I used to smoke cigarettes, and I still miss them. But I'll stick with my pipe."

Martin loaded his pipe. "By the way, do you know what Karl Barth said about smoking and theologians?"

Kate shook her head.

"Well, he said that you can tell what kind of a theologian somebody is by what they smoke. If they smoke cigarettes, they're liberal; if they smoke cigars, they're orthodox; and if they smoke a pipe, they're neo-orthodox. Then somebody asked Barth, 'What if they don't smoke?' And he said, in his heavily accented English, 'Then they're no theologian.' "

Kate laughed and said, "That reminds me—I have something for you." She took the pipe lighter out of her handbag and gave it to him.

He took it with a look of surprise and examined it. "It's really very fine. Thank you. You know, it's been a long time since anybody gave me a smoking gift—my kids wish I would stop. But I like smoking. I've always felt there's something communal about smoking with another person—almost intimate."

"You're pretty introspective, aren't you?" Kate asked.

"I'm sure I am. Sometimes I wonder if it's accentuated by living alone. Much of the time, the only person to talk to is myself. But I think I'd be this way even if I weren't single. I think I've always noticed impressions more than details. That might be a bit obscure. You know—what gets recorded in my mind is the impression something or someone is making on me rather than the particulars in the scene? I've kind of always been this way."

Kate said, "Close your eyes."

"Well—okay," Martin said and shut his eyes.

"Keep them closed. Now, tell me, what color are my eyes?"

"I don't know," he said after a brief pause. "I'm sorry. I'm a little embarrassed not to know."

Kate laughed.

Martin opened his eyes and looked closely at her. "Okay, they're gray shading toward blue. And they go wonderfully with your dark hair."

"Thank you," said Kate, feeling flattered. "And you see, I do know what you're talking about. I'd bet that if you tell a friend about our time together, you'll be able to tell him a lot. But if he asks, 'What color are her eyes?' or 'What was she wearing?' you wouldn't know. That's all right—we have a name for your condition: you're an extreme intuitive introvert."

"Is that bad?"

Kate said, "No, no. You folks are a bit less than 2 percent of the population. But if people don't understand that about you, they'll think you're weird, the better they get to know you. It's not pathological—you don't need to go on meds. You just need to be careful who you hook up with. If they don't understand that about you, there'll be trouble."

"You know," Martin said, "I went through my young adulthood, from my teens through my twenties, with a piece of advice about how to initiate relationships and be a good conversationalist. I read it in Ann Landers, I think. It was very simple, and not bad: draw them out—keep it focused on them. Find out what their interests are and ask about them. I think that's decent advice, and it worked pretty well for me. It took me years to realize that it also had a downside. I could draw lots of people out—but when they drew me out and I got comfortable enough to talk about how I see things, they would say, 'What?' So it is nice to learn that a small percentage of the population is like me. I wish I had known that when I was young."

"Really?"

"Well, it would have changed my mate-selection process."

Kate looked at Martin and smiled. "Your mate-selection process? Sounds pretty formal."

Martin smiled. "Yeah, you're right. Not really the right phrase. But what I mean is that if I had understood this earlier, I might not be alone now."

Kate was silent. Then, thinking about her own life, she said, "You sounded sad just now. Is being alone hard for you?"

Now Martin was silent. Then he said, "Well, my life is good, and I'm grateful—it's turned out better than I imagined. But, yes, it would be good to be with someone I love. I miss that."

Kate paused, wondering at the direction this conversation had taken. Then she said, "Me too."

Martin looked at his watch. "We need to leave for the airport soon. But I'd like to ask you a question. If you're our choice, will you accept? I don't mean to put you on the spot, but I'm curious. You've seen us now, or at least seen as much as you can in a short visit. And I know your college's decision has created a real dilemma. But what do you think? Or is my question premature?"

Kate thought about what to say and smiled to herself as a comic option occurred to her. "Oh yes," she could say breathlessly, "oh yes, Martin, oh yes." She thought not. Instead, she said, "I'd like to. But honestly, I don't know."

26

Back at Wells Kate felt the last week in February crawl by. She knew that next week Scudder would make its decision and, depending upon what it was, she would have to make her own decision. She dreaded it.

In her classes and with students she was able, mostly, to be present and involved. But when she was alone, the decision gnawed on her. And she gnawed on it.

And she dreamed. One of her dreams woke her up, and she wrote it down in her journal, remembering Martin's practice.

I am walking Bob the dog. He is on a leash. We are in my hometown, walking on a sidewalk in front of a house that I remember in our old neighborhood. A tall hedge separates the house from the sidewalk. Bob tugs on the leash and leads both of us into some calf-high grass between the sidewalk and the street. Bob is enjoying sniffing the tall grass and nibbling at it. Then a stern voice comes from behind the hedge: "Stay on the sidewalk, please." I can't see who is saying it. The voice wakes me up.

The first week in March went even more slowly. On Friday, although she had no classes, she spent the morning in her office at the college. She thought it important to be there in case any students came by and to show up in the department even when she didn't need to be on campus.

In the early afternoon, Kate drove home. Soon settled in her study, she opened her e-mail and immediately saw a message from Scudder. For the past few days, she had been checking e-mail more often than usual. She called it up on her screen:

Dear Professor Riley,

We are pleased to offer you our one-year visiting appointment in New Testament. We hope you will accept.

A letter and contract have been sent by postal mail today, but we want you to know as soon as possible of our offer. The formal contract will spell the terms out in greater detail, but to review:

- *A salary of $72,000 and benefits.*
- *Professional travel allowance.*
- *Housing at no cost in a faculty apartment.*
- *Teaching load of two courses each semester, including our two-semester Introduction to the New Testament.*

Finally, we hope to have your decision by a week from today. As I know you are aware, it is getting late in the year to hire faculty. If this schedule is difficult for you, we are willing to talk about it, but it would ease our situation if we could hear from you within the week.

Yours truly,
Alberto Gomez
Academic Dean

Kate saved the message and put her computer on standby, got up from her desk, and walked to her kitchen. She turned on the electric kettle to boil water. Deciding not to preheat the teapot, she popped two bags of PG Tips into it and then added a third.

While the water was heating, she leaned against the kitchen counter. She lit a cigarette and thought she wouldn't count it in her daily ration of six. One arm wrapped around her waist and the other extended only slightly farther away, her cigarette between her first and second fingers, she thought about how she felt.

Not really surprised, she realized—she had thought she had a pretty good chance.

And pleased. She knew that she would have been disappointed if the offer hadn't come.

But oh my. The water boiled, and Kate poured it in the teapot. As the tea steeped, she continued smoking, trying to do so slowly, as she thought about what else she felt. Troubled. *Oh yes.* Very much aware of a shadow, a cloud.

The tea now ready, she poured a cup, added milk and artificial sweetener, and returned to her study. She decided to make a list of things to do.

1. Call Geoff and Fredrika. Tell them I want to talk to them.
2. Meet with Vincent and let him know. Not looking forward to that. Wait until Monday.
3. E-mail Scudder.
4. Be in touch with Martin, phone or e-mail.

Kate looked at her list and added another item:

5. Need to decide.

Oh my.

She decided that the first thing to do was to write an e-mail to Scudder:

Dear Dean Gomez,

I am very pleased to learn that Scudder has decided to offer this position to me.

I appreciate your deadline. I will let you know my decision not later than a week from today. Among other things, professional courtesy requires that I let my department chair and dean know before I give my answer to you.

You will hear from me again by Friday.

Thank you,
Katharine Riley

Then she wrote to Martin:

Dear Martin,

A very quick note to let you know I've been offered the position—and I realize that you may already know this.

I've e-mailed Dean Gomez to tell him I'll give him a definite answer by a week from today. I've got a lot to figure out.

More later. All the best—and have a good weekend.

Kate

Fredrika paused, her mouth full of Geoff's Provençal stew. "Well, Kate, what I want to ask is why you're even thinking about this. Why do you want to go to Scudder so badly? Or perhaps I should say, so much? I mean, on one level, this is a no-brainer—give up an almost certain permanent position for a one-year temporary appointment in a seminary? Are you crazy?" She smiled.

"Maybe," Kate said. She had invited Geoff and Fredrika to an emergency dinner summit, which Geoff had generously agreed to host. "But I do puzzle about that a lot. You know, I love teaching at Wells. And I think what I do here matters. I get to introduce my students—these bright young people—to the big questions. You know, like the nature of reality, and what we're like, and how we should live, and how religions have addressed those questions. I mean, what could be more important?"

Oh my, she thought, *I'm becoming a bit grand.* She continued, "So why am I so interested in Scudder? I think I've figured it out. I'd like to know what it's like to be able to talk about these questions in an intentionally Christian context like a seminary—what it would be like to be with people who are wrestling all the time with what this means for Christians. I wonder if maybe that's my real vocation."

Fredrika and Geoff were quiet for a few moments. Then Geoff spoke. "Kate, I think you want to do this. I've thought so for a long time, ever since you got the invitation to apply back in January. And how you've just answered Fredrika's question confirms that. So why wouldn't you? As I see it, it boils down to two facts." He raised one finger. "You have no guarantee that you can return to Wells." He raised a second finger. "You're not sure what the senior faculty in the department think of you—whether they want to keep you or not. And if you go to Scudder, then a year from now they'll be the ones deciding whether to rehire you."

"Right," Kate said, realizing that she was slightly miffed about having the obvious so clearly put.

"So, maybe we should talk about the reasons you don't just say yes to Scudder."

Kate said, aware of a note of irritation in her voice, "You've just stated them,"

"Well," Geoff said, "not really. Those are just the facts of the situation. They don't have to be reasons unless you make them reasons."

Kate looked puzzled. Geoff said, "What I mean is that maybe

it would be helpful to think through why you give so much weight to those facts. Do you know what I mean? What I'm suggesting is that it might be helpful to talk about why those facts loom so large for you."

"Okay," Kate said, hesitation in her voice.

"Well," Geoff said, "let's talk about whether you want to be at Wells the rest of your teaching career. If you stay here, you're almost certainly going to get tenure. And you know how it is in the academic world—once you get tenure someplace, you rarely get to move on unless you become famous enough to get a senior appointment elsewhere. So, do you want to be here forever?"

Kate ate another spoonful of stew and reflected. "I don't know. I haven't thought of it that way."

Once again they lapsed into silence. Then Fredrika said, "Kate, I'm wondering how much your conflict and confusion are driven by security issues. We all have them—nothing to be ashamed of or embarrassed about."

She paused. "I'm going to say something obvious. From what I know about your life, you've been alone for a very long time. You were, what, seventeen or eighteen when your parents died?"

"Seventeen—almost eighteen."

"And even before that, you were basically responsible for earning your own spending money? I remember your telling me that your folks didn't have much money—that your dad's business failed when you were about ten."

"More than spending money," Kate said. "Clothes money, money for hot lunches at school, anything I needed beyond eating and sleeping at home."

Fredrika continued, "So for more than half of your life, and all of your adult life, you've been alone and financially on your own."

She paused and then asked, "What's the longest you've lived anywhere since your parents died?"

Kate thought for a moment. "Do you mean in the same town? That would be five years—four years in college and then a year in the same town afterwards."

"No," Fredrika said, "that's not what I mean. I mean in the same living space—you know, the same apartment or house? And that probably wasn't in college—I imagine you moved to a different dorm or apartment every year or almost every year?"

"Yeah, that's right. I did."

"So, what's the longest time you've lived in the same space?"

Kate thought about it for a moment. She thought she knew where Fredrika was going. "Here," she said. "I've been in the same house since I got here four and a half years ago."

Fredrika looked down at her lap and then up at Kate. "I'm wondering if Wells represents security for you. Think about it. If you decide to stay here rather than going to Scudder, you're almost certain to get tenure. You'll have an institution committed to your financial security for the rest of your life. And you can settle down, buy a house, maybe find a place that you can call home.

"I wouldn't exactly call Wells your family, but I'm wondering if it taps into your yearning for what family sometimes provides—you know, a lifelong community, and one that will take care of you. If you stayed here, you'd never have to move or worry about financial security again."

Kate nodded. "You know, I have started to realize through this process how much I depend upon Wells for not only security, but also my sense of self. If I leave, then the year after next, instead of being a professor close to being tenured, I could be unemployed. I think I see what you're saying. If I were prudent, I should say no to this. If I didn't go to Scudder, I'd probably be guaranteed to get tenure here. I could even use saying no to Scudder as a positive. You know, even though I had an opportunity to be a visiting professor at a pretty good school and with a larger salary, I chose to stay here because of my commitment to Wells and to educating undergraduates in a liberal arts setting. What could Vincent and the college do if I decided that?"

"You're probably right," Geoff said. "But I don't think that's the point Freddie—Fredrika—and I are trying to make."

"Oh?" Kate responded.

"Well, yeah," Geoff said, looking at Kate and then Fredrika. "I think we both know you'd like to go to Scudder. But you're afraid to."

"Afraid?"

They were silent. "Well," Geoff said, "that's what we've been talking about. I know, I know—it sounds like a judgment. But it's not. You're so good at what you do." Again looking at Fredrika, he said. "We can't imagine that if you go to Scudder, it could be the end of your teaching career."

Fredrika said, "That's right. You'll land on your feet whatever you decide."

"Agreed," Geoff added.

"Well," Kate responded, "it's all very well for you two to say that. But . . ." She stopped.

After a few beats, Fredrika said, "But?"

Kate frowned. "Well, I thought of saying that I'm not afraid. And then I realized that I am. So I thought about justifying my fear—I mean, you've already said it, Fredrika. I am alone, and nobody's going to take care of me if I blow this. You're right. I do have security issues—or insecurity issues, I guess."

There was silence as they all took another mouthful of the stew. Then Fredrika said, "Well, to ask that old standard question.

What's the worst that could happen to you if you went to Scudder for a year?"

"I might not get rehired at Wells—and even if I do, I might not get tenure."

"And?"

"And?" With frustration in her voice, Kate said, "That's pretty serious. I wouldn't have a job."

Fredrika was quiet. Then, looking directly into Kate's eyes, she said, "You know, I just don't think that's going to happen. I've seen you teach, and you're one of the best teachers I've ever known—maybe even the best. I don't think God's going to throw you away if you go to Scudder."

Fredrika continued to hold Kate's gaze. "Are you supposed to get tenure at Wells? I don't have a clue. But I'm confident that you have a role in God's providential purpose. I can't imagine otherwise. So don't decide this on the basis of security concerns."

Kate felt a bit beaten up. But as she thought about what Fredrika and Geoff were saying, she realized they might be right.

Geoff said, "I know you worry a lot about what Vincent and Fred and Paul really think of you. If you do accept the position at Scudder, you'll find out. If they do rehire you, that will tell you a lot. And if they don't—well, would you really want to be tenured here?"

Fredrika added, "And one more thing. You know that biblical phrase, 'Fear not,' 'Do not be afraid'? Somebody told me that it occurs 365 times in the Bible—one for each day of the year. I've never checked it out, but if that's true, I might have to change my understanding of inspiration. But I know it's in the Bible a lot for a good reason."

"So," Kate said, looking at both of them, "you're saying I shouldn't be prudent about this?"

"Well," Geoff said, "prudence is one thing. But being afraid is something else."

Then he added, "You know, for selfish reasons, I hope you stay here—I'll miss you if you go to Scudder. But I don't want you to stay here because you're afraid of leaving."

Again silence. Then Fredrika asked, "What do you think God is calling you to do?"

27

Sunday morning at St. Columba's, Kate sat in her usual pew. She listened as Fredrika read the collect for the day: "Gracious God, whose blessed Son Jesus Christ came down from heaven to be the true bread which gives life to the world: Evermore give us this bread, that he may live in us, and we in him; who lives and reigns with you and the Holy Spirit, one God; now and forever." Kate joined the congregation's murmured "Amen."

Fredrika began her sermon: "Our gospel text today is about blindness and seeing. And so is my sermon. Blindness and seeing are central not only to our text, but to Jesus and the gospels as a whole."

She quoted familiar sayings about people with eyes who

do not see and spoke about how sighted people are often blind. She spoke about her own twenty years of marriage and how she had blinders on for most of that time. Kate listened attentively. It was not often that Fredrika spoke about herself in her sermons; she had told Kate she worried it was narcissistic, so when Fredrika did use a personal example, Kate always took special note.

Then Fredrika developed the gospel story about Jesus opening the eyes of a blind man in John 9 with its affirmation of Jesus as the "Light of the World." She emphasized how Jesus came to give everyone sight. At the end of the service, the congregation sang "Amazing Grace" with its line from the same story, the exclamation of the blind man to whom sight was given by Jesus, "I once was blind, but now I see."

Kate went home still conflicted. She spent the rest of Sunday and Monday alone.

She prayed. She spoke out loud to God. "Lord, if going to Scudder is about me—about the extra money or ambition or a feather in my hat—I don't want to have anything to do with it. But if this is about you, then help me out."

She did the evening service from the *Book of Common Prayer,* lingering over the words of the ancient prayer for light, the *Phos Hilaron:*

O gracious light,
pure brightness of the ever living Father in heaven,
O Jesus Christ, holy and blessed!
Now, as we come to the setting of the sun,
and our eyes behold the vesper light,
we sing your praises, O God: Father, Son, and Holy
Spirit.
You are worthy at all times to be praised by happy voices,

O Son of God, O Giver of life,
and to be glorified through all the worlds.
Amen.

Monday night, well after midnight, she was startled awake by a dream. She turned on the lamp next to her bed and wrote it down:

I am about ten years old. I am running. My parents are running with me, and something behind us is gaining on us. I can't run very fast—my legs are heavy and clumsy. They don't work very well. Even so, my parents are falling behind me. I slow down, and they call to me, "Keep running! Keep running!" I do, and they fall farther behind. I look back over my shoulder and realize I can't see them anymore. I know I need to get to a large house across a meadow strewn with stones and boulders. Whatever is chasing me is getting closer. I wake up, terrified.

She put down her journal and decided to leave her bedside lamp on. As she tried to go back to sleep, she wished she were not alone. It would be good to have somebody in bed with her. Not for the first time, she thought of a dog. A dog might be perfect.

Tuesday morning, she sat in her office thinking that she should see Vincent. She dreaded doing so and decided to put if off. There was no point in telling him about the offer from Scudder if she wasn't yet sure what she would decide.

Last night's dream continued to haunt her. She didn't know how to understand it. Did it mean, "Don't do this"? Don't make a foolish mistake like her dad had made long ago? Or was it about her fear—and was she supposed to honor her fear? What did it mean to "keep running" from whatever it was that had swallowed up her parents? And was she supposed to keep running, or perhaps stop to face what was chasing her?

There was a light knock on her partially open door. Kate looked up and smiled warmly. "Hi, Fiona." Fiona Amundson was a favorite of hers, bright and extremely hardworking. She'd grown accustomed to seeing her face in at least one of her classes each semester and suspected that Fiona had recruited quite a few others into her classes as well.

"Kate," she said and broke off with a timid smile. "It's still a little hard for me to call you by your first name even though that's how I think of you. Do you have a few minutes? I don't have an appointment."

"Of course," Kate said. "Come in."

Fiona sat down in the leather seat facing Kate and smoothed her long red hair back from her face in a nervous gesture "The reason I'm here is that I heard that there was a petition about denying you tenure next year."

Kate blinked. She'd expected Fiona to have a question about a paper or a topic they'd covered in class. It probably wasn't surprising, however, that Fiona had heard about the petition. Clearly someone had been contacting Wells parents about it, although the last time Kate had checked there were no new signatures, and she'd hoped the thing had died a natural death.

Fiona seemed to mistake her expression. "I didn't have anything to do with that petition," she said hastily. "I think it's horrible. I mean, you're my favorite teacher. In fact, you're the favorite teacher of just about everyone I know."

"Thank you, Fiona. I really appreciate that. I don't want you to worry about the petition, though—"

"That's not why I'm here," Fiona interrupted. "I—well, Allison and I, thought it was so awful that someone would do that to you that we started a petition of our own." Reaching into her bag, she pulled out a sheaf of papers and handed them to Kate.

The pages were also printouts from petitiononline.com, but this petition was titled "Give Kate Riley Tenure," and it had pages of signatures. Kate thumbed through them with astonishment, recognizing some of the names as current students and their parents and even some as the names of former students who had already graduated.

"We used the religious studies alumni e-mail directory," Fiona said. "We've got 307 signatures and counting. I'm on my way to take them to Professor Matthison, but I wanted to show you first."

Kate couldn't speak; she was so moved by Fiona's gesture and the amount of time and effort she and Allison must have put into gathering so many names. She turned back to the first page and read the paragraph under the title. "We, the undersigned, find Professor Katharine (Kate) Riley to be an outstanding addition to the Religious Studies Department at Wells College. Her knowledge, passion, and enthusiasm have enlightened and inspired us. Frankly, we believe that it would be insane for Wells not to grant her tenure." Where tears had been threatening to fall, Kate was now able to laugh.

"Fiona," she said, "I can't thank you and Allison enough. I am truly moved by your support. Nothing could mean more to a teacher."

She looked at the young woman seated across the desk from her and came to a decision. "But I need to be honest with you. I've been offered a position to teach next year at Scudder Divinity School, and I'm seriously thinking about taking it. I haven't fully made the decision yet, and so of course I hadn't planned to say anything to any students until I had, but in light of this very kind gesture, I thought you deserved to be aware of the possibility."

Instead of disappointment, however, Fiona beamed a thousand-watt smile. "Scudder? Really?"

Kate nodded, a bit perplexed.

"But Josh and I were just talking about how much we'd both like to go there. I was going to ask you for a letter of recommendation. Their application deadline is April 1. Oh my gosh, that'd be fantastic if you were a teacher there!"

Kate couldn't help but return Fiona's smile even as she cautioned her. "Well, I don't know for sure that I'll be going, and even if I do accept their offer, it'll most likely only be for a year."

But Fiona was already gathering up her bag. "Wait until I tell Josh. This is so great!"

"Just remember; it's not for sure yet!" Kate called after her as Fiona swept out of the room with a hurried good-bye. In her haste she had forgotten the petition with its pages of signatures.

Kate looked down again at the petition. Funny how these pieces of paper made her feel so much more honored than the flattering offer from Scudder. And even more confused.

At the start of class that afternoon, Kate distributed another handout. "Today, we move into a new topic on the syllabus," she announced, " 'The Impact of the Enlightenment on Faith.' Now, in a sense we've been treating that topic all term—the impact of the Enlightenment on the Bible and thus on Christianity as the dominant religion of Western culture. But our topic today is more specific—namely, the impact of the Enlightenment on the meaning of the word 'faith.' Because faith is central to Christianity, as well as to other religions, it matters what we think the word 'faith'—and its sibling or at least cousin 'believing'—means.

"The central claim of your readings for today is that the dominant meanings of 'faith' and 'believing' have undergone a radical change in Western culture, and thus Western Christianity, since the Enlightenment."

Kate paused. "But before we turn to talking about the readings,

I want to begin by inviting you to think about a question. Think about the word 'believe.' I'm not asking you how you would define it, or what you think it should mean, but how you hear it being used in everyday language today. When do you hear people using the word 'believe'? When do you use it? What meanings are implied by how people use the word? Take a couple minutes to think about that and jot something down."

Kate set her timer as her students began to ponder. She looked at them as they thought and wrote and was struck by how dear their faces were. After three minutes, she asked, "So what did you come up with?"

A young man named Alex was the first to reply. "Well, I thought about the difference between knowing and believing. You know, there are some things you can know, and other things you can only believe in."

A student named Sarah said, "Maybe my comment is the same as what Alex just said. But what I thought of is that people use the word 'believe' when they're not sure about something. Like, if you asked me, 'What's the capital of Kansas?' and I didn't know for sure, I might say, 'I believe it's Wichita—or is it Topeka?' " There was a chuckle of recognition from the class. She continued, "I do that all the time on multiple-choice questions—I'm not sure about the answer, but I believe it's this one."

Another student, Noreen, said, "I think for Christians, believing—and I need to say that this is an impression, because I don't know very much about Christianity—is what they turn to when something seems kind of far-fetched. Like God creating the world in six days or conceiving Jesus in a virgin. I mean, people who aren't Christians don't think those kinds of things happened, so I think faith for Christians means believing things that you otherwise maybe wouldn't."

She took a breath and concluded, "At least that's how I hear some of my Christian friends use the word. You know, they say, 'You just need to believe it.' "

Kate noticed that Erin looked particularly struck by that comment.

Jonathan said, "Yeah, I hear the word used that way too. But my comment is a bit different. I started thinking about what we mean when we say 'I believe you' and when we say 'I believe *in* you.' It occurred to me that they're not the same. 'I believe you' means 'I believe you're telling the truth and not lying,' and 'I believe in you' means more than that. Like I trust your integrity, or that you've got what it takes, or something like that. So I'm thinking that 'believe in' means something more than 'believe.' "

Erin said, "I want to say something about the last two comments. I hear my Christian friends using 'believe' in both of these ways. They—we, I guess—do believe some things that people who aren't Christian don't—like Jesus is the Son of God and he was born of a virgin and he died for our sins. And we also talk about believing in Jesus. So I think there is some difference between 'believe' and 'believe in,' but I don't think they're completely different. Doesn't the second include the first—you know, even though believing in Jesus means more than believing some things about him, it also involves believing that what the gospels say about him is true? Can you separate the two?"

Kate waited to see if somebody in the class would pick up on Erin's comment or take the discussion in a different direction.

Fiona spoke. "Well, I think I agree that the meanings are related, but they still seem pretty different to me. Like if I say to Josh," she gestured at him, " 'I believe in you,' that's a whole lot different from saying 'I believe you.' You know, the second one basically has to do with information—like I'm accepting the truth of what he's telling me. He's a good source of information. But with 'believe in'—I don't know, it's hard to put into words—there's some kind of combination of trust and commitment. You don't say 'I believe in you' casually. Believing is about information; believing in somebody seems real different."

Allison jumped in. "And not just believing in somebody, but also believing in something. Like, if I say, I believe in democracy, I don't mean simply that it exists—I mean that I'm committed to it as a form of government, maybe even as the best form. So 'believing in' is about a lot more than believing a set of facts."

Andrew, his navy wool beret at a forty-five-degree angle to his head, said, "Like what Mark Twain said when asked if he believed in infant baptism. Believe in it? Hell, I've seen it." Almost half the class groaned—they had heard Andrew say it before.

A few more students spoke variations on what had already been said. When the time Kate had set aside for class responses had passed, Kate said, "Okay, good. Nicely done."

She continued, "Now, I want to relate what you've just been talking about to today's readings. The main points are on your handout, so you don't have to be too concerned about taking notes. But I want to supplement and elaborate those points. So sit back while I talk you through this.

"Your first readings were from two books by Wilfred Cantwell Smith, *Faith and Belief: The Difference Between Them* and *Belief and History.* Smith was a professor of religion and theology at Harvard for many years until he died about a decade ago. Basically, Smith's argument is that the meaning of the word 'believe' began to change dramatically in the 1600s, the century in which the Enlightenment began and a century after the Protestant Reformation. Both played a role in changing the meanings of the words 'believing' and 'faith.'

"He develops his argument with a wonderfully detailed study of how the word 'believe' was used in English-language texts from before the year 1600 and then in the centuries afterward. His conclusion was that before the seventeenth century the verb 'believe' consistently had a person for its direct object; in the seventeenth century it began more and more often to have a statement as its direct object.

"This is a significant difference," Kate continued. "It's the difference between 'believing in' somebody and 'believing' a statement to be true. A couple of you have already commented about that. And the reason for the change in meaning? Exactly what we've been talking about in this course: the conflict between the Christianity of the time and the new knowledge of the Enlightenment. When Enlightenment thinking differed from conventional Christian beliefs, Christians responded by invoking 'believing,' and the primary meaning of the word 'faith' began to be 'believing' that a claim, a biblical statement, a doctrine, or a dogma is true.

"The Protestant Reformation also contributed to this development. The Reformation spawned not just one version of Christianity in opposition to the Roman Catholic Church, but a number of denominations. So Protestant groups not only differentiated themselves from Catholics, but also from each other by what they 'believed.' Infant baptism or adult baptism? Predestination or not? The Lord's Supper—the Eucharist or the Mass: transubstantiation or consubstantiation or remembrance?

"I don't want to go into the details of these differences. I'm simply illustrating Smith's point that, over the last few centuries, the primary meaning of faith for many Western Christians has become believing in the truth of a set of statements, biblical or doctrinal or both. Its dominant meaning became 'believing the right things.'

"The other part of Smith's argument is what the word 'believe' meant in English language texts before about 1600. Then, before the collision with the Enlightenment, as I mentioned a moment ago, the direct object of 'believe' was consistently a person, not an object. In a Christian context, this meant God as known in Jesus. So believing wasn't about seeing a set of statements about God and Jesus as true, but believing *in* God and Jesus. Think about what you've already said about believing in a person compared to believing that a statement is true.

"Then the final step—Smith's suggestion that we best understand the pre-1600 meaning of believing by thinking of it as 'beloving.' Indeed, that's even the etymology of the word in English—'believe' comes from a medieval English word that means 'to belove.' Thus to believe in God and Jesus meant to belove God and Jesus. Think about that—it's the difference between believing that a set of statements about God and Jesus are true and beloving God and Jesus. This is the difference between 'believing that' and 'believing in.' Smith's claim is that faith as the former is a Western innovation of the last few centuries. The gist of his claim is that in only one of the world's religions, and only for a couple hundred years, have 'believing' and 'faith' meant accepting a set of statements to be true. That's pretty stunning."

Kate looked at her class to see if eyes were glazing over. She noticed Erin in particular was sitting up very straight, her eyes bright. Satisfied that her students were still engaged, she continued, "Okay, a couple minutes more of me, and then I'll invite you back into conversation."

She paused. "Now to relate Smith's argument to your other reading for today, the excerpt from H. Richard Niebuhr's *The Responsible Self.* A summary is on your handout, so you can simply listen while I make some comments about it. According to Niebuhr, there are three primary meanings of 'faith' in the history of Christianity. To use the Latin words to name these meanings, they are *assensus, fidelitas,* and *fiducia.*

faith as assenting to the truth of a claim or a set
'believing that' a statement or set of statements is
ning of faith that, according to Smith, has been
ed since the Enlightenment.

"The second, *fidelitas,* means faithfulness, as in our word 'fidelity.' It means faithfulness to a relationship. Fidelity isn't just about 'not straying.' Positively, it means commitment, loyalty, allegiance, steadfastness, presence, attention. In a Christian context, this is faith as faithfulness to God—not to statements about God, but to God."

Kate paused and looked at her class, scanning for puzzled faces. Seeing none, she continued. "The third meaning of faith, Niebuhr says, is *fiducia.* The best English equivalent is the verb 'trust'—faith as 'trust.' Think about what 'trust' means. In a Christian context, and more generally in a religious context, faith as *fiducia* means trusting in God—or if the word 'God' is a problem, a trusting relationship with 'what is.'

"The opposite of faith as trust," Niebuhr says, "is anxiety. Think about that for a moment—the opposite of faith as trust is not doubt or skepticism or unbelief, but anxiety, worry, and fear. Now think about the amount of anxiety, worry, and fear in your life. I won't ask you to share, but just think about that for a minute."

When a minute had passed, Kate continued. "To return to Niebuhr's point, anxiety, worry, and fear all flow from lack of trust. But faith as trust progressively diminishes anxiety and at its deepest level casts it out. This is what Jesus meant when he said, 'Why are you anxious, you of little faith?' Anxiety and little faith, little trust, go together. A century and a half ago, Kierkegaard put this meaning of faith this way: faith is like floating in seventy thousand fathoms of water. Think of the image. Faith is trusting that the water will buoy you up. If you do, you'll float. But if you thrash around or become rigid with fear, you'll sink.

"The same image is at the center of a poem by Denise Levertov, a poet who died a few years ago. It's called 'The Avowal,' and I'm using it to illustrate this meaning of 'faith.' Listen to how the language works:

As swimmers dare
to lie face to the sky
and water bears them,
as hawks rest upon air
and air sustains them;
so would I learn to attain
freefall, and float
into Creator Spirit's deep embrace,
knowing no effort earns
that all-surrounding grace.

After a few moments of silence, Kate said, "I'm going to read it again, partly because it's short, and partly because I think we often hear a poem better the second time through."

After the second reading, Kate was silent for about a minute, caught up in her own thoughts. Then she said, "If we had faith as *fiducia,* as trust in God, as trust in 'what is,' we wouldn't be anxious or worried or fearful. Think of how great that would be. Think of what the anxiety-free life would be like. Think of how free you would be. Faith as trust generates, to use a phrase from Niebuhr's contemporary Paul Tillich, 'the courage to be.'"

Kate paused again, longer than she had anticipated. She noticed Erin nodding and wearing a huge grin. It looked like something had really connected with her. Kate pulled herself back to the readings. "Now, finally, to make the obvious connection
readings from Smith and Niebuhr: over the past coup
the primary meanings of the words 'believing' and

become *assensus*—giving your mental assent to a set of statements, biblical or doctrinal. But before Christianity and the Enlightenment collided, the most important meanings of 'faith' and 'believing' were *fidelitas* and *fiducia*—faithfulness to God and trust in God."

Kate stopped and looked at her class and then at her watch. "Well, that took a bit longer than I thought it would—but we do have about ten minutes left for conversation about all of this. Let me suggest two possible focal points. First, any questions or comments about the claims Smith and Niebuhr make and how they develop them? How persuasive, or unpersuasive, are they? How clear or muddled? Second, the 'so what' question—what do you think about the implications of their argument or connections to things you've observed or thought about?"

As Kate waited for students to respond, she thought about what she had just said about anxiety and trust, worry and freedom, fear and courage. And she realized she couldn't put her decision off any longer. Right after class she would go to Vincent's office.

28

Later that day, at six thirty, she arrived at Geoff's. He greeted her and said, "You look a bit weary—or maybe bleary? Have you been at Murphy's?" he asked in a tone of mock accusation.

"No," Kate said, "but you're right about weary."

"So," Geoff said, "will our evening be a time for celebration? Or a time for hand-wringing? I can do either—I just need to know whether to get out the bubbly or the tissues."

Kate smiled. "Let's wait for Fredrika before we do any of that."

"What about me?" came a voice from the foyer. "I'm here—and excited about my second dinner at Chez Cooper in one week." Fredrika appeared in the kitchen, her face bright. "So, is this a celebration or what?"

"Well, I did make my decision," Kate said.

"And?" Geoff and Fredrika said in unison.

"Well, before I tell you, let me tell you how I got there." Both of them groaned, and Kate smiled again. "Just wait. One of my favorite students came to see me today and showed me a petition she'd created about how I should be granted tenure. It had more than three hundred signatures. She was going to deliver it to Vincent, but forgot it when she left my office. I was so touched, and what surprised me was that you'd think something like that would have made me want to stay at Wells for certain, because it went a long way toward reassuring me that I could have tenure here if I wanted it. But with that fear gone, or at least dissipated, I realized that I wasn't at all sure that I wanted tenure. It reinforced for me that I really want to teach at Scudder.

"And then in my afternoon class, the readings I had assigned way back in January when I drew up the syllabus before the term began were about the various meanings of faith. And to illustrate the third one, faith as trust, I read them Denise Levertov's poem 'The Avowal.' I hadn't planned to include it in the class period—but it was on the floor in my study when I was getting ready to leave the house this morning. It must have fallen out of my poetry file, and so I picked it up and tucked it into my class file. Do you know that poem?"

Both Fredrika and Geoff nodded. "You shared it with me once before, and I even used it in a sermon. But maybe you were away that Sunday," said Fredrika.

"I had forgotten that," Kate said. "Anyway, when I looked over my class notes, there it was, and so I decided to use it in class. When I finished reading it to my students, I was surprised by how powerfully it affected me. I had to stop for about a minute before I could continue. I think my students thought I wanted them to think about it. One of them, a woman named Erin, actually came up after class and told me that the class and poem had helped her decide to trust God no matter where it took her. But it was really about me. And that poem has stayed with me—it's kept coming back to me ever since."

Kate paused. "So I've decided to go to Scudder. I must admit that I'm not completely at peace about it. I'm still a bit scared. But," she took a breath, "I'm going to do this."

Both Geoff and Fredrika beamed at her. "Kate, I think this is great," Fredrika said. "And you know what else? I don't think you need to be afraid."

She reached in her purse and pulled out her notepad. "I was hoping you were going to decide this. So I brought this quote from Frederick Buechner that I think fits what you've been going through really well. It goes like this: 'Listen to your life. Listen to what happens to you because it is through what happens to you that God speaks. . . . It's in language that's not always easy to decipher, but it's there, powerfully, memorably, unforgettably.' "

"That's perfect," said Kate, her eyes brimming with tears.

"None of that, my dear!" said Geoff. "This is a celebration. And I have a little something for you too." He went to the other room and returned with a bouquet of roses, then to the refrigerator, from which he pulled out a bottle of champagne. "An Argyle Brut from Oregon," he announced. "We're going to celebrate you."

Kate smiled, noticed a card attached to the roses, opened it, and read, "Darling, you've done it. You've said *Yes.* I'll miss you. Love you, Geoff."

Looking up at Geoff, aware that her eyes were tearing even more, she said, "Thank you. Thank you very much."

"You're welcome," Geoff said as he worked the wire loose from the top of the bottle. The cork suddenly popped and hit the ceiling. Geoff expertly turned the bottle to a horizontal position and poured the frothing liquid into a champagne flute. He handed it to Kate and filled two more flutes for Fredrika and himself.

"To you," he said, raising his glass, "and all that this might mean for you." They sipped.

"Mmm," said Fredrika. Kate realized it was very good champagne.

"Geoff, you're wonderful. You treat me so well." Then, smiling, she said, "If only I could find a straight guy like you. Alas. Thank you, both of you, for being here." She lifted her glass, and they all sipped again.

"So have you told Scudder yet? Or your department chair—what's his name. Vincent? Or Victor?" Fredrika asked.

"I haven't told Scudder yet. I thought I'd e-mail them tonight. But I did tell Vincent, right after my class today."

"How'd that go?" Geoff asked.

"Well, he did say he was glad for me, but his next words were that he'd have to get a replacement search started right away, because I hadn't given them much time." She smiled ruefully. "I guess I had hoped he would say something like, 'We'll really miss you. And we hope you'll come back to us—that's all we want.' Instead, his parting words were, 'Well, that's it then.' "

"Hmmm," said Fredrika.

"Not the most thoughtful thing to say," said Geoff.

"No," Kate agreed. "He's hard to read. But I guess I did get the parting shot. Before I walked out, I dropped the student petition on his desk."

Geoff grinned. "Nice. Always excellent to have the last word. And it never hurts to have more than three hundred seconds. So on that note, let's move on to dinner. I will be serving filet mignon cooked just the way Kate likes it—medium rare, but more rare than medium. Trust me to get it right."

Kate smiled, "I do. You know I do."

"And with the main course, a bottle of Fieldstone Alexander Valley cabernet—only the best."

"Are you trying to get us drunk?" Fredrika asked.

Geoff paused, looked at Kate and Fredrika in turn, and said with an exaggerated leer, "I've been wanting to have my way with you two ladies for a very long time."

They both laughed. Kate scrunched up her face. "I wish."

The next morning, just after her breakfast of coffee, toast, and cheese, she spent half an hour rereading John O'Donohue's *Eternal Echoes.* She knew he had recently died, an aneurysm taking him away in his fifties in the middle of the night. She thought of the lecture she had heard him give a few months before his death: the awakening of the mind to the sacred is the great adventure. *Yes.*

Last night she had decided to wait until now to respond to Scudder, because she didn't want to write her response when she was tipsy. She turned on her computer and began to write:

Dear Dean Gomez,

I am pleased to accept your offer of a position as visiting professor of New Testament during the next academic year. At your convenience, let me know what needs to be done next.

I look forward to being part of the Scudder community.

Yours truly,
Katharine (Kate) Riley

She glanced at what she had written and hit "Send."

Walking from her study to the kitchen to refill her coffee cup, she felt a lightness of being. She had loved the phrase ever since seeing the movie *The Unbearable Lightness of Being.* Its wonderful and fearful juxtapositions of luminosity and fragility, beauty and ephemerality, intensity and mortality had moved her. But now it was more than a metaphor. She felt it.

Back in her study, she lit a cigarette, her second of the day. Sitting back, sipping her coffee, inhaling deeply, she looked out the window at sunlight on March snow.

Looking at her watch, she saw that she needed to leave for campus in fifteen minutes. And she wanted to brush her teeth after the cigarette. But first she wrote one more e-mail.

Dear Martin,

I said yes.

Kate

SUGGESTIONS FOR READING GROUPS

Some reading groups discuss the whole of a book in one session with participants reading all of it before they gather to talk about it for an hour or two. Some schedule many sessions on a book, reading it section by section over an extended period of time and meeting to discuss the portion they have just read.

If your group is in the first category—one session that presumes that participants have read the whole novel by then—you might consider the following questions:

1. The main characters are Kate Riley, Martin Erickson, and Erin Mattson. What do you think of each of them? What are their issues? Do they change—and if so, in what way and why?
2. The didactic theme of the novel is different understandings of what it means to be Christian today—how to understand Christianity in an Enlightenment and post-Enlightenment world. These differences include how to understand the Bible, Adam and Eve and "original sin," the Christmas stories, Jesus and the gospels, the Bible's teachings about homosexuality, the meaning of "believe" and so forth. What do you make of the differences presented in the novel? What did you find persuasive, or not? What was new? Was anything unsettling or disturbing? Did the novel change your understanding of Christianity (or religion) in any way?
3. Reflect on the novel's title, *Putting Away Childish Things.* It echoes words from the apostle Paul in I

Corinthians 13.11: "When I was a child, I spoke like a child, I thought like a child, I reasoned like a child; when I became an adult, I put an end to childish ways." How do you see this applying to the novel? To the main characters? What "childish ways" do you see in their thoughts and behaviors? To what extent do you think they have "put an end to childish ways"?

If your group is in the second category—meeting for several sessions and reading an assigned number of chapters before each session, you will do things quite differently. Group leaders—ideally a man and a woman—will need to decide how many sessions and thus how to divide the novel into assigned chapters.

If this is a "new group" rather than a continuing group in which people already know each other, you might spend much or all of the first session on "group formation" by providing participants an opportunity to begin to know each other.

If the group is small (fifteen or fewer?), you could keep them together as they share their responses to the questions below. If the group is larger, you may want to divide them into small groups of four or five. Interaction in which everybody speaks is the goal—if not in a large group, then at least in small groups. Invite them to introduce themselves with brief answers to the following questions:

- Where were you born and where did you grow up?
- What was your religion/denomination (or lack thereof) as you grew up?
- What religion/denomination (or not) are you now?
- And a question that Kate asks her class: what was your impression of the Bible by the end of childhood? And now?

Encourage them simply to share this information as they go around the group—no conversation until all have had their say. Once everybody has been heard from, then conversation can begin for as much time as has been set aside for it. Participants can respond to what they have heard from others or ask questions about what they've heard.

In subsequent sessions, you may want to invite the group to think about and then share with each other their responses to the religious/theological issues encountered in the novel. Examples:

- Chapter 3: what do you think of what Kate says during her radio interviews about her book on the Christmas stories? About these stories as "parables"?
- Chapters 9 and 10: how would you respond to the question about what you imagine it would have been like to live within the pre-modern worldview? What do you think about the students' responses? And what do you think about Kate's handout explaining that all religions are human products, human constructions?
- Chapter 12: what do you think of Martin's "outline" for his lecture on "Mysticism and the Christian Path"? Do you feel like you understand what he's talking about?
- Chapter 14: how would you respond to the question about whether Adam and Eve were real people? About creation stories as myths? About what this might mean for the notion of "original sin"? What do you think of what the students say as they puzzle about this?
- Chapter 18: Erin and Kate talk about homosexuality in the Bible. What do you think of Erin's concerns? What do you think of Kate's interaction with her and the understanding that she suggests?

- Chapter 21: what do you make of the distinction between the pre-Easter Jesus and the post-Easter Jesus? Does it make sense to you? Is it illuminating? Or confusing, perplexing?
- Chapter 22: Martin and Margaret Bardwell talk about David Friedrich Strauss and his understanding of gospel stories that include spectacular events. What do you think about this—about whether it's important that spectacular events really happened back then, or whether it makes more sense to think about them as symbolic or parabolic stories?
- Chapter 27: Kate's class about the meanings of "believe" and "faith." What are the pre-modern and modern meanings of these words? Do you find them illuminating? What do you think of how deeply Kate was affected by what she presented in class?

Finally:

- In a concluding session or two, you could consider the "large" questions above in suggestions for a group that meets only once to talk about this book.
- You might also discuss whether this novel has changed—or underlined—the way you think about what it means to be Christian today.

Speaking Christian

CHAPTER ONE

"Speaking Christian," by which I mean knowing and understanding Christian language, is in a state of crisis in North America. I suspect the crisis extends to other parts of the world as well, but I write about the cultural terrain I know best. The crisis is twofold. For many, an increasing number, Christianity has become an unfamiliar language. Many people either do not know the words at all or, if they have heard the words, have no idea what they mean.

But Christian illiteracy is only the first part of the crisis. Even more seriously, even for those who think they speak "Christian" fluently, the faith itself is often misunderstood and distorted by many to whom it is seemingly very familiar. They think they are speaking the language as it has always been understood, but what they mean by the words and concepts is so different from what these things have meant historically, that they would have trouble communicating with the very authors of the past they honor.

So why do I express this crisis as a problem of language? Because language is the medium through which people participate in their religion. To be part of a religion means being able to speak and understand its language. Every religion has a basic vocabulary: its "big" words and collections of words, spoken and heard in worship, embodied in rituals and practices.

Thus to be Jewish means "speaking Jewish"; to be Muslim means "speaking Muslim"; to be Buddhist means "speaking Buddhist"; and so forth. By "speaking" I do not mean merely knowing either the ancient languages of these religions or their modern descendants. I mean something more basic: the way practitioners use the concepts and ideas from their religion as a lens through which to see the world, the way they use them to connect their religion to their life in the world.

To use an illuminating phrase from recent scholarship, religions are "cultural-linguistic traditions."[1] What this means is both simple and important. Every religion originated in a particular culture and thus used the language of that culture, even if in ways that radically challenged it. If a religion survived over time, it became a cultural-linguistic tradition in its own right, with its own language, its basic vocabulary, sacred texts and stories, rituals and practices. These are often organized into comprehensive systems of thought—what Christians call theology, including doctrines and dogmas.

In this respect, being Christian (or Jewish or Muslim) is like being French (or Turkish or Korean). One of the criteria for being French is the ability to speak French. Another is being able to understand French. We would not think someone fluent in French if that person could only speak it, but not understand it. In the same way, literacy means more than simply being able to make sounds out of written words. It also involves having some understanding of what the words mean. Christian literacy means not simply the ability to recognize biblical and Christian words, but also to understand them.

Of course, being Christian is about more than words, just as being French is about more than fluency in French. One doesn't become French simply by learning the language. Being French also involves membership in a community and an "ethos," a way of life. So also being Christian is about being part of a community and an ethos, a way of life. It is about more than language, but not less.

Christian language is grounded in the Bible and postbiblical Christianity. It includes the words used, heard, sung, and prayed in worship, devotion, teaching, and community. To be Christian is to know, use, and be shaped by this language—to live one's life with God within the framework of this language.

AN UNFAMILIAR AND MISUNDERSTOOD LANGUAGE

Christian language is becoming unfamiliar for an obvious reason. Over the last half century, the percentage of people growing up Christian has decreased significantly in North America and even more so in Europe. Many born after the mid-1960s have had little exposure to biblical and Christian language, except what they may have picked up from a culture in which Christianity is a strong presence.

I became vividly aware of this shift thirty years ago when I moved from teaching in Minnesota, where Christian language was in the air that we breathed, to teaching in Oregon, the least churched state in the country. On the first day of my first class, an introduction to the New Testament, I said that we couldn't understand the New Testament without understanding that early Christianity was rooted in Judaism. A hand went up: "What's Judaism?"

Good question. What is a one- to five-minute response to somebody who doesn't know anything about Judaism and wants to know what it is? As I sought to define Judaism, I mentioned Moses, and another hand went up: "Who's Moses?" Another good question. How do you say who Moses was to somebody who has never heard of him?

I knew that I wasn't in Minnesota anymore. Many of my students in Oregon had little familiarity with the Bible and Christianity. I began to ask them on the first day of courses to write a ten-minute essay on the topic "Me and the Bible" or "Me and Christianity." Some questions they had to answer were: What has been your exposure to Christianity and the Bible? Did you grow up in a church? And whether you did or not, what have you heard about the Bible and Christianity? What's your impression?

Here is a sampling of what I read and learned:

> "I don't know much about the Bible, but I think there's a story in it about a guy in a fish."
>
> "I don't know much about Christianity, but I think that Christians are really against trespassing."
>
> Half had never been to a church service, except for a wedding or funeral, and not all had experienced even that.
>
> More than half described Christians as literalistic, anti-intellectual, judgmental, self-righteous, and bigoted.
>
> One who had never been to a Christian worship service happened to attend what may have been the only snake-handling church in Oregon. He said that he hadn't known that Christian worship included snakes, and he thought that was pretty interesting.

The problem wasn't the intelligence of my students; they were bright. But they were harbingers of a future that is becoming more and more present. Many Americans under forty have grown up with little or no involvement in a church. Of those born since 1980, 25 percent describe themselves as having no religious affiliation.

Unfamiliarity with Christian language—its important words and the sacred texts and stories in which those words are embedded—is widespread among Christians as well. Polls indicate that less than half of American Christians can name the four Gospels. Only a third know that the Sermon on the Mount is in Matthew. Two-thirds think that the saying "God helps those who help themselves" comes from the Bible (it doesn't). Most know only a few stories from the Old Testament, often in garbled form. Stories from the New Testament fared only slightly better. Thus, even for many Christians the language of the Bible and Christianity is like a foreign language.

The problem is not simply unfamiliarity. Many of us have heard Christian language since childhood. If we are still part of a church, we continue to hear it in biblical readings, sermons, hymns, prayers, liturgies, and creeds. We are steeped in it.

The problem is that it is often misunderstood. It has acquired meanings that are very different from their biblical and ancient meanings. Sometimes the issue is diminishment, the reduction of rich and multiple meanings to one particular meaning. Often the issue is even more serious, not just diminishment, but distortion and serious misunderstanding.

There are two major reasons why the Christian language is frequently misunderstood today. First, a particular common and widely shared understanding of what Christianity is has created a framework within which biblical and Christian language is most often understood. I call it the heaven-and-hell framework. The second reason we misunderstand Christian terms is the result of the "literalization" of biblical and Christian language. This is my name for the process by which many have come to assume that the most faithful way to understand Christian terms is as literal and absolute representations of the inerrant revelation of God. In this chapter, we will tackle the heaven-and-hell framework and take up the literalization of Christian language in the next chapter.

THE HEAVEN-AND-HELL FRAMEWORK

Words have their meanings within frameworks. Frameworks are large interpretive contexts that shape the meanings of words. *Elephant* means something very different in the framework of a visit to a game park in Africa from what it means in the framework of a political cartoon. Frameworks matter.

The large framework shaping the meaning of Christian language for many today is the heaven-and-hell Christianity of not so long ago. I have puzzled, indeed struggled, with what to call this, seeking to avoid terms that sound pejorative or patronizing, yet still wanting to use ones that give an accurate description. By *heaven-and-hell Christianity,* I mean simply an understanding of Christianity that most Protestants and Catholics shared in common and thus took for granted not very long ago.

Suppose that you had been asked at the end of childhood, at age twelve or so, the following questions: What is Christianity about? What is the heart of its message, "the gospel"? Why should people be Christian? The questions are relevant not only for those who grew up Christian. Virtually everybody who grew up in a Western culture acquired some impression of Christianity by the end of childhood.

At that age, my single-sentence answer, the impression that formed in my mind as I grew up Christian a half century ago, would have been: Jesus died for our sins so that we can be forgiven and go to heaven, if we believe in him. Of course, I learned that being Christian was about more than that. It also meant seeking to lead a changed life by obeying God's commandments, especially the commandment to love one another. It was about behavior as well as belief. But its core was clear. We have been bad and deserve to be punished, even to the extent of eternal torment in hell. But God sent Jesus to die for us so that, if we believe in him, we can be forgiven and go to heaven.

This understanding was not idiosyncratic to my Scandinavian Lutheran childhood. Rather, it was widely shared by Protestants and Catholics. With varying degrees of conviction, it continues to be seen as the core of Christianity by millions, within and outside the church. It is the framework within which many understand Christian language.

The heaven-and-hell framework has four central elements: the afterlife, sin and forgiveness, Jesus's dying for our sins, and believing. They are all there in my childhood memory and present in the minds of many Christians. What is already in our minds shapes what we experience, including how we hear words.

The Afterlife: Heaven is the reason for being Christian. Life after death was so important in the form of Christianity that I absorbed growing up that if somebody had convinced me when I was twelve or so that there was no afterlife, I would have had no idea what Christianity was about or why I should be Christian.

This is the understanding held by many Christians today. Some belong to churches that explicitly emphasize the hope of heaven and the threat of hell. Others belong to churches that seldom or never mention hell. But even for many of them, the hope of a blessed afterlife is what Christianity is most centrally about. How important has the promise of heaven (and perhaps the threat of hell) been to the forms of Christianity that you have experienced or heard about?

Sin and Forgiveness: Sin is the central issue in our life with God. Forgiveness is the solution. Because we are sinners, we deserve to be punished. Consider how often sin and forgiveness appear in Christian worship. Most services include a confession of sin. In my childhood, every Sunday morning we said, "We poor sinners confess unto thee that we are by nature sinful and unclean, and that we have sinned against thee by thought, word, and deed, wherefore we flee for refuge to thine infinite mercy, seeking and imploring thy grace, for the sake of our Lord Jesus Christ." That's pretty intense, though not as severe as some I have heard. Confessing sins wasn't just Protestant; my Catholic friends had to go to confession every Saturday and confess in person to a priest.

Most worship services also include a threefold appeal for God's mercy: "Lord, have mercy upon us. Christ, have mercy upon us. Lord, have mercy upon us." We need God's mercy because we are sinners. The words of the Eucharist (also known as the Lord's Supper, Mass, or Communion) commonly emphasize our sinfulness and Jesus as the sacrifice who makes forgiveness possible. Take time to reflect on how central sin and forgiveness were to your impression of Christianity.

That heaven-and-hell Christianity is "sin-ridden" is often more apparent to non-Christians than Christians. Some years ago I heard a Buddhist teacher say with a twinkle in his eye, "You Christians must be very bad people—you're always confessing your sins and asking for forgiveness."

Jesus Died for Our Sins: Within this framework, what is most important about Jesus is his death. He died for our sins in our place, paid the price of our disobedience, and thereby made our forgiveness possible. This understanding is widespread not only among the many who affirm it, but also among many who have misgivings about it or reject it.

Recall Mel Gibson's blockbuster movie *The Passion of the Christ*. It focused on the last twelve hours of Jesus's life, from his arrest through his torture, suffering, and death, and portrayed all of this as Jesus's bearing the sins of the world. Recall its enthusiastic reception by many conservative Christians. Even Pope John Paul II endorsed it; he said, "It is as it was." The message was clear that what matters most about Jesus is his death as a substitutionary sacrifice for the sins of the world.

The connection between an afterlife and Jesus dying for our sins is insisted upon by conservative Christian voices in America today. For example, Albert Mohler, president of the flagship Southern Baptist Theological Seminary, said in 2010: "Did Jesus go to the cross as a mere victim? If so, then we have no gospel, we have no hope of everlasting life. Did Jesus go merely as a political prisoner, executed because he had offended the regime? Well, if so, that's a very interesting chapter of human history, but I'm not going to stake my life on it, much less my hope for eternity."[2]

Note how his statement combines the "gospel," the "hope of everlasting life," and the "hope for eternity" with Jesus being more than "a mere victim," more than "a political prisoner executed because he had offended the regime." For Mohler and many Christians, what matters about Jesus is that he died for our sins, so that we can be forgiven and go to heaven.

Believing: The final element that makes up the heaven-and-hell framework is believing, understood as affirming a core set of statements to be true. Believing, or "having faith," is what God wants from us and what makes it possible to go to heaven. For about half of Protestants, this means not only believing that Jesus died for our sins, but much more, including that the Bible is the inerrant revelation of God, literally and absolutely true. For other Protestants and most Catholics, what is to be believed is not as rigorously detailed. But there is common agreement that affirming a set of beliefs matters. For many, this has become the primary meaning of "faith."

The framework created by these four elements decisively shapes the meaning of many "big" Christian words, giving them meanings very different from their biblical and ancient Christian ones. To illustrate:

Salvation now refers to life after death; it is about going to heaven. But in the Bible, it is seldom about an afterlife; rather, it is about transformation this side of death.

Saved now means to be saved from our sins. But in the Bible, it is about much more than this, and often not about sin at all.

Savior now refers to Jesus as the one who saves us from our sins. But in the Bible, *savior* is used long before Jesus and most often has nothing to do with being saved from sin.

Sacrifice now refers to Jesus's death on the cross as payment for our sins. But in the Bible, sacrifice is never about substitutionary payment for sin.

God now refers to a personlike being separate from the universe. God's character is both loving and punitive. God loves us enough to send Jesus to die for us, but God will also judge and punish those who don't believe or behave as they ought. But the Bible also contains a very different understanding of God, both of what the word refers to and of God's character.

Mercy is now about God forgiving us, even though we are sinful and deserve to be punished. But in the Bible, the ancient words translated into English as *mercy* often do not mean what *mercy* means in modern English.

Repentance is now remorse for sin and resolving to live a better life. But in the Bible, its meanings are quite different: to return from exile and "to go beyond the mind we have."

Redeemer, redeem, and *redemption* (like *savior, save,* and *salvation*) now refer to Jesus as the redeemer who redeems us from our sins and brings about our redemption. But in the Bible, these words are not about being saved from sin, but about being set free from slavery.

> *Righteousness* is now primarily about individual virtue—about being a righteous person. But in the Bible, it is often a collective or social virtue. It is about justice and whether societies are just or unjust.
>
> *Peace* is now primarily understood as an individual internal state—peace of mind and being at peace with God. But in the Bible, peace is more than internal peace. It is a major part of God's dream for the world, a world of nonviolence and the end of war.
>
> *Faith* now means believing a set of statements about God, Jesus, and the Bible to be true, often literally true. But in the Bible and premodern Christianity, faith and believing are not about affirming the truth of statements. Rather, they are about commitment, loyalty, and allegiance, and not to a set of statements, but to God as known especially in Jesus. Perhaps the best single synonym for *to believe* is *to belove.*

All of these words and more will be treated in this book. For now, the point is that the common heaven-and-hell framework is like a black hole that sucks the meaning of Christian language into it, changing and distorting it.

Because much of this book is a critique of how this framework has narrowed and distorted the meaning of much of Christian language, I want to emphasize that it has worked and still works for millions. By *worked,* I mean that it had good effects in their lives.

My own parents, born over a century ago, are an example. I think they and many in their generation lived within the framework of conventional heaven-and-hell Christianity all their lives. So far as I know, it didn't create problems for them—though I wish I had thought to ask them while they were still alive. In part, it worked for them because it was taken for granted and was thus "softer" than its hardened contemporary forms. It didn't require willed affirmation and vigorous defense. For them and for many, it was a means of grace whereby the Spirit of God worked in them, producing the fruits of gentleness, decency, and compassion. God's Spirit can and does work through many means.

But in our time, the meaning of Christian language within the heaven-and-hell framework of conventional Christianity has become a problem for many. For some, it renders much of Christian language opaque and deprives it of its richness. For others, the issue is more than deprivation; Christian language has become an obstacle, an intellectual stumbling block, sometimes so large that taking Christianity seriously becomes very difficult.

Redeem or Replace?

So serious is the problem that some have concluded that Christian language is beyond redemption and needs to be replaced by language that actually communicates what we want to communicate. If *salvation* means something very different from what most people think it means, can we use the word without being misunderstood? If *God* means something very different from what it means to most people, can we use the word without being misunderstood? So also with many others, like *saved, mercy, righteousness, repentance,* and so forth.

A powerful case for the need to replace Christian language is made by Gretta Vosper, a pastor in the United Church of Canada, president of the Canadian Center for Progressive Christianity and author of *With or Without God: Why the Way We Live Is More Important Than What We Believe.*[3] She invites her readers to imagine what a visitor to a typical mainline worship service experiences:

> Readings from the Bible that are not only unfamiliar, but sometimes disturbing, concluding with "The Word of the Lord," followed by "Thanks be to God."
>
> Prayers that presuppose that God can be persuaded to intervene.
>
> A liturgy that emphasizes that we have been sinful, but Jesus paid the price by dying for us.

Language about bread and wine as the body and blood of Jesus given for us.

What does this language mean to outsiders, or, for that matter, to insiders, to Christians? Vosper's book makes a bracing case for changing our language that needs to be taken seriously by all who are concerned with the viability of Christian language today.

But I choose the second option, to redeem rather than replace Christian language. One reason is personal. As an Episcopalian, I belong to a denomination saturated with Christian language. Every Sunday, we hear four biblical readings, more than most other Christians do. Our liturgies and prayers from the Book of Common Prayer are filled with biblical and Christian language. For me to abandon this language would mean leaving a biblical and liturgical denomination that has been and is profoundly nourishing.

The second reason is more than personal. It is the premise of this book that religions are like languages. If we take this seriously, it means that being Christian means speaking Christian. To cease to speak Christian would mean no longer being Christian—just as ceasing to speak French would mean no longer being French. Speaking Christian is essential to being Christian.

I do not want to be misunderstood. People can live a good life without knowing or using Christian language. And by "a good life" I do not mean simply a happy life or decent life, but a transformed life that embodies virtues enshrined in Christianity. Christianity is not the only path of goodness and transformation. But Christianity has repeatedly shown itself throughout its history to be an effective path for goodness and transformation—a path that is affirmed by millions and still has the potential to be a powerful force for our future. That is why I think it is worth redeeming rather than replacing Christian language. We have too much to lose.

What it means to redeem Christian language is illuminated by the primary biblical meaning of *redeem:* to set free, to release from bondage.

Christian language needs to be set free, released, reclaimed from its captivity to its conventional modern meanings.

Redeeming Christian language includes reclaiming individual words and short phrases like *salvation, saved, sacrifice, redemption, repentance; God, Jesus, Trinity; righteousness, mercy, justice, grace, the kingdom of God; eternal life; Jesus* as *Lord* and *Savior,* as *the Way and the Truth and the Life,* and more. We need to ask afresh: What does this language mean? What does it means to use these words? It also means redeeming collections of words heard in Christian worship: biblical readings, the Lord's Prayer, creeds, the liturgy, especially the Eucharist.

The language of the Bible and postbiblical Christianity is much richer and broader than commonly supposed. The latter includes language used by saints, mystics, and theologians like Augustine, Thomas Aquinas, Francis of Assisi, Julian of Norwich, Catherine of Sienna, Teresa of Avila, John of the Cross, Martin Luther, John Calvin, and many others. The tradition also includes the imaginative enhancement of Christian language in Christian art, music, hymnody, and poetry.

Thoughtfully understood, Christian language is perceptive, persuasive, and powerful. Its insights about the human condition illuminate the way we commonly experience our lives. It points to an alternative vision and way of life centered in God and God's passion for a different kind of world. It has power. For many it has been and continues to be a sacrament of the sacred, a means of grace, a way the Spirit of God speaks to us, a vehicle whereby our lives are changed. But how we understand this language matters.

Notes

1 George Lindbeck, *The Nature of Doctrine* (Philadelphia: Westminster, 1984).

2 "Jesus, Reconsidered: Book Sparks Evangelical Debate," interview on NPR's "Morning Edition," March 26, 2010. (Interviewer was Barbara Bradley Hagerty.)

3 Gretta Vosper, *With or Without God: Why the Way We Live Is More Important Than What We Believe* (Toronto: HarperCollins, 2008).